GRANTA

GRANTA 70, SUMMER (Winter in Australia) 2000
www.granta.com

Granta, 2-3 Hanover Yard, Noel Road, London N1 8BE
Tel 020 7704 9776 Fax 020 7704 0474
e-mail for editorial: editorial@grantamag.co.uk

Granta US, 1755 Broadway, 5th Floor, New York, NY 10019-3780, USA

TO SUBSCRIBE call 020 7704 0470 or e-mail subs@grantamag.co.uk
A one-year subscription (four issues) costs £24.95 (UK), £32.95 (rest of Europe) and £39.95 (rest of the world).

Granta is printed in the United States of America. The paper used in this publication meets the minimum requirements of American National Standard for Information Sciences—Permanence of Paper for Printed Library Materials, ANSI Z39.48-1984. ∞

Granta is published by Granta Publications and distributed in the United Kingdom by Fourth Estate, 6 Salem Road, London W2 4BU, and in the United States by Granta Direct Sales, 1755 Broadway, 5th Floor, New York, NY 10019-3780, USA.

Design: Random Design
Cover paintings by Roger Law, courtesy of the Rebecca Hossack Gallery

ISBN 0 903141 36 1

A NEW WORLD

'Chaudhuri writes about India like no one else'
ROBERT McCRUM, *OBSERVER*

From the author of *Freedom Song*

AMIT CHAUDHURI

PICADOR
www.picador.com

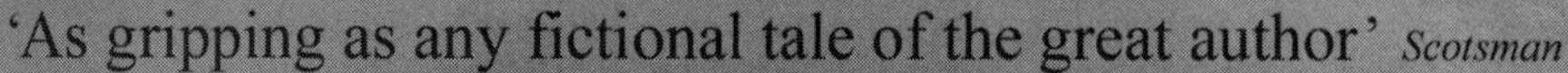

One of the most acclaimed books of 1999

THE LIGHTHOUSE STEVENSONS

BELLA BATHURST

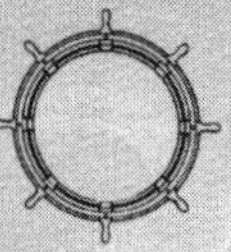

'A world of science and culture is condensed into a slim highly-focused narrative'

Financial Times

'Bathurst's fluent and scholarly biography spins a gripping dynastic yarn around a murky corner of history'

Guardian

flamingo

www.fireandwater.com

GRANTA 70

Australia

Ian Jack	INTRODUCTION	7
Peter Conrad	NEW NEW WORLD	11
Tim Winton	AQUIFER	39
Robyn Davidson	MARRYING EDDIE	53
Peter Carey	TRUE HISTORY OF THE KELLY GANG, FIRST PART	69
Les Murray	THE NEW HIEROGLYPHICS	101
David Moore	GROWING UP	105
Ben Rice	POBBY AND DINGAN	133
Howard Jacobson	THE WEEPING POM	181
Paul Toohey	THE ROAD TO GINGER RILEY'S	199
Polly Borland	GROG	231
Georgia Blain	THE GERMAINE TAPE	263
Frank Moorhouse	WAR WORK	277
Kate Grenville	MATE	293
Murray Bail	VOYAGE SOUTH	305
Thomas Keneally	MY FATHER'S AUSTRALIA	331

NOTES ON CONTRIBUTORS 351-2

Glossary

Akubra quintessential bush hat, made of felt (brand name)
Battlers' blocks parcels of land given out after the Second World War to returned soldiers; any piece of land too small and scrubby to be profitable
Backblocks remote country
Coolabah *Eucalyptus microtheca*; a common variety of Eucalypt
Coolamon a shallow wooden dish which can carry food, water or babies
Dag matted sheep turd; term of endearment or mild abuse
Damper unleavened bread cooked in the ashes of a camp fire
Dingo wild dog
Drongo an inept, awkward or embarrassing person
Dunny outside toilet
Esky portable ice box (brand name)
Fossick to search for something
Galah a kind of parrot; an idiot
Heeler from Blue Heeler; an Australian cattle dog
Hooroo goodbye
Jarrah *Eucalyptus marginata*; a rare and sought-after hardwood
Jumbuck sheep
Melaleuca paperbark tree
Mullock heap spoil tip
Nobby opal
Noodling hunting on a spoil tip for gems, particularly opals
Ringer champion shearer
Roo as drawn by Roger Law below; leading marsupial of 120 species
Snagger old shearer
Squatters nineteenth-century settlers who paid the government a lease fee to graze sheep on crown land (sometimes ruining it for cultivation)
Stubby small, squat beer bottle; pair of shorts
Ute truck (from utility vehicle)
VB Victoria Bitter, a popular beer
Wilcha windbreak

Introduction

Later this year Australia will set out to demonstrate its credentials as the world's most successful sporting nation. There is a national strategy in place: the Sydney 2000 Gold Medal Plan, which aims to secure sixty medals, twenty of them gold, by the time the Sydney Olympics end on 30 September. In the last Olympics in Atlanta, Australia won forty-one medals, or 2.28 for every million Australian citizens. No other country in the world came close to such a high ratio of medals per head of population. At the same games, the US won 101 medals, which is 0.37 of a medal for every million Americans. In every sport which Australia takes seriously—inside and outside the Olympic framework; cricket, Rugby League, Rugby, tennis, hockey, surfing, swimming—its teams and individual athletes and players are at or very near the top.

Sport matters in Australia, though the importance of the Sydney Olympics to Australia runs well beyond medal counts or revenue from television rights. Soon after the location of this year's games was decided in Monte Carlo in 1993, Paul Keating, then Australia's Prime Minister, said that the decision sent a message home to his fellow Australians that 'you people can travel on your own, under your own steam'. As the English writer, Michael Davie, observes in his new book *Anglo-Australian Attitudes*, this seemed a most extraordinary thing to say, because, as Davie writes, 'under whose steam did Keating think Australia had been travelling thus far?' Surely not Britain's; these days Australia's old imperial master has barely enough steam for itself. And hardly America's; Australia may have been strategically dependent on the US in the half-century between the fall of Singapore and the end of the Cold War, but it has never seen itself socially in hock or subservient to it. The deeper implication of Keating's remark—what he must have been getting at—was that there was still something unresolved about Australia, both in its identity and its place in the world; an island continent of 19 million people, mainly of European ancestry, as geographically remote from the North American and European societies it most resembles as it is possible to be.

As with Olympic medals, there was also in the 1990s a national strategy to win a new identity and a new role. Australia would take its place among the nations of Asia. It would finally abolish the British monarch as its head of state and become a republic. It would formally apologize to its original, pre-colonial inhabitants, the 350,000 Aborigines whose old way of living colonization had in one way or another ruined, and embark on a programme of reconciliation between natives and settlers, who now included increasing numbers of 'New Australians' who had migrated from south and east Asia. The strategy would be fulfilled to coincide with Australia's hundredth anniversary as a unified nation—Australia became a Commonwealth of the British Empire on 1 January 1901, but the enabling legislation was passed in London the previous year. And there to advertise this new national clarity and resolve on a thousand million television screens would be the Olympics in newly-burnished Sydney, which even unburnished is one of the most beautiful cities in the world ('Sydney is the city that San Francisco thinks it is'—Gore Vidal).

It went wrong, in many ways. Asia's economic boom turned to slump, and though the Australian economy was immune—in fact, grew—Asia no longer seemed quite the most promising political destination. The electorate replaced Keating's administration with a more conservative government. No national apology was offered to the Aborigines. In 1999, the referendum to secure a republic failed. And so Australia remains in an ambiguous condition and continues to argue with itself; a good place, though not only for those reasons, to be a writer.

At first sight, it seems an unlikely country for introspection and social division. The visitor from Europe or North America flies for more than twenty hours south across civilizations which can be only half understood through years of study—to arrive in a city which apparently replicates the one he or she just left behind in London or New York, equally prosperous and made unfamiliar mainly through its welcome bonus of gregariousness, physicality and hedonism: sun, chilled wine, beaches, surf, the barbecue. Of course, nowhere, not even *Australia Felix*, the lucky country of the south, is quite so easy. The arguments become evident. Queen v. President is simple enough, until it becomes complicated by subdivision: what kind of president, how elected? The cities are liberal multicultures, or like to be thought of in that way, but what about the country, the bush? Much less so, if at all; forgetting the Aborigines for a moment, racism has been endemic here since gold diggers rioted against their Chinese fellows in the great gold rush of the 1850s. Then again, does the bush matter any longer, other than as a piece of historic iconography? Sheep farms and country towns have emptied, wool has nearly vanished from the scale of Australian exports. Australian culture as male and working class—the celebrated 'mateship' of sheep runs, wool wharves, xenophobia and beer—is under threat from something smoother and, in terms of class if not race and gender, less egalitarian. Male bonding might one day be better observed at Sydney's annual gay and lesbian Mardi Gras.

Some of these arguments can be glimpsed in this issue of *Granta*; a lot of Australian writing returns sooner or later to the question of the historic

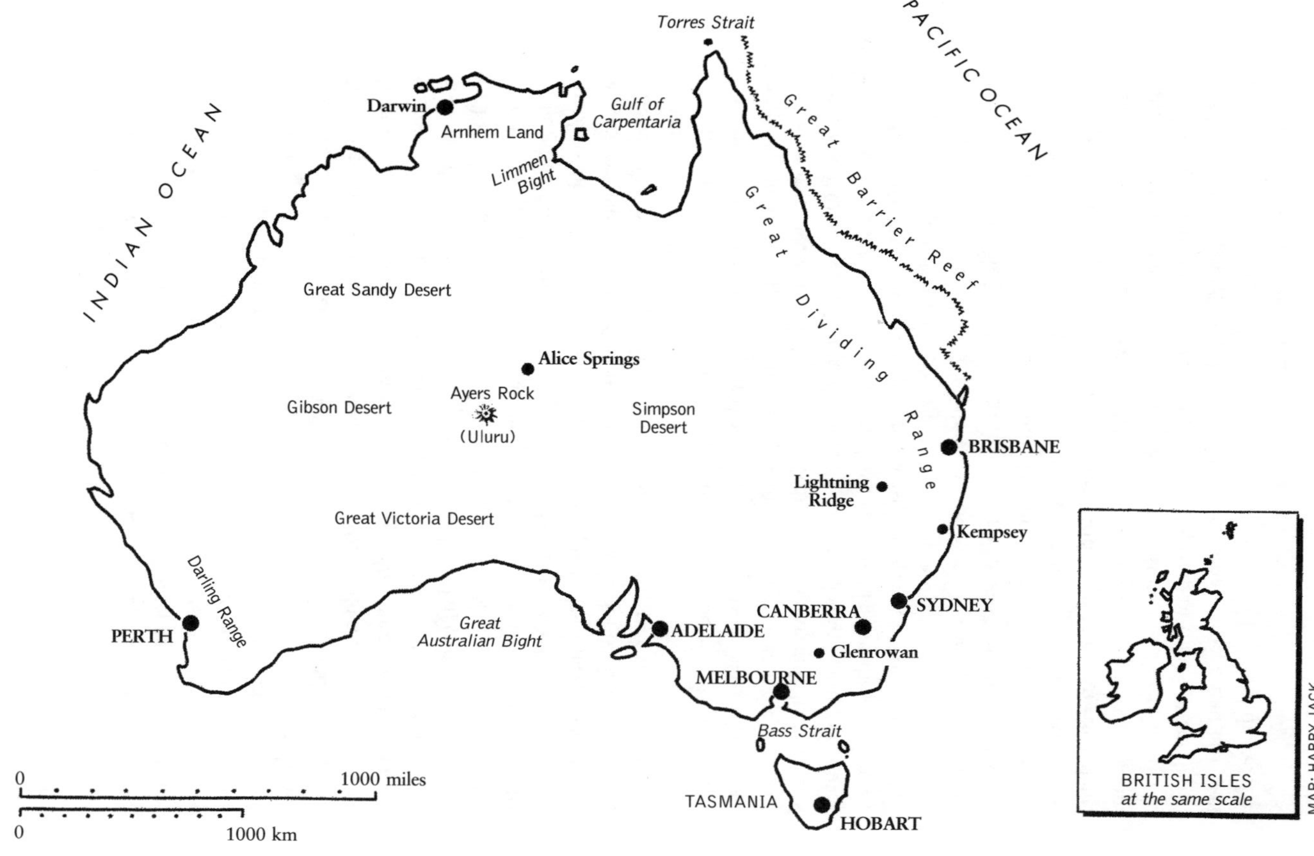

MAP: HARRY JACK

relationship between the individual and his/her nation (as you might expect from a society with harsh and improbable origins as a far-flung British prison). Sooner or later, too, the Aboriginal question often inserts itself. 'Aborigine' is a broad term for many different clans with different customs and languages, but taken together indigenous Australians form only about two per cent of the population. Colonial history has nothing to be proud of here, but, considering Aborigines as a demographic statistic, the prominence of shame and intrigue about them in modern Australian writing and among the Australian intelligentsia is a remarkable thing. You could travel a long way in North America and in North American literature before encountering this level of concern about native peoples, though the history of their treatment by colonists there is no less terrible. On the one hand, the larger hand, this speaks well of Australia. On the other and smaller hand, it sometimes seems as if a stiff humbugging piety has caught hold of the place, in which Aborigines to some white Australians are an unpunishing version of Catholicism; the sacred suppliers of art, mystery, tourism, identity and guilt. They have risen in the writerly imagination to the size and height of Ayers Rock (aka Uluru, a sacred Aboriginal site). The well-being of their future in the real world, however, remains problematic.

It may now be pointed out that this Australian issue of *Granta* contains no writing by Aborigines, or for that matter by any Australians without an Anglo-Celtic-sounding surname. They may be 'represented'; they do not represent themselves (other than in their own spoken words in Polly Borland's interviews). Quite right: *Granta* is primarily concerned with writing, on which terrifying and contentious judgements have to be made. But the fact that we could find no Aboriginal writing to fit the issue does not of course mean that no good Aboriginal writing exists.

A New New World? Certainly in Australia's still widespread sense of promise and optimism; but in Australian writing also in two particular ways. The first is its frequent concern with the natural environment—count the landscapes and the number of plants and animals encountered in the average Australian novel compared with its British or American equivalent. The second is the long experience it brings to bear on the identity question: who are we and what shall we become? The erosion of national identity is now a worldwide phenomenon. Muddle is the state of things. Australians, while thinking themselves behind in the old national game, are in fact well ahead in the new one. Other than in sport, the clarity of flags and the resolve of anthems belongs more and more to the last century. IAN JACK

GRANTA

NEW NEW WORLD

Peter Conrad

Peter Conrad with his father in Tasmania, 1950s

I left Australia at the age of twenty, carrying with me everything I thought I would need. It did not amount to much: a suitcase of clothes and a tea chest of books. I congratulated myself on how light-hearted I felt as my parents drove me to the airport in Hobart. Unlike Adam when ushered out of Eden, I did not look back. My mother cried. 'She's a bit emotional,' my father said, then shook my hand as if concluding a business transaction.

That afternoon in Melbourne, I boarded a ship which spent the next month toiling uphill towards the northern hemisphere; I was on my way to take up a scholarship at Oxford. Once or twice during the voyage, I checked on my tea chest in the rattling hold, to make sure that my skimpy library of English literature was intact. The books were my passport and my bank account—my entitlement to a place in an imaginary England, where I had actually been living ever since I learned to read.

Thirty years later I made the journey in reverse once more, though the month afloat is these days abbreviated to a groggy, elongated day in a jet. It must have been my tenth trip back. This time, however, no one met me at the airport in Hobart. I took a taxi to a hotel and scribbled a London address in the register. Next day—I needed the interval to get up the courage for the last, brief leg of the journey—I went out to my parents' house in the northern suburbs. It was empty. My father had died while watching football on television a decade before. He suddenly absented himself from his body, which went on sitting in its customary chair, wide-eyed. Shortly before my arrival, my mother, too, had slipped quietly out of life, not wanting to make a fuss. Over time she had learned to be less emotional: there were no goodbyes.

As their only child, the disposal of their house and its contents fell to me. I was now more or less the age they had been when I set off so nonchalantly for England, leaving them to spend the rest of their lives on this patch of ground. They had grown up in rural poverty during the Depression, and this flimsy suburban house was the only proof of success in life they ever asked for. It demonstrated that they had escaped from the harsh valleys where they spent their childhoods. My father always thought of the house, along with the thousands of others hurriedly constructed by the government after the war, as his handiwork: he was a painter by trade. When they married, he told my mother that she would never need to take a job. The house and its garden occupied her for the rest of her life. The lilies and roses she grew were her repudiation of the bush; my father did his best to tame wildness by mowing the lawns.

I needed less than a day to sort through their accumulated chattels: his tool box and her sewing kit, his beer tankards and her sherry glasses, and the white hats they wore when they went bowling. Two polished boxes contained their memories, which they seldom revisited. The smaller box, still in its accustomed place on the mantelpiece, held the family photographs. Beside their bed, the larger box, almost a trunk, contained memorabilia of the war. In it, I knew after raiding it in childhood, were the letters my father wrote to my mother from New Guinea, where the army sent him in 1945. Snooping all those years before, I soon put them back in their tattered envelopes. The graveyards of crosses which stood for kisses alarmed me. Who knew what primal scene I might stumble on if I continued reading?

Of course I packaged up the photographs and letters, ready to be posted to myself in England. In my pocket I took another memento, a curio I had always coveted. On every trip back I made sure that it was still in its usual place, hidden among jars of home-made preserves in a kitchen cabinet. It was a chipped china ornament, modelled on one of the pylons which anchor the Sydney Harbour Bridge; it commemorated the opening of the bridge in 1932, with sketchily painted glimpses of the blue harbour. Supposedly it dispensed salt and pepper, but I never knew it do anything so humdrum. Over the course of time, my parents had forgotten who gave it to them. I often had to plead with them not to throw it away.

In childhood, I thought of that shaker almost as a magic lamp, which might have telekinetic powers if you rubbed it. Apart from my books, it was the only emblem of elsewhere in the house. The bridge, a thousand miles to the north, did more than span the harbour. It made grander promises—to abbreviate all distances, to shrink the seas which estranged Tasmania from the mainland and Australia from the other continents. Beneath the bridge, I knew, was the terminal from which the ocean liners departed, festooned with streamers thrown between passengers on deck and the families who waved goodbye from the shore. The streamers maintained a connection for a few minutes, while the ships manoeuvred away from their berths. Soon, like cut umbilical cords, they snapped. That was the moment, surely, when you were set free.

I could not have been more wrong. You grow back into the past, just as surely as you turn into the parents who once seemed so puzzlingly unrelated to you. I found a place for the ornament in my London kitchen, where it joined an assembly of Sydney souvenirs—a panoramic photograph of the harbour bristling with sails on the day of Australia's bicentenary; the architect's sketches for the fins of the opera house; a coat hanger in the shape of the coat-hanger-shaped bridge; and a cushion with a street map printed on it which, propped on an empty chair on the other side of the table, allows me to go on leisurely strolls around the foreshore while I eat my dinner. When I was a child, that chipped pylon symbolized the romance of everywhere I had not been. Now it marks a different gateway, probably debarred. Having got to the end of the voyage out, I find my desires backtracking. Why is it that we can only imagine paradises which are lost?

My father had a defensive refrain, a mantra he chanted whenever I dreamed of worlds elsewhere. 'Well, I'm happy enough here,' he always said. Having struggled from their starveling farms to the edge of the city, he and my mother had been granted as much happiness as they had the right to ask for. They found it hard to understand why my ambitions were so far-fetched. They might have been proud of a son who sometimes got his name in the local paper after winning a sports trophy. But a scholarship overseas took me out of their ken, and even made the bonds of kinship fray. No wonder they looked askance at my success in exams at school: they must have known that I was preparing myself to escape at the first opportunity. They had no other child, though both of them had come from tribes of eight or ten siblings, incubated annually to work on the land. If only I could have left a brother or sister behind me, to be happy, well-adjusted, content. Instead, my desire to get away meant the ruthless withdrawal of affection from my parents, and from the country to which they—by what I could only think of as an administrative error—had relegated me.

Looking back, I wonder where my cold determination came from. I can't avoid owning up to ingratitude, but part of the blame also belongs to the seditious books in that tea chest which I took to England with me. I had a colonial childhood; it was English literature which alienated me from Australia. How could I have loved the place I grew up in, when the books from which I derived my mental map denied its existence, or saw it as a faint, estranged copy of a reality that was impossibly far away?

In those days, we inhabited what the Australian poet James McAuley described as a 'land of similes'. Metaphors assert a similarity between two things which are actually not at all alike; colonial Australia relied on similes to make connections with a so-called motherland which it did not resemble. In Tasmania, these outlandish similes used to be written all over the map. The parts of the state were originally named after British counties, though in a garbled order, with no concern for topography. The north-eastern tip of Tasmania supposedly corresponded to south-western England, with counties called Dorset, Devon and Cornwall; our south-west belonged to a county known as Kent, which straggled off into the wind-battered horizontal shrubbery and toppling cliffs of Port Davey, where the earth runs out. Long after the names were changed, teachers who had never been further afield than Melbourne continued to insist that Tasmania looked just like England. Yes, we had hop kilns, orchards, and a lot of rain—but what about Mount Wellington, the un-English extinct volcano that reared above Hobart, or the dripping, matted rainforests behind it? A few odd correspondences could not atone for the bereft misery of distance. When, after two years in Oxford, I was elected to a fellowship at All Souls, my new colleagues expressed sympathy about my origins. One of them once said that Tasmania must be just like the Isle of Wight, only 12,000 miles from London.

How could we not have grown up with a low opinion of ourselves? Australia's founding narrative is about rejection, not (like America's) about aspiration. The Pilgrim Fathers boarded the *Mayflower* in pursuit of an ideal which their descendants today call 'Personal Growth'. The convicts on the First Fleet, which arrived in

Sydney in 1788, did not choose to make the trip, and entertained no grandiose hopes about their destination.

Australia began as an imperial amenity, a tip for Britain's human refuse, and it remained a place of last resort, literally a terminus. During the 1950s, the country still officially classified its interior as a nullity, good for nothing except rehearsing apocalypse. Robert Menzies, the anglophile Prime Minister, gladly gave Britain permission to test its atomic weapons in the outback. Nevil Shute's novel *On the Beach* described a local version of Armageddon. Forever exiled from the action, Shute's Australians wait to be killed off by fallout from a nuclear combat in the northern hemisphere. The sickly cloud drifts down the east coast, expunging Brisbane, Sydney and Melbourne. Tasmania, being an island, is granted a fortnight's grace before the dysentery and the cancerous lesions appear; then the human race is officially annihilated. Traipsing through the streets of Hobart after I read the novel, I remember thinking—as I looked up at the mountain brooding above the town and down across the grey harbour with its chilly hackles which opened the way to the Antarctic—that this was where the world would end. Or had it done so already, without our being told? In those days before television, news travelled slowly. Perhaps Shute's doleful beach, where the hollow men gather together and avoid speech, was Sandy Bay, the scene of my infantile paddling.

My reading acquired a secret sub-plot: a desperate desire to be reassured that the rest of the world knew we existed. I was not sure whether to be pleased when I found a glancing mention of Tasmania in *Gulliver's Travels*. The story begins with Gulliver 'driven by a violent storm to the north-west of Van Diemen's Land' (as the penal colony was first known); Lilliput lies somewhere in the vicinity. Much later, I discovered that Joyce had played linguistic games with us in *Finnegans Wake*. Glugg gives Tasmania as the answer to a riddle: it is the kind of place only quiz contestants would know about. Warped into tossmania, it becomes a nasty winter ailment, which Ondt thinks he might have caught. For Swift, we clung to the edge of known reality. Beyond us, there was only fantasy. For Joyce, we were one of the more improbably recondite entries in the dictionary—a word no one but he or his crazed punsters would ever think of using.

Otherwise, there were only glancing disparagements. Charles

Darwin made brief landfalls in Sydney and Hobart in 1836, while travelling round the world on the *Beagle*. In Sydney he congratulated himself on being 'born an Englishman', because the settlement testified to 'the power of the British nation'. When he looked beyond the Georgian sandstone village, he winced. He disliked the miserably thin pasture and the 'extreme uniformity of the vegetation', just as Mark Twain, when he arrived, bewailed the prospect of a country populated exclusively by the lower orders. Darwin chided the Aborigines, who obstinately refused to be civilized. Why didn't they build houses, or 'take the trouble of tending a flock of sheep'? He also disliked Australian evergreens, and pitied people who missed the chance to witness 'the first bursting into full foliage' of a deciduous tree. It did not matter to him that this momentary spectacle had to be paid for by the penance of a denuded, fluey winter (probably with a long bout of tossmania). Darwin's field trip almost turned him into a cosmic Manichaean. Australia's marsupials and its unruly gum trees, which kept their leaves but shed their bark, made him entertain the possibility of an alternative creation: these freaks could not have been dreamed up by the same god who designed the northern hemisphere.

Stopping briefly in Hobart, Darwin considered it 'very inferior to...Sydney; the latter might be called a city, this is only a town'. He congratulated the colonists on their policy of genocide, which left Tasmania with 'the great advantage of being free from a native population'. He admired the potato fields, though he was disconcerted by the 'fewness of the large houses, either built or building'. So was I in the 1950s, and I still am. The suburb I grew up in was unpacked from boxes on a newly razored hill; though the roads were eventually tarred and the backyards disappeared under layers of concrete, we were squeezed between shaggy, indomitable mountains. Darwin clambered up Mount Wellington, cursing a 'stupid' guide, but at least he made the acquaintance of a few patrician plants on its slopes—a 'noble forest' of eucalypts, and man ferns whose fronds opened into 'elegant parasols'.

Earlier, as he set out across the Tasman Sea, he remarked: 'We were all glad to leave New Zealand.' He was no less glad to leave Australia, which he did 'without sorrow or regret.' Those were my emotions exactly at the airport in 1968—or rather I studiously refused to indulge in emotion, leaving that to my mother.

Darwin did give the gawky country a pat on the head in parting: 'Farewell, Australia! You are a rising child, and doubtless some day will reign as a great princess in the South.' But do princesses reign? A few years after Victoria's accession, Darwin could not conceive of Australia queening it, and added a chastening admonition: 'You are too great and ambitious for affection, yet not great enough for respect.' When I first read *The Voyage of the 'Beagle'*, I missed the unease and intimidation in his phrasing. Now I imagine a nerdy Brit whose inept advances are laughed off by a bronzed Bondi siren, 'too great and ambitious' to accept his love.

In 1930 the photographer E. O. Hoppé spent ten months in Australia, taking pictures for a volume entitled *The Fifth Continent.* Though he conscientiously documented the bush, and lined up the so-called 'wild men' to compose a 'dusky background' for his images, he expected more of the country than eroding plains, mosquito-ridden swamps and lunar deserts. 'The spiritual home of the white races,' he declared, 'is naturally in the cities built up by their vigour and vision.' Hoppé considered urbane Melbourne virtually Bostonian, but in Canberra, the new federal capital, the government buildings looked as if they still had price tags on them. In Sydney he saw only verdure, not signs of vigorous, visionary human effort: he called Taronga 'the happiest zoo in the world', because 'its boundaries come right to the ocean edge and make a natural home for water-loving denizens of the animal world', while across the harbour lay the Botanic Gardens, 'Mecca of typists in the lunch hour'. The typists could be considered fauna, nibbling their sandwiches among the flora. The gardens for them were Mecca, a place of pagan worship. Where, however, was the white, shining, spiritual citadel? In 1930, no one imagined that an opera house might one day be anchored on the foreshore.

Every so often, ambassadors for the white races arrived, sent to redress the balance between nature and culture in our benighted land. Laurence Olivier and Vivien Leigh came out on tour with the Old Vic in 1948. They even visited Hobart, and performed *The School for Scandal* across the road from the hospital where I had been born a couple of months earlier. I treasured the coincidence when I was growing up, and told myself that it was at least theoretically possible that I might have been taken to a performance—that is, if my parents had been theatre-goers, and if the theatre had admitted fractious babes in arms. Stepping ashore in Perth, Olivier announced: 'We know practically nothing about Australia.' Wanting to be polite, he said he was eager to see a black swan, and wondered why there were none on view at the docks. Leigh enquired, with a tinkling giggle, 'What *is* a billabong?' She and Olivier had been studying the words to 'Waltzing Matilda' during the voyage across the Indian Ocean, but they were none the wiser about billabongs, swagmen, jumbucks, tucker bags, or the identity of Matilda herself. They found Australia as bewildering as Lewis Carroll's invented land of the Jabberwock, with its Jubjub bird, Bandersnatch and slithy toves—a realm of regression, whose official language was baby talk.

Kenneth Clark, following the Oliviers in 1949, declared the Australian landscape unreal. It was useless for pictorial purposes, he thought, because it lacked 'dark woods'. Nature, to his eye, should compose a shady background to society, like the park beyond the ha-ha in a Georgian country house; there were no such elegant gradations between light and shade in Australia. Clark added that he did not consider 'the jungle'—by which I suppose he meant the bush—to be 'authentically Australian', though he gave no further reasons for this whimsical decision. He was not even sure that the laws of physics retained their force in this nether realm. Gravity was confounded by 'bounding kangaroos' and by flying foxes which slept suspended from the branches of trees. Fruit bats outraged other protocols: they used the same aperture for eating and excreting.

The last continent lay not just at the bottom of the known world but outside normality, like another planet which had lunged into the Southern Ocean. Australia came to seem an extraterrestrial destination. The cartoonist Hergé sent his boy reporter Tintin there in 1966 in *Vol 714 pour Sydney*. The purpose is to attend an astronauts' conference; Tintin and his dog Milou have already travelled to the moon, which is apparently more accessible than Australia—or at least more conceivable, because at the end of the story, after an accident-prone Indonesian detour, they still haven't arrived in Sydney.

Australia's remoteness from reality came in handy. Even after the closure of the prison colony, it was a convenient place of stowage for those who could not be accommodated in the stricter society of England. At the end of *David Copperfield*, Dickens sent the improvident Micawber to Australia, where—what kind of comment was this on colonial standards?—he immediately made good. More recently, the film publicists who wanted to conceal Merle Oberon's Eurasian ancestry fudged the issue by putting it about that she was born in Tasmania. She had never set foot there, but this hardly mattered. Tasmania was a non-place; no one would ever check. Sadly, Tasmanians believed the story, which connected them to a parallel universe of fame and glamour. People used to claim that they went to school with Merle, or escorted her to dances. Some even hinted that they had enjoyed her favours.

Australian troops were always available to die in Britain's wars. At Gallipoli, they were used by the imperial generals as cannon fodder, and lined up to be massacred. In the 1960s, still cheerfully belligerent, Australia volunteered to join a newer empire, and its army followed the Americans into Vietnam. Diminished and sidelined by history, Britain now consoled itself by ridiculing the former colony. In 1966 Michael Powell directed a film version of *They're a Weird Mob*, based on a phoney memoir about an Italian immigrant—the kind of alien being (given to gesticulation, unlike the laconic locals, and fond of spicy food) whom we used to call a 'new Australian'. The book, a best-seller during the 1950s, was written by the Irish humourist John O'Grady, though it purported to be the autobiography of Nino Culotta, who undergoes a humbling initiation when he lands in Sydney. Nino is bewildered by Australian slang and has trouble with pub etiquette; he is mocked by his workmates and victimized by their practical jokes. But he knows that this harsh treatment is a rite of passage, a tribal blooding. He accepts it without complaint, and is ultimately acclimatized and naturalized. How could a story so ingratiating, so determined to flatter the myths of a virile frontier and the tough love known as mateship, fail to succeed? Even my father, who usually confined himself to the sports pages of the newspaper, read a borrowed copy of *They're a Weird Mob*.

The novel was written from inside Australia, appealing to local foibles; Powell's film snootily looked at the country from outside. His adaptation begins with a survey of indigenous manners. A narrator describes Australia as 'a nation of sportsmen'; on the screen, incompetent hunters stagger through the bush, firing at one another or puncturing beer cans. We eavesdrop on a dispute at a racetrack, conducted in that florid rhetoric Australians employ when affectionately abusing each other. 'They call this English,' groans the narrator.

During the credit titles, a choral anthem warns of the brutal levelling which awaits the educated, fastidious newcomer Nino. As his migrant ship crosses Sydney Harbour to dock at Circular Quay, baritonal voices chant the rugged national creed:

> There are many manly things that must be done,
> A man's gotta prove he's a man,
> Wear your shorts, bare your chest, get a tan, build a barbecue,
> It's a man's country, sweetheart,
> From the chain marks on its ankles right up to its short back and sides.

The Hitler Youth might have marched to such a tune. But, though it hurts me to admit it, this brutish manifesto does sum up the country's values in those cruder and more innocent days. At school we were always being lectured about behaviour which was 'un-Australian'. My desire to spend sports periods in the library was often cited as an example. The shorts and the bared chest remind me unpleasantly of the preening gymnast Chesty Bond, a virile icon who advertised athletic vests in the 1950s. One of Sydney's beaches was named Manly in homage to the strapping natives who were doing manly things there when the ghostly white visitors arrived. My parents had a barbecue on their manicured suburban lawn; it enabled them to pretend they were living in the bush. By 1966 the Beatles had liberated English locks, but the short back and sides was still, according to Powell's testosterone choir, the only haircut in the repertoire of Australian barbers, as compulsory as the shearing which effaces individuality when you join the army or go to prison.

A while ago, Prince Charles reminisced in a speech about the initiation he had to undergo during his term at Geelong Grammar School in Victoria. Like Nino in *They're a Weird Mob*, who smiles gamely while his workmates call him a dago or a drongo and add that he is not fair dinkum, Charles remembered being mocked as a

Pommy bastard. One weekend he was sent on a sixty-mile hike through the bush, which involved climbing a peak called Mount Buggery. Bastardizing and buggery—these were the inductions which awaited the neophyte in the man's country. Charles has no choice but to smile fondly at the folk ways of a country which he no doubt hopes will nominally belong to his family for a while longer. My memories are less forgiving. The hymn in Powell's film, declaimed from the air above that incoming liner, reminds me why I was so anxious to board a ship headed in the opposite direction.

As soon as Nino steps ashore in Sydney, Powell nastily disparages the ideology of brawn. A quick survey of nightclubs in King's Cross shows what has become of women in this masculine land. In a dressing room at Les Girls, a peroxided dolly bird preens and frizzes her beehive in front of a mirror. Then this spurious girl reaches for an electric razor to shave her jaw. In the man's country, the women are also men. Australia's fate, in this view, is inversion. *They're a Weird Mob* begins with a montage of Sydney scenes, projected upside down. 'Australians live down under,' comments the narrator, marvelling that, 'Like flies on the ceiling, they never fall off.' At last the supercilious northerners had found something to admire: we were credited with the sticky-legged agility of domestic pests.

In retrospect, I can understand the indignant patriotism of my parents' generation, though it used to infuriate me. On the mantelpiece in our house, a boomerang lolled. It was made of pine, and had been smoothed and polished in a factory. No one ever tried out its magic by throwing it. But even so, stationary and de-tribalized, it remained a weapon, brandished against the rest of the world. And why not? That lofty other world either snubbed or satirized my parents, and it enticed me to betray them by doing the same. Though all I thought I wanted from their house was the pylon, I found myself unable to bin the boomerang. Maybe one day I will use it to concuss a London burglar.

My parents never left the country; whenever my father fell ill, he blamed that involuntary wartime expedition to New Guinea, and convinced the government that gout, sciatica and indigestion should be classified as war wounds. They did go on holidays to what they superstitiously called 'the other side', meaning the mainland, and brought back beer mats from a poker palace in Surfers' Paradise or a gravy-spattered menu from a Murray River cruise boat. They also kept my dog-eared school atlas, geopolitically obsolete, on top of the television set—but only in order to check up on where the latest, distant, irrelevant wars were happening. Once they made vague plans to visit me in England, but then they thought better of it. My father cited his gouty toe or his turbulent stomach, which might act up overseas.

Of course my world view was the opposite of theirs. Australia seemed vacant, vacuous: it had a 'dead heart', which is how we used to describe the rust-coloured desert which occupies most of our land mass. In those days, no lines of force led to Ayers Rock, that scarlet omphalos at the mid-point of the continent. The arrows my imagination followed were those which tracked the paths of liners, ploughing across oceans and wriggling through the Panama or the Suez Canals to reach countries I considered more real than ours because I had seen pictures of them and read books about them. The postcards I sent home to my parents reported on triumphant sightings of cathedrals and skyscrapers which meant little to them. They tactfully pretended to be interested, and filed the cards in albums. I found these in the house after my mother's death, and burned them. All those journeys were detours, an excuse for running away.

After I left, Australia decolonized itself. Taking stock of my life, I can only see myself as a quaint historical specimen—like my salt-and-pepper shaker, a damaged antique. At school, we were taken to the museum in Hobart to look at the mummified remains of Truganini, allegedly the last of the Tasmanian Aborigines. Perhaps there is a glass case waiting for me somewhere, with a label identifying me as the end of another line: here you see the last expatriate—the final victim of a delusion which made so many people renounce their parentage and repudiate their household gods.

No young Australian will ever again feel as isolated, needy and inadequate as I did. Australia's self-confidence has expanded to fill up the continent; instead of harrying its restive dreamers in exile, it awards them grants to write novels or direct films. It even honours those who have their own dissident definition of the 'man's country'. This year the University of Tasmania hosted an exhibition called 'Material Boys: (un)Zipped', with work by 'nine male textile artists who identify as gay/queer' addressing 'questions of equity: the legal, social and moral status of gay men'. That may seem a heavy burden to lay on textiles. All the same, I felt very old when I read about the show.

As it painstakingly redefines itself, reclaiming its history and implanting a home-grown culture, Australia has come to be envied by a world which once ignored its existence. Dreams now travel in a different direction, gravitating back from the deracinated northern hemisphere to the earthy, enchanted south. Last November in Antwerp, I noticed a shop devoted to the sale of Australian Home-Made Ice Cream. It remained open during a sodden, windy winter, because what it sold was a charm, an elixir, for which there is a demand in all weathers.

In England, the advertising agencies have transformed Australian holidays into existential quests, adventures in self-transformation. One television campaign tells a series of short, therapeutic stories. We see British visitors frolicking or vegging out in the usual Australian resorts. Then a phrase flashes on to the screen: the invidious nickname they were given, before they made this life-changing expedition, by their friends and colleagues back in Britain. A man gleefully bungee jumps off a cliff in the Blue Mountains. He is then identified as Scaredy Cat. Another man fries in sensual stupor on a beach. He used to be known as Workaholic. Someone else plunges into a pool beside a waterfall, allowing a gang of Aboriginal kids to splash him. The caption tags him as Control Freak. A young woman in an empty landscape leans on the windscreen of an open jeep and stares in rapture at a distant revelation. A moment later, we see what she is transfixed by: Ayers Rock. Then comes her label which, with the healing, silent intercession of the outback, she has now lived down. She is, or once was, Chatterbox. Like a Wordsworthian mystic, she has been subdued to quietness by the contemplation of Australian nature, so much more sublimely untamed than the domesticated scenery of the English Lakes.

A single catchphrase unifies all these case histories. First we are given a word to ponder, the name of a rebranded country: Australia. Then comes the slogan designed to catch the clients: 'Discover the other side of yourself'. Not, any longer, the underside, the hindquarters of the globe, as unsightly as a monkey's rump. Australia promises the possibility of acquaintance with your other side, your true but secret self.

'Down under' no longer refers to a topsy-turvydom where men mimic flies; nowadays it designates an erogenous zone. Early in 1999, Channel 4 broadcast a snazzy serial called *Queer as Folk*, about the erotic tribulations of some fictional gay men in Manchester. One of the characters, Vince, a supermarket manager, bags a handsome Australian lover, Cameron. When he shows off his prize in a bar, an effeminate friend flaps an appreciative wrist and drools: 'Oooh, Australia, *niiice*—down under, didgeridoos, all sorts of possibilities!' Cameron is an accountant, owns a house, buys Vince a car, and even tantalizes him with brochures advertising a trip to—of all places—Melbourne. (Poor Vince is not good-looking enough to be presentable in Sydney.) Taking stock of his pallid complexion, his oily hair and his meagre physique, Vince wonders why Cameron bothers with him: 'I mean, I can't be the best shag he's ever had. After all, he's Australian!' That remark, I thought when I heard it, is epochal. In 200 years we have never been paid a finer or a more intimately welcome compliment.

Australians are currently on top; the former colonials do the colonizing, in bed and out of it. Subscribing to English comics when I was at school, I had to wait two or three agonizing months while each issue dawdled across the water from London. Christmas numbers, with luck, turned up at Easter. Ours was an unsynchronized, woefully belated life. In fact we were ahead, not behind; we got the sun before those laggard countries to the north. Australia's priority, its claim to the first and freshest light, was officially recognized last New Year's Eve. The twenty-first century, after a swift warm-up in New Zealand, began in Sydney.

I watched Sydney celebrating midnight on television while I ate my lunch in Portugal. The span of the harbour bridge wore a neon smile, and boomerangs scudded harmlessly through the air leaving vapour trails of colour behind them. Cascades streamed down the sky, and flowers made of fire exploded into bloom. I remembered a visit I made a few months before to the old observatory on a bluff beside the harbour bridge. One of the displays narrates an ochre-coloured Genesis, attributing the moulding of the earth to the sun, Jingdu, rather than the grim and jealous Christian God. Another room charts Captain Cook's trip to the southern hemisphere to witness the transit of Venus in 1769. Australia, according to astronomers, is the best place for viewing Magellanic clouds. Look up on an average night, and you see straight into the galactic centre, while beneath your feet is the oldest, newest continent. On New Year's Eve, the solar system seemed to be still in riotous, creative eruption above the blue-black water of the harbour.

While galaxies combust and dilate in the sky, the globe we cling to is forever being redesigned. The Surrealists published an idiosyncratic world map in 1929, enlarging or dwarfing terrain in accordance with their aesthetic principles. The area beneath the equator was for them subliminal and savage, like the human body below the waistline; their cartography favoured places with luridly irrational histories. New Zealand was expanded, because it had earthquakes and cannibals. Easter Island, with its stone totems, grew as big as South America. Australia, boringly British, dwindled to the size of the New Hebrides. If this subjective map were redrawn today, Australia would have to be inflated, pushing aside all those upstart Pacific islands. Nicknamed Oz, and situated as far from flat-minded, monochrome Kansas as you can get, it has become a magnet for the fantasies of the upper hemisphere. A German book published in 1997 even called Australia *Heimat der Träume*. The dreams are those of the Aborigines: a globalized world has come to venerate this stubbornly unassimilated race and its guarded wisdom.

Australia's new popularity gratifies but also alarms me. The blithely hospitable country has welcomed a new race of colonizers who do not want to annex its land but to appropriate the gods interred in its landscape. I find myself resenting these adoptive, part-time Australians—perversely, I suppose, since why shouldn't they covet the patrimony I discarded when I left? Nevertheless, I think that their motives are suspect, their methods slipshod.

Bruce Chatwin, for instance, went to Central Australia looking for 'the most abstract desert I could find anywhere'. The desert is only abstract—featureless, a red blank—if you fail to look at it closely. When you get to know it, you find that it seethes with life, with sunken watercourses and prickly but edible plants. Chatwin never saw beyond the pre-imagined abstraction. In *The Songlines*, he simply unpacked the baggage of preconceptions he brought with him. As a boy, he leafed through a book illustrated with pictures of koalas, kookaburras and kangaroos, dingos and Tasmanian devils. A great-aunt warned him that Australians were Upside-downers. When he asked how come they didn't fall off the earth, she credited gravity, rather than likening them to flies. There is something plaintively British in the young Chatwin's reverie about the continent's sacred name: 'I never heard the word "Australia" without calling to mind the fumes of the eucalyptus inhaler and an incessant red country populated by sheep.' The eucalyptus inhaler is a poignant symptom of that pinched and stuffy northern-hemisphere malady, sinusitis. The other image is simply wrong. Australia does indeed have many woolly citizens, but they need to graze, so that part of the country where they congregate is green, not red. More at home in literary pastoral than on a farm, Chatwin called the character who guides him through the lineal maze of aboriginal lore Arkady, wishfully transforming Australia into an idyllic English Arcadia.

A brisk collector of ideas and countries, Chatwin always had his eye on the next stop. When Murray Bail took him to the Blue Mountains, he glanced at the wooded gulf as if clicking a camera, then announced: 'This time next week I'll be at the base camp of Everest.' Salman Rushdie, who travelled to the Northern Territory with Chatwin after a publicity junket to the Adelaide Writers' Festival, made a virtue out of his high-speed passage through the region. 'Shanghai! Montevideo! Alice Springs!' sighs the narrator of Rushdie's *The Moor's Last Sigh*. 'Do you know that places only yield up their secrets, their most profound mysteries, to those who are just passing through?' The rhetorical question anticipates our agreement, but this is an instamatic creed, the self-delusion of an over-scheduled tourist. Rushdie arranges a facile global reunion of mythologies at the end of his novel, equating 'Australia's ancestors, the Wandjina, [who] take their ease underground', with Arthur asleep in Avalon, Barbarossa in his cave, Finn MacCool slumbering in the Irish hills, and Walt Disney's Sleeping Beauty in her glass coffin. Such multinational mergers only work if you blur the details. For the record, Wandjinas—after imprinting a trace of themselves on rock—do not go to ground but dissolve into clouds.

Chatwin, a chatterbox who was not silenced by the desert, interrogated the Aborigines, unable to comprehend the occult nature of their society. Rushdie similarly hints at spoliation when he comments on the way places like Alice Springs 'yield up their secrets'. A yield is a profit, forcibly tugged from the earth. Colonizers used to want Australia's minerals or its primary produce. Now, employing the same violent and negligent methods of extraction, they have come back to plunder its myths. Rushdie could not be more wrong about Alice Springs, which protects its secrets with sullen ferocity. A few years ago, a drunk eyeballed me in the main street, just off the desiccated river bed where the Aborigines gather. He must have smelt the blood of an alien, because he barked: 'Where the fuck have you come up from, mate?' To get to Alice Springs, you have to come up from somewhere further south; for local chauvinists, the phrase implies that the new arrivals have undergone a promotion, which not all of them deserve. I didn't know what to answer. Was I up from Hobart, or down from London? Instead of replying, I dodged out of the way, and left him to berate a Japanese couple.

Imperialism today conducts its assault with cameras, not gunboats; annexation is achieved by framing and capturing an image, which stills life as suddenly as a bullet. In *Until the End of the World*, the apocalyptic road movie filmed by Wim Wenders in the Australian outback, some Aborigines object to the video contraptions—substitutes for seeing—which a gaggle of New Age tourists have trained on them. 'You think we want you tramping through our dreamings with your fancy cameras?' their leader demands. Their protest comes too late. Another small fable appeared on British television during 1999. It began with a gliding overhead view of the Queensland coast—fuzzy mangrove swamps and white, untrodden beaches—accompanied by the lulling monotone of a didgeridoo. A somnolent, smiling face then appeared. After that, words slid across the screen, transforming the images into a sales pitch. The first phrase announced that: 'The average person dreams only two hours per night,' then added a qualification—'except in Qantas Business Class.' Finally, the product responsible for the beatific expression of the businessman was identified: 'The Qantas Dreamtime Seat', a recliner which allegedly lowers you into the collective unconsciousness when you press a lever. A well-fed snooze while cruising between international engagements is hardly what the Aborigines mean by Dreamtime. And come to think of it, you do not often see tribal people in Business Class on Qantas.

Nevertheless, the dream's appeal is contagious. In London in 1996 I went to a chamber music concert at the Wigmore Hall. The Brodsky Quartet—whose members, despite the Russian-sounding name of their group, are dumpy Mancunians—accompanied a favourite singer of mine, the Swedish mezzo-soprano Anne Sofie von Otter. To my delight, the concert included a piece the quartet had commissioned from Peter Sculthorpe, who was born in Tasmania. Its title, stroking the same buzzword used by Qantas, was 'Island Dreaming'. The classical string players did their best to reproduce the whining and droning of Aboriginal instruments, while von Otter, an arctic blonde, vocalized a tribal incantation and declaimed a refrain about rowing out to the edge of a tropical reef (though she looked as if she might have been more at home ice-skating on a frozen lake).

When I consulted the programme, I found that the words she sang supposedly came from 'the Tallest Straight Islands north of Australia'. I speculated briefly about where these tall, straight islands might be, and what they looked like—presumably they resembled von Otter, who is a six-footer with the posture of a birch tree and spikily upright hair. Then I realized that Tallest Straight was a mishearing of Torres Strait, just off Cape York at the conical tip of Queensland. Someone at the Wigmore Hall was dozing, rather than dreaming. Perhaps the writer of the programme notes had telephoned Sculthorpe in Sydney on a crackly line and was befuddled by his accent. I would not have been surprised to read that he was born in Tossmania.

Growing up, I cherished the idea of Sculthorpe, even though I knew little of his music: it seemed important that there should be such a thing as a Tasmanian composer. Our world was harsh, raw, only too recently and precariously settled. Gusts of wind regularly blew the roofs off houses in the suburb where I lived. One summer the southern half of the state was charred by a bush fire. A friend of mine remembers lying in the road beneath a wet blanket with her mother, waiting for the flames to pass over them. Her mother told her not to squeal if her skin got singed. Artists, surely, could help to tame this volatile, combustible place, like Orpheus pacifying wild beasts with his lute. There is magic in the act of representation, whether it uses notes or words or lines and colours. Reality becomes more habitable with the help of fiction.

In the early Sixties, Sculthorpe set a portion of my adolescent life to music—at least I thought until very recently that he had done so. At the age of thirteen, I had a part in a children's film called *They Found a Cave*. With a Blytonesque gang of siblings I pretended to go bush, running away from home to be a cave-dweller. I did not have far to go, since the cave, made of plaster, was installed in a shed just across the highway from my parents' house. In one way, the pretence was in deadly earnest: I played a little English boy, evacuated to Tasmania during the Blitz. I did not have to bother apeing the accent, since my voice was dubbed by a menopausal contralto. Sculthorpe, who had just returned to Tasmania after studying at Oxford, composed a score for the film, with a jaunty waltz which Larry Adler, gracing us with a little international credibility, played on his harmonica. The tune stuck in my memory, encapsulating the mood of the film and of my Tasmanian boyhood: bucolic, chirpy, yet somehow bereft, going round in circles before it trailed away into depression.

A while ago in Sydney I found a compact disc of Sculthorpe's music, and was startled to hear the waltz again—except that it turned out to have nothing to do with Tasmania, or with me. Its proper title is 'Left Bank Waltz', and when Sculthorpe first composed it in 1958 he was evoking the atmosphere of a Paris café. Three years later, he simply recycled it for the film, and replaced the swooning strings with a harmonica. It was some consolation to learn that, in 1958, Sculthorpe had never been on the left bank of the Seine. This makes the waltz, after all, a piece of inadvertently Australian music: an effort to imagine, or eavesdrop on, an unattainable elsewhere.

That other, older world is now within easy reach. But when we leave home, we still tend to wear cultural camouflage. Only the costumes have changed: rather than hoping to be mistaken for browner and lankier Brits, we are more likely to present ourselves as ersatz Americans. For a few Australians, it has turned out to be a profitable imposture: Nicole Kidman transformed herself into a Jamesian heiress for *The Portrait of a Lady*, Judy Davis duplicated the tics and jitters of a Manhattan neurotic in *Celebrity*. Guy Pearce and Russell Crowe slipped effortlessly into the skins of two morally abraded cops in *LA Confidential*. We have not entirely dismantled McAuley's 'land of similes', but now when searching for similitudes, America is where we find them.

Perhaps my own estrangement was a symptom of a more general, abiding sense of displacement. I could not believe that I belonged in Australia, and Australia still has difficulty acknowledging that it belongs in south-east Asia. Joan Sutherland—a monarchist who lives in Switzerland, which despite being a republic has convenient tax laws—made a maladroit contribution to the recent debate about constitutional change. She indignantly remembered that, when she last renewed her Australian passport at the post office in Sydney, she had to submit to interrogation by a Chinese person! It did not occur to her that the postal employee, though of Chinese extraction, might be a native Australian and a lifelong resident. Anglo-Australia has always lived in fear of Asian usurpation: hence the happy collusion with the Americans in Vietnam. Do the 'white races', as Hoppé called them, still feel deracinated in Australia, bewildered by the country's need to befriend Indonesia and Malaysia? It remains advisable to cultivate an extra identity, to show how readily you can be re-assimilated by the wider, whiter, richer world.

Even the landscape has got in on the act. Australia itself regularly impersonates America; it is cheaper than the original. In the dopey television series *Flipper*, Queensland pretends to be Florida, with a few indigenous beach boys hired to play foreigners in their own country. *Baywatch*, that ludicrous and lubricious carnival of flesh, dressed up a Sydney beach as Malibu for a few seasons, then during 1999 announced a move to Avalon on the Gold Coast (though these negotiations were merely a ploy to extort a better deal from Hawaii). Rupert Murdoch, himself an Americanized Australian, has expelled the prize steers, home-made pies and wood-chopping champions from the agricultural showgrounds in Sydney and opened a film studio there. The production which inaugurated the premises was *The Matrix*, a parable directed by the Wachowski brothers about a future when the actual world will be supplanted by deluding images, in which Sydney plays a virtual Chicago. (Only at the very end, when we glimpse the span of the harbour bridge for a few seconds between blocks, is the hoax obliquely admitted to.)

This traffic in deceptive, ingratiating images is conducted by those who should know better. 'New Worlds from Old', a comparative exhibition of nineteenth-century Australian and American landscape paintings, opened in Canberra in 1998 and travelled to Washington the following year. The curator Patrick McCaughey wrote an essay on 'The American-Australian Experience' for the catalogue: note that hybridising hyphen, and note also the order in which the countries are named. McCaughey's piece is a tourist promotion in the guise of art history, and it entices mid-Westerners to visit Australia by assuring them that what they will find there is the America of the 1950s. Encouraging a side trip to Melbourne, he promises that 'the streets are safe and clean' and 'well-maintained parkland provides a...garden-like experience'. The suburbs of Carlton and Fitzroy can be sampled with impunity, because 'the older, inner-city residential areas have been almost universally gentrified', while 'the impoverished and dangerous ghetto is uncommon'. All this, and no need to struggle with a foreign language or an unfamiliar currency! I only hope that those retirees with their synthetic pastels and their expensive video cameras don't stray into stewing Brunswick, or the Aboriginal district of Redfern in Sydney.

Diverging into pathos, McCaughey confesses the longing of Australian artists and writers 'to be recognized in America', and hopes that 'the opening of the American mind' might occur as a result of his exhibition. That mind, however, remains clamped resolutely shut. It embarrassed me to read the review of 'New Worlds from Old' in the *Sydney Morning Herald*, headlined 'Big Brother is Watching Us'. The article quoted Orwell's motto without taking heed of its warning. In *Nineteen Eighty-four*, freedom, autonomy and privacy involve escaping the totalitarian scrutiny of Big Brother. In the Sydney paper, the baleful phrase has become a cry of glee and gratification that our existence has been noticed and validated overseas.

Australia is not a poor man's America. Its dreams are different—not epics of belligerent triumph, mechanically subjugating the wilderness, but elegies which stoically accept man's necessary defeat by inimical nature. Americans are fanatical optimists, while Australians are laconically, humorously tragic. The American dream deludingly promises to deliver whatever you wish for, and when it fails to do so, the result is disillusionment, fury, a craving for revenge. The dreaming of the Australian Aborigines has nothing to do with fame and riches, swimming pools and high rises; it is a reverie, a morose reminder of our earthly mortality.

I worry about an Australia which is so keen to manoeuvre itself nearer to America. As a boy, I often dismayed myself by measuring the oceans in my atlas with a ruler. Inches, when you checked the scale, translated into thousands of miles. How long would it take to get across the Pacific, or over the Indian Ocean and then up the Atlantic? And how inconceivably much would the journey cost? Whenever would I be old enough to go? Distance has now been abolished by jet planes, satellites, and the instant electronic gossip of computers. But at the same time we have lost the sense of difference. Perhaps, after all, we should be grateful for isolation, our protective cordon.

Even though the oceans have been abridged by air travel, a trip to Australia is an ordeal—and so it should be, because your arrival must be earned. Monsoons over India, thunderstorms around Singapore, the inevitable jolting above the equator. The insomniac vigil as the plane bores on. The dumbfounding thought of the Pacific, with no land underneath for 6,000 miles if you fly from Los Angeles. On the Asian route, the five hours spent diagonally travelling across the desert after you reach the north-western corner of Australia. Touching down at last, I even used to relish the pause for purgation before you were allowed to disembark. Public-health officials in shorts would board the plane and march up the aisles, grinning as they sprayed you with aerosol cans. (Nowadays the disinfection happens more discreetly, while you're in transit.) Even after surviving the discomforts of the journey and its meteorological upsets, you still had to be cleansed before you stepped out to greet the dazing light.

D. H. Lawrence saw the country as an open door, framing blueness. 'You just walk out of the world,' he said, 'and into Australia.'

To describe my own life, I have to rewrite the sentence. I walked out of Australia into the world, and impolitely slammed the door as I left.

On that last trip to Hobart, I felt like a ghost, haunting only myself. But I must have been visible, because when I got to my parents' house, someone challenged me. The woman next door glared suspiciously through a window, then came out to growl at me. 'Looking for someone?' she demanded.

'No,' I said, though the correct answer would have been, 'Myself.' Why should I seek her authorization? I had lived in the house for twenty years; she moved in a few weeks ago. One of my cousins had told me about her. She received visits from a man in a dented truck, who virilely slammed the doors of his vehicle on arrival. She also occasionally helped herself to the pile of firewood my mother had bought for a winter she did not live through.

Stepping sideways over a low fence, she cut me off. 'There's no one home,' she said, and crossed her arms over her robust chest.

'I know. It's my mother's house,' I said. It did not occur to me to say it was mine.

I waited for her to tell me that my mother was dead. Instead she unclenched her arms and backed off, but kept me under surveillance. There she was, whenever I carried out any rubbish, on duty behind a ragged curtain. I suppose it was my sense of guilt that made me think she looked reproachful.

Inside the house, I felt even guiltier as I took inventory of my inheritance. 'It'll all be yours when I go,' my mother used to say to me during her decade as a widow. Now it all was, and I had no use for it. Plates whose floral patterns had been scrubbed off, spoons with tarnished apostles at their tips, a clock which had ticked itself to a stop: they went to the tip, carted off after I left. Memories proved less easy to dispose of. Leaning on a shelf was a photograph of me with my mother on my last visit, just a few months before. We were gamely grinning in the garden which her health had forced her to neglect. But only half of the photograph remained: my mother, with a pair of scissors gripped at a jagged angle in her arthritic hands, must have cut herself out of it. Another tidy preparation for her exit, along with the advance payment for her funeral?

I spared myself from having to look through the drawers of clothes. But in the middle of the day, I opened the packet containing my father's letters. The household objects, so useless and so indestructible, oppressed me. I wanted to hear a voice, even if it was silent. The letters, smelling of scent and face powder, brought my mother back to life, too. But the voice which resounded from them was my father's, salty and sardonic. Homesick in New Guinea, he jeered at an enemy he called the Nip, and moaned about the itchy, drenching tropics. My mother, a nurse in Hobart, relayed a complaint by one of his brothers: when they celebrated victory over the Japanese, there was plenty of beer but no glasses. 'Tell Bill he should have used the thunder mug,' wrote my father. 'Hope you know what I mean.' A few weeks later, still awaiting repatriation, he reported on a night at the pictures: 'When they put "God Save the King" on the screen, the boys all sung out "What about Joe?" meaning Stalin.'

At the end of another letter, before the compulsory cuddles and the rows of crosses, he sighed, 'I will be quite happy to spend the rest of my life in good old Tassie.' I remembered a remark he made in this very room during one of my first trips back from England. 'You don't have to live over there, you know,' he told me. Oh yes I do, I thought. Couldn't he see that it was not an exile or a penitential foreign posting, like the weeks he spent in New Guinea? He was saying, of course, that I was still welcome in his house. I ignored the shy, indirect invitation.

The letters chronicled his impatience as successive troopships sailed away without him. Eventually he volunteered for a civilian job which was guaranteed to get him out of the jungle: builders and painters went back first, since Australia needed suburbs to house the demobbed soldiers who were randily queuing to marry their sweethearts. A telegram announced his arrival in Sydney, another his return from there to Hobart. Home he came to marry my mother, to have a child, to paint his brand-new house and live in it for the next forty years. His letters stopped when he began to live happily—or happily enough—ever after. There was no further need to write: writing is a compensation for absence, or for loss. During the final days of separation, he rejoiced at the prospect of the future he and my mother were going to share. Unfortunately for them, that future contained me, and my rejection of their world. And unfortunately for me, this rejection was followed by a remorseful bid for acceptance, probably too late.

At the end of the day, I fiddled clumsily as I locked the back door. My cousin had found the key in my mother's purse; its stem was fragile, its teeth worn, and I had no time to learn the knack of using it. I left the roof to rust and the weeds to grow. The entire suburb had outlived its usefulness, like a Pompeii of weatherboard and corrugated iron. Mount Wellington confronted me as grumpily as ever. A good thing that its supply of lava long ago ran dry.

The nosy neighbour came out to say 'See yer then,' though both of us knew that would never happen. I took away with me a china pylon, a pine boomerang, and a lifetime of regrets. □

SHORTLISTED FOR THE 1999
WHITBREAD FIRST NOVEL AWARD

'This book is alight with wonder.'
Time Out

'The finest debut I've read in years.'
The Times

The Great Ideas is a gripping mystery like no other, and a quest for knowledge that will delight anyone with an enquiring mind.

FOURTH ESTATE

GRANTA

AQUIFER

Tim Winton

Tim Winton

One evening not long ago I stirred from a television stupor at the sound of a familiar street name and saw a police forensic team in waders carry bones from the edge of a lake. Four femurs and a skull, to be precise. The view widened and I saw a shabby clique of melaleucas and knew exactly where it was that this macabre discovery had taken place. Through the open window I smelt dead lupin and for a long time forgot my age. Life moves on, people say, but I doubt that. Moves in, more like it.

Cast adrift again from middle age, I lay awake all night and travelled in loops and ellipses while an old song from school rang in my head.

I love her far horizons,
I love her jewelled sea,
Her beauty and her terror,
The wide brown land for me.

Before dawn and without explanation, I rose, made myself coffee and began the long drive back to where I come from.

The battlers' blocks, that's what they called the meagre grid of limestone streets of my childhood. Suburban lots scoured from bush land for an outpost of progress so that emigrants from Holland, England and the Balkans and freckly types like us, barely a generation off the farm, could participate in the Antipodean prize of home ownership. Our street wound down a long gully that gave on to a swamp. A few fences away the grey haze of banksia scrub and tuart trees resumed with its hiss of cicadas and crow song. Houses were of three basic designs and randomly jumbled along the way to lend an air of natural progression rather than reveal the entire suburb's origins in the smoky, fly-buzzing office of some bored government architect. But our houses were new; no one had ever lived in them before. They were as fresh as we imagined the country itself to be.

As they moved in people planted buffalo grass and roses and put in rubber trees which brought havoc to the septics a decade later. From high on the ridge the city could be seen forming itself into a spearhead. It was coming our way and it travelled inexorably but honestly in straight lines. The bush rolled and twisted like an unmade bed. It was, in the beginning, only a fence away.

Aquifer

The men of our street went to work and left the driveways empty. They came home from the city tired, often silent. They scattered blood and bone on their garden beds and retired to their sheds. All day the women of the street cleaned and cooked and moved sprinklers around the garden to keep things alive. Late in the morning the baker arrived in his van, red-cheeked from civilization, and after him the man with the veggie truck. At the sound of their bells kids spilled out into the dusty street and their mothers emerged in housecoats and pedal pushers with rollers in their hair. Everyone was working class, even the Aborigines around the corner whose name was Jones, though it seemed that these were Joneses who didn't need much keeping up with. We were new. It was all new.

At night when I was a baby my parents went walking to get me to sleep and while they were out they foraged for building materials in the streets beyond where raw sandy lots lay pegged out between brickies' sheds and piles of rough-sawn jarrah.

The old man built a retaining wall from bricks he loaded into the pram that first summer. A lot of sheds went up quickly in our street. All those jarrah planks, all that asbestos sheeting, those bags of Portland cement. It was all taxpayers' property anyway. Great evening strollers, the locals.

I grew up in a boxy double brick house with roses and a letter box, like anyone else. My parents were always struggling to get me inside something, into shirts and shoes, inside the fence, the neighbourhood, the house, out of the sun or the rain, out of the world itself it often seemed to me. I climbed the jacaranda and played with the kids across the street and came in ghosted with limestone dust. I sat on the fence and stared at the noisy blue bush and in time I was allowed to roam there.

When the road crew arrived and the lumpy limestone was tarred the street seemed subdued. The easterly wind was no longer chalky. In July and August when it finally rained the water ran down the hill towards the reedy recess of the swamp. Down the way a little from our place, outside the Dutchies' house with its window full of ornaments, a broad puddle formed and drew small children to its ochre sheen. The swamp was where we wanted to be, down there where the melaleucas seemed to stumble and the ducks skated, but our parents forbade it; they talked of quicksand and tiger snakes, wild roots and submerged logs and we made do with the winter puddle outside the van Gelders'. I remember my mother standing exasperated in the rain with the brolly over her head at dusk while I frog-kicked around in my speedos.

Eventually the road crew returned to put a drain in and my puddle became less impressive. Then a red telephone box appeared beside it. I suppose I was five or six when I learned to go in and stand on tiptoe to reach up and dial 1194 to hear a man with a BBC voice announce the exact time. I did that for years, alone and in company, listening to the authority in the man's voice. He sounded like he knew what he was on about, that at the stroke it would indeed be the time he said it was. It was a delicious thing to know, that at any moment of the day, when adults weren't about, you could dial yourself something worth knowing, something irrefutable, and not need to pay.

When I was old enough I walked to school with the ragged column that worked its way up the hill for the mile or so it took. From high ground you could see the city and the real suburbs in the distance. You could even smell the sea. In the afternoons the blue bush plain was hazy with smoke and the dust churned up by bulldozers. On winter nights great bonfires of trees scraped into windrows flickered in the sky above the yard. Beyond the splintery fence cicadas and birds whirred. Now and then the hard laughter of ducks washed up the street; they sounded like mechanical clowns in a sideshow. When summer came and the windows lay open all night the noise of frogs and crickets and mosquitoes pressed in as though the swamp had swelled in the dark.

The smallest of us talked about the swamp. Down at the turnaround where the lupins took over, we climbed the peppermint to look out across that wild expanse, but for the longest time we didn't dare go further.

Bruno the Yugo went to the swamp. He had a flat head and he was twelve. He ranged down through the reeds until dark, even though his oldies flogged him for it. Across from Bruno lived the Mannerings. They were Poms with moany Midlands accents. I could never tell when they were happy. Their house smelt of fag smoke and kero and they didn't like open windows. George the father had very long feet. He wore socks and plastic sandals. His son Alan waited for me after school some days to walk behind me and nudge me wordlessly with a knuckle for the full mile. He was twelve and scared of Bruno the Yugo. I never knew why he picked me from all the kids in our street. He never said a thing, just poked and prodded and shoved until we came down the hill to within sight of our homes. He was tall and fair, Alan Mannering, and though I dreaded him I don't think I ever hated him. When he spoke to someone else beyond me his voice was soft and full of menace, his accent broadly local as my own. Some days he threw his schoolbag up on to the veranda of his place and headed on down to the swamp without even stopping in and I watched him go in relief and envy. Mostly I played with the Box kids across the road. There were seven or eight of them. They were Catholics and most of them wet the bed though it was hard to say which ones because they all had the same ammonia and milk smell. I liked them, though they fought and cried a lot. We slipped through the bush together where there were no straight lines. Beyond the fence there were snarls and matted tangles. We hid behind grass trees and twisted logs and gathered burrs in our shirts and seeds in our hair. Eventually the Boxes began to slip off to the swamp. I always pulled up short, though, and went back to dial 1194 for reassurance.

Another Pom moved in next door. I saw him digging and stood to watch, my shadow the only greeting. I watched him dig until only his balding head showed. He winked and pointed down until I shuffled over to the lip and saw the damp earth beneath my sandals.

'The water table,' he said in a chirpy accent, 'it's high here, see. Half these fence posts are in it, you know.'

The rank, dark stink of blood and bone rose up from his side of the fence. I climbed back over the fence doubtfully.

'Looks dry this country, it does, but underground there's water. Caves of it. Drilling, that's what this country needs.'

I went indoors.

Someone hung a snake from our jacaranda out front. It was a dugite, headless and oozing. My mother went spare.

Across the road one night, Mr Box left his kids asleep in the Holden and went indoors with his wife. It was for a moment's peace, my oldies said but a moment was all they had. The station wagon rolled across the road, bulldozed the letter box and mowed down our roses.

George Mannering with the long feet mowed his buffalo grass every week with a push mower. He liked grass; it was the one thing he'd not had in England though he reminded us that English grass was finer. My mother rolled her eyes. George Mannering bought a Victa power mower and I stood out front to watch his first cut. I was there when two-year-old Charlie lurched up between his father's legs and lost some toes in a bright pink blur. All the way back inside to my room I heard his voice above the whine of the two-stroke which sputtered alone out there until the ambulance came.

I forget how old I was when I gave in and went to the swamp. It felt bad to be cheating on my parents but the wild beyond the fences and the lawns and sprinklers was too much for me. By this time I was beginning to have second thoughts about the 1194 man. My parents bought a kitchen clock which seemed to cheat with time. A minute was longer some days than others. An hour beyond the fence travelled differently across your skin compared with an hour of television. I felt time turn off. Time wasn't straight and neither was the man with the BBC voice. I discovered that you could say anything you liked to him, shocking things you'd only say to prove a point, and the man never said a thing except declare the plodding time. I surrendered to the swamp without warning. Every wrinkle, every hollow in the landscape led to the hissing maze down there. It was December, I remember. I got off my bike and stepped down into dried lupin like a man striding through a crowd. Seed pods rattled behind me. A black swan rose from the water. I went on until the ground hardened with moisture and then went spongy with saturation. Scaly paperbarks keeled away in trains of black shadow. Reeds bristled like venetian blinds in the breeze. Black water bled from the ground with a linoleum gleam.

From the water's edge you couldn't even see our street. The crowns of tuart trees were all I saw those early years before jacarandas, flame trees, and cape lilacs found their way to water and rose from yards like flags. I found eggs in the reeds, skinks in a fallen log, a bluetongue lizard jawing at me with its hard scales shining amidst the sighing wild oats. I sat in the hot shade of a melaleuca in a daze.

After that I went back alone or in the company of the Box kids or even Bruno. We dug hideouts and lit fires, came upon snakes real and imagined. I trekked to the swamp's farthest limits where the market gardens began. Italian men in ragged hats worked on sprinklers, lifted melons, turned the black earth. Water rose in rainbows across their land. I went home before dark amazed that my parents still believed me when I swore solemnly that I hadn't been down the swamp.

At school I learned about the wide brown land, the dry country. Summer after summer we recited the imperatives of water conservation. Sprinklers were banned in daylight hours and our parents watered glumly by hand.

One summer my mother announced that she'd come upon some Cape Coloureds at the nearest market garden. I thought she meant poultry of some kind. I met them on my own one day and was confused by their accents. We threw a ball for a while, two girls and me. Their skin had a mildness about it. They didn't seem as angry as the Joneses. The Joneses were dark and loud. Even their laughter seemed angry. I never had much to do with any of them. I rode past their house careful not to provoke them. They gave my little brother a hiding once. I never knew why. His nose swelled like a turnip and he nursed this grievance for the rest of his life. It made his mind up about them, he said. I kept clear. I already had Alan Mannering to worry about.

The Joneses never went near the swamp. I heard they were frightened of the dark. Their dad worked in a mine. Bruno said vile things to them and bolted into the swamp for sanctuary. It was his favourite game the year Americans went to the moon.

One sunny winter day I sat in a hummock of soft weeds to stare at the tadpoles I had in my coffee jar. Billy Box said we all begin as tadpoles, that the Pope didn't want us to waste even one of them. I fell asleep pondering this queer assertion and when I woke Alan Mannering stood over me, his face without expression. I said nothing. He looked around for a moment before pulling his dick out of his shorts and pissing over me. He didn't wet me; he pissed around me in a huge circle. I saw sunlight in his pale stream and lay still lest I disturb his aim. When he was finished he reeled himself back into his shorts and walked off. I emptied my tadpoles back into the lake.

What did he want? What did he ever want from me?

I was ten when people started dumping cars down the swamp. Wrecks would just appear, driven in the back way from behind the market gardens, stripped or burned, left near the water on soft ground where the dirt tracks gave out.

Alan Mannering was the first to hack the roof off a car and use it upturned as a canoe. That's what kids said, though Bruno claimed it was his own idea.

I was with half a dozen Box kids when I saw Alan and Bruno out on the lake a hundred yards apart sculling along with fence pickets. Those Box kids crowded against me, straining, big and small, to see. I can still remember the smell of them pressed in like that, their scent of warm milk and wet sheets. The two bigger boys drifted in silhouette out on the ruffled water. One of the Boxes went back for their old man's axe and we went to work on the scorched remains of an old F. J. Holden with nasty green upholstery. One of them came upon a used condom. The entire Box posse was horrified. I had no idea what it was and figured (correctly as it turned out) that you needed to be a Catholic to understand. Before dark we had our roof on the water. We kept close to shore and quickly discovered that two passengers was all it took. Some Boxes went home wet. I suppose nobody noticed.

Next day was Saturday. I got down to the swamp early in order to have the raft to myself for a while and had only pulled it from its nest of reeds when Alan Mannering appeared beside me. He never said a word. I actually cannot remember that boy ever uttering a word meant for me, but I don't trust myself on this. He lived over the road for ten years. He all but walked me home from school for five of those, poking me from behind, sometimes peppering my calves with gravel. I was in his house once, I remember the airless indoor smell. But he never spoke to me at any time.

Alan Mannering lifted the jarrah picket he'd ripped from someone's fence and pressed the point of it into my chest. I tried to bat it away but he managed to twist it into my shirt and catch the flesh beneath so that I yielded a few steps. He stepped toward me casually, his downy legs graceful.

'You're shit,' I said, surprising myself.

Alan Mannering smiled. I saw cavities in his teeth and a hot rush of gratitude burned my cheeks, my fingertips. Somehow the glimpse of his teeth made it bearable to see him drag our F. J. Holden roof to the water and pole out into the shimmering distance without even a growl of triumph, let alone a word. I lifted my T-shirt to inspect the little graze on my chest and when I looked up again he was in trouble.

When he went down, sliding sideways like a banking aircraft out there in the ruffled shimmer of the swamp's eye, I really didn't think that my smug feeling, my satisfied pity about his English teeth had caused the capsize. He didn't come up. I never even hated him, though I'd never called anyone shit before or since. After the water settled back and shook itself smooth again like hung washing, there wasn't a movement. No sign.

I went home and said nothing.

Police dragged the swamp, found the car roof but no body. Across the road the Mannerings' lawn grew long and cries louder than any mower drifted over day and night.

That Christmas we drove the Falcon across the Nullabor Plain to visit the Eastern States which is what we still call the remainder of Australia. The old man sealed the doors with masking tape and the four of us sat for days breathing white dust. The limestone road was marked only with blown tyres and blown roos. Near the border we stopped at the great blowhole that runs all the way to the distant sea. Its rising gorge made me queasy. I thought of things sucked in, of all that surging, sucking water beneath the crust of the wide brown land.

Back home, though they did not find his body, I knew that Alan Mannering was in the swamp. I thought of him silent, fair, awful, encased in the black cake mix of sediment down there.

The next year, come winter, the night air was musky with smoke and sparks hung in the sky like eyes. Bulldozers towing great chains and steel balls mowed down tuart trees and banksias.

I learned to spell aquifer.

Three doors up, Wally Burniston came home drunk night after night. His wife Beryl locked him out and if he couldn't smash his way in he lay bawling on the veranda until he passed out. Some school mornings I passed his place and saw him lying there beside the delivered milk, his greasy rocker's haircut awry, his mouth open, shoes gone.

New streets appeared even while the bush burned. I listened to the man from 1194 in the phone box that stank of cigarettes and knew that he was making the time up as he went along.

I saw the rainbow mist of the market-garden sprinklers and felt uneasy. I thought of Alan Mannering in that mist. He'd have been liquid long ago. I was eleven now, I knew this sort of thing.

As our neighbourhood became a suburb, and the bush was heaved back even further on itself, there was talk of using the swamp for landfill, making it a dump so that in time it could be reclaimed. But the market gardeners were furious. Their water came from the swamp, after all. Water was no longer cheap.

The van Gelders divorced. Wally Burniston was taken somewhere, I never found out where. One Sunday afternoon I found myself in the van Gelders' backyard scrounging for a companion when I came upon Mrs van Gelder at the back step. She had kohl around her eyes and a haircut that made her look like Cleopatra as played by Elizabeth Taylor and her short dress showed legs all the way up to her dark panties. She raised her chin at me, tapped ash from her cigarette, narrowed her eyes against the smoke that rose from her lips. I coasted near her on my bike preparing half-heartedly to ask where her son might be but she smiled and stopped me asking. From where I sat on my old chopper I saw the alarming shadow between her breasts and her smile broadened. Half her buttons were undone. She seemed sleepy. I stood against the pedals, preparing to take off, when she reached down and pulled out a breast. Its nipple was startling brown and it wore a green vein down its fuselage like a fuel line. I popped an involuntary wheelstand as I hurtled back out into the street. The slipstream of a car tugged at my shirt and tyres bawled on the fresh bitumen as someone braked and stalled. A woman began to cry. People came into the street. I swooped through them and coasted down our driveway, trembling, and hid in the shed. Months later I woke from a dream in which Mrs van Gelder leaned before me so that her cleavage showed and I stared but did not touch as dark water slurped against the plump banks of her flesh. I sat up in bed wet as a Catholic.

From one summer to the next water restrictions grew more drastic and people in our neighbourhood began to sink bores to get free unlimited groundwater. The Englishman next door was the first and then everyone drilled and I thought of Alan Mannering raining silently down upon the lawns of our street. I thought of him in lettuce and tomatoes, on our roses. Like blood and bone. I considered him bearing mosquito larvae—even being in mosquito larvae. I thought of him in frogs' blood, and of tadpoles toiling through the muddy depths of Alan Mannering. On autumn evenings I sat outside for barbecues and felt the dew settle unsettlingly. At night I woke in a sweat and turned on the bedside light to examine the moisture on my palm where I wiped my brow. My neighbour had gotten into everything; he was artesian.

At the age of twelve I contemplated the others who might have drowned in our swamp. Explorers, maybe. Car thieves who drove too close to the edge. Even, startlingly, people like the Joneses before they became working class like us. The more I let myself think about it the less new everything seemed. The houses weren't old but the remnants of the bush, the swamp itself, that was another thing altogether. Sometimes the land beyond the straight lines seemed not merely shabby but grizzled. I imagined a hundred years, then a thousand and a million. I surveyed the zeroes of a million. Birds, fish, animals, plants were drowned in our swamp. On every zero I drew a squiggly tadpole tail and shuddered. All those creatures living and dying, born to be reclaimed, all sinking back into the earth to rise again and again: evaporated, precipitated, percolated. Every time a mosquito bit I thought involuntarily of some queasy transaction with fair, silent, awful Alan Mannering. If I'm honest about it, I think I still do even now.

I knew even at ten that I hadn't willed him to die, good teeth or bad. I pulled down my T-shirt and saw him slip sideways and go without a sound, without a word. I faced the idea that he did it deliberately to spite me but he looked neither casual nor determined as he slipped into the dark. It was unexpected.

The brown land, I figured, wasn't just wide but deep too. All that dust on the surface, the powder of ash and bones, bark and skin. Out west here when the easterly blows the air sometimes turns pink with the flying dirt of the deserts, pink and corporeal. And beneath the crust, rising and falling with the tide, the soup, the juice of things filters down strong and pure and mobile as time itself finding its own level. I chewed on these things in classroom daydreams until the idea was no longer terrifying all of the time. In fact at moments it was strangely comforting. All the dead alive in the land, all the lost banking, mounting in layers of silt and humus, all the creatures and plants making thermoclines in water lit and unlit. I wasn't responsible for their coming and going either but I felt them in the water. I have, boy and man, felt the dead in my very water.

Not long after my thirteenth birthday we left the neighbourhood. We sold the house to a man who eventually married and then divorced Mrs van Gelder. News of the street trickled back to me over the years. I met people in malls, airports, waiting rooms. The man next door murdered his wife. Up the road, near the ridge, a man invented the orbital engine and the Americans tried to ruin him. Bruno went back to Serbia to burn Albanians out of their homes; someone saw him on television. One of the Box kids became a famous surgeon. Girls got pregnant. Families began to buy second cars and electrical appliances that stood like trophies on Formica shelves. The suburb straightened the bush out.

Years went by. So they say. For the past five the state has endured a historic drought. The metropolitan dams look like rock pools at ebb tide and it has long been forbidden to wash a car with a running hose. Unless they have sunk bores people's gardens have crisped and died. With all that pumping the water table has sunk and artesian water has begun to stink and leave gory stains on fences and walls. And our old swamp is all but dry. I saw it on the news because of the bones that have been revealed in the newly exposed mud. All around the swamp the ground is hardening in folds and wrinkles. The mud is veinous and cracks open to the sun.

From the moment I arrived in my air-conditioned Korean car I began to feel sheepish. Police were pulling down their tape barriers and a few news trucks wheeled away. The action was over. I sat behind the little steering wheel feeling the grit of fatigue in my eyes. I didn't even get out. What had I been expecting to see, more bones, *the* bones perhaps, have them handed over for my close inspection?

Would that suddenly make me sanguine about Alan Mannering?

The swamp has a cycleway around it now and even a bird hide. Around the perimeter, where the wild oats are slashed, signs bristle with civic exhortations. Behind the pine log barriers the straight lines give way to the scruffiness of natural Australia. The sun drove in through the windscreen and the dash began to cook and give off a chemical smell. Down at the swamp's receding edge the scrofulous melaleucas looked fat and solid as though they'd see off another five years of drought. I pulled away and drove up our old street running a few laps of the neighbourhood in low gear. I took in the gardens whose European ornamentals were blanching. Only a few people were about, women and children I didn't recognize. They stood before bloody mineral stains on parapet walls with a kind of stunned look that I wondered about. A man with rounded shoulders stood in front of my old house. The jacaranda was gone. Somebody had paved where it stood to make room for a hulking great fibreglass boat. No one looked my way more than a moment and part of me, some reptilian piece of me, was disappointed that no one looked up, saw right through the tinted glass and recognized me as the kid who was with Alan Mannering the day he drowned down there on the swamp. It's as though I craved discovery, even accusation. There he is! He was there! No one said it when it happened and nobody mentioned it since. People were always oddly incurious about him. He was gone, time, as they say, moves on. They all went on without him while he rose and fell, came and went regardless. And they had no idea.

It's kind of plush-looking, the old neighbourhood, despite the drought: houses remodelled, exotic trees grown against second-storey extensions. Middle class, I suppose, which is a shock until you remember that everyone's middle class in this country now. Except for the unemployed and the dead. The city has swept past our old outpost. The bush has peeled back like the sea before Moses. Progress has made straight the way until terracotta roofs shimmer as far as the eye can see.

As I left I noticed furniture on the sandy roadside verge around the corner. Some black kids hauled things across the yard in Woolworths bags under the frank and hostile gaze of neighbours either side. An Aboriginal woman raised her fist at a man with a mobile phone and clipboard. I pulled over a moment, transfixed. Another man with a mobile phone and aviator glasses came over and asked me to move on. They were expecting a truck, he said; I complied obedient as ever, but as I gathered speed and found the freeway entry I thought of the Joneses being evicted like that. I was right to doubt the 1194 man on the telephone. Time doesn't click on and on at the stroke. It comes and goes in waves and folds like water; it flutters and sifts like dust, rises, billows, falls back on itself. When a wave breaks the water is not moving. The swell has travelled great distances but only the energy is moving, not the water. Perhaps time moves through us and not us through it. Seeing the Joneses out on the street, the only people I recognized from the old days, only confirmed what I've thought since Alan Mannering circled me as his own, pointed me out with his jagged paling and left, that the past is in us, and not behind us. Things are never over. □

MARRYING EDDIE

Robyn Davidson

Robyn Davidson with some of Eddie's relatives beside his grave, June 1998

Until I was in my twenties, I had never seen an Aborigine. Black Australians constituted one per cent of the population, and that one per cent was mostly located on reserves outside rural towns, or in outback government and mission settlements.

They were out of sight, though not always out of mind. Among my family photos is one of 'The Blacks' Camp'. It must have been taken at the turn of the century on one of the cattle properties settled by my forebears. Scattered through a stand of untidy gum trees are twenty or so 'humpies', shelters made of saplings and canvas sheeting. There are three black women dressed in Victorian skirts and high collars, a man in a stockman's outfit and a few children. They are all looking towards the camera, but from a hundred yards' distance. In spite of the familiar gum trees I could never escape the feeling that I was gazing into foreign territory. That hundred yards was a zone of separation between two worlds; worlds which shared the same space, but were entirely unconnected.

My first ever encounter with Aborigines occurred in the early Seventies, in Alice Springs, where I had gone to prepare for a journey west across the continent, alone, with camels. I had just got off the train from Sydney. I had a dog, six dollars, a small suitcase and one packet of tobacco.

As I was wandering about in a daze looking for a cheap place to stay, an old Aboriginal man stopped me and asked for a cigarette. I handed him the tobacco pouch, which he pocketed along with the papers and matches, thus demonstrating the shrewd adaptability of nomads everywhere, but hunter-gatherers in particular: the skilful milking of the natural environment—in this case, guilt-ridden whitefellas.

That long-ago Alice Springs did not quite reach one-horse standards. There were two pubs, a cafe—of the tea, white bread and mixed grill variety—and an Italian lunch joint called Sorrentino's. Or perhaps Sorrentino's came later. I remember that first year as if it is obscured by billowing dust: dry river beds, blacks' camps, river red gums, heat, barking dogs, corrugated iron, ugliness, loneliness, racial tension.

I found a place to stay a few miles out of town—an abandoned, roofless stone house, bound together by fig trees and alive with snakes. On the other side of the river bed was one of the several Aboriginal fringe camps that were situated on the outskirts of town. Its residents were the traditional owners of the country around and to the north of Alice. They lived under sheets of plastic and corrugated iron, or inside abandoned cars. They had no water tap.

I had made contact with some of them, and one in particular, old Ada Baxter, I counted as a friend. I would sometimes stay with her, watching as she drank herself into oblivion, or breaking up another fight with one of her succession of white, no-hoper boyfriends. Sometimes women would visit me from the camp, professing concern at my being alone and unprotected. I tolerated their company, was sometimes glad of it, but I didn't kid myself that I understood their world any more than I expected them to understand my pleasure in solitude.

Quite by chance I had arrived in the Alice just ahead of the first shock waves detonated by the Land Rights Act, under which untenanted stretches of desert in the Northern Territory could be claimed by Aboriginal clans, provided they could prove before a white tribunal that their 'ownership' was authentic. Suddenly the town was invaded by 'southern do-gooders'—young, urban, left-wing teachers, lawyers, doctors, anthropologists, linguists, artists, who had come to lend their skills to the Aboriginal cause. The Central Land Council, a little grass-roots organization, had been set up to administer the Act. Tiny bureaucracies began to form around specific issues—health, housing, education, communications. These were nominally led by Aborigines, but various kinds of expertise were needed and these were provided by the 'do-gooders'. The city had infiltrated the bush.

The backlash was predictable: 'Rights for Whites' graffiti and a pathetic little equivalent of the Ku Klux Klan. But the real battle was (as it still is) with the Northern Territory government, the Federal government, and the mining and pastoral lobbies.

Initially I kept my distance from this new group, which at the time numbered no more than twenty. I had come to the Alice for different reasons, and although my sympathies lay with them, my mind was on other things. But slowly they wore down my resistance until I came to depend upon them. These were friendships forged in extraordinary times, and destined to last. By the time I left on my journey, in March 1977, Alice was already transformed.

It is one of the great unsolved mysteries—why we are drawn to one individual more than another. When a shared language and shared sensibilities are involved, it is easier to explain. But why did I instantly respond to Eddie, like him, more than the people he was with?

I had been travelling west with my camels for about three months and had entered a drought area. The camels were thirsty. I arrived at a well to water them, but the well was dry. It was a week's walk to the next one. I was on Pitjantjatjara lands now, south-west of Ayers Rock, in the sand hills. The chances of coming across another human being were zero. The water drums were just about empty. I was very frightened. One night I heard a car in the distance, a clapped-out car without muffler or suspension—an Aboriginal car. The men in it had seen my fire and driven through the scrub to my camp. They were elders who had been to a land rights meeting and were on their way home to a tiny settlement—Wingelina.

Eddie is the only one who stands out in my memory of that night. He handed me some par-cooked rabbit, which I ate. His face got lost in wrinkles when he smiled. He was wearing a huge Adidas running shoe on one foot, and a woman's slipper on the other. He was a couple of inches shorter than me. He looked to be about seventy years old. He spoke no English and my Pitjantjatjara was rudimentary. I said my name was Robbie, which he pronounced 'Raaapie'.

In the morning, when I packed up to leave, it was Eddie who fell in beside me, announcing that he would escort me into Wingelina—two days' trudge away. I will never know why he chose to do that. I don't know whether the affinity I felt was reciprocated, or whether they had all discussed it when I was asleep and Eddie had got landed with the job; whether the escort was to protect me, or to protect the sacred places I might stumble into; or whether, on a whim, he felt like a walk—an unusual thing for these old nomads who now preferred to do their hunting in cars. Perhaps Eddie was, inside his own context, an unusual man.

He ended up staying with me for a month, escorting me several hundred miles beyond Wingelina into Western Australia. During that time we struggled to communicate with each other, were irritable with each other, resorted to laughter or eloquent silence. He gave me pituri, native tobacco, to chew so I wouldn't feel tired. My hunting skills broke his heart. Several times I missed kangaroo, but managed to shoot him some rabbits. He was half-blind with trachoma, so couldn't use the rifle himself, but he insisted on carrying it. He was solicitous and protective of me. At night he would build the wilcha, indicating where I should roll out my swag, and wake in the night to see if I was all right, building and stoking the fire. Or if by chance we came across a carload of strangers along a lonely track, Eddie, despite his size, displayed the rifle to maximum effect. He gave me two small pieces of stone, and to this day I have no idea if they were significant in any way. Often he broke into song as we walked along—singing up his country through which we were travelling. He tried to explain these ideas to me. He was dingo. This was where dingo had travelled, where dingo still is. He was singing dingo. I understood very little of Aboriginal philosophy then, but I certainly understood that when this old man talked of country, of his place, his whole being was transfused with something like joy. He was utterly at home. Often I would catch him looking at me sideways, trying to figure me out. I suppose that we posed the same questions to each other. Who are you? How do I make sense of you? How can I accommodate what you know?

Eddie probably saw his first whitefella when he was in his forties. Since then there would have been minimal contact—a missionary perhaps, an Afghan trader with his camel team, more recently a white lawyer or 'adviser'. Of course, even these remote Western desert cultures had been shaken by the tremors of invasion. They had already undergone rapid adaptation. But Eddie's consciousness had been formed by a tradition that stretched down into the very root of the continent, and that meant that his mind and mine were about as different as it is possible for minds to be. In the fundamentals—conceptions of time and space—we were mutually uninterpretable. My world was anchored in history, his in geography. His country—dingo—was 'conscious' and he, being a particle of that country, was therefore also conscious. He was not sundered from phenomena, as I was—an observer looking in at the world as if I were not quite of it.

By the end of our journey together we had signally failed to understand each other, yet an unlikely, even unprecedented connection had formed.

Alice Springs, 1988. Of the town I knew, bits remained like old stage props incorporated into a new play. There were now shopping malls, wide bitumen roads, a Woolworths, a Sheraton hotel, stop lights. Even the fringe camps had houses and ablution blocks. Aboriginal bureaucracies were housed in large buildings and employed large staffs. There was an Aboriginal radio station, Aboriginal rock bands, an Aboriginal women's refuge, a couple of cooperative galleries selling dot-dot paintings.

The subculture inhabited by my friends had changed, too. For a start, it had expanded. Within the group there was now room for variant ideologies, around which smaller subgroups had coalesced. There were a few more communists, a new ghetto of lesbian feminists and a couple of my old friends had joined the New Age camp. Despite its internal divisions, the little community remained powerfully bound together—its ethos was founded in the Sixties and Seventies, and its raison d'être was still Aboriginal politics. Almost everyone, it seemed, had lucrative consultancies or well-paid jobs in Aboriginal organizations. 'Nigger farming', as the more cynical urbanized blacks termed it, was a flourishing industry.

But some things were unchanged: the beauty of the Macdonnell ranges in contrast to the vileness of the town; Aboriginal drunks in the Todd river bed, Aborigines in bandages, Aborigines cadging from tourists, or trying to sell paintings for cash with which to buy more grog, Aboriginal health statistics—among the worst in the world.

I went to visit my friends in the fringe camps. The redoubtable Ada was just the same, only the boyfriend had changed. Joanie, a young girl from across the creek, who had once said, 'What have I got to look forward to? Getting drunk and beaten up every night?' had been prescient, as it turned out. I visited her in the morning and she was already swigging from a flagon. Ten years before, she would dress up in my clothes and fantasize about being a model. Now there was scar tissue where her top lip used to be.

A week later I was in a tiny aeroplane bumping along the heat shimmer 7,000 feet above the desert. The pilot squinted at the horizon, looking for Ayers Rock. There it was—a blue bump—and to the right of it, Lake Amadeus, a sheet of frosted glass fractured into patterns of icier white. Round islands of orange sand in the middle of the lake were covered in stubble, and criss-crossing the salt-ice were stitchings of animal pads. The landscape was a dot-dot painting.

Half an hour later I saw a pinprick of light in that vast canvas—one small corrugated-iron roof at the end of a four-wheel-drive track leading back to vanishing point. It was an Aboriginal outstation. Outstations, we all believed, were one of the uncontestable successes of the whole land rights struggle. Having gained freehold title of their land—thousands of square miles of it—the Pitjantjatjara were involved in a reverse diaspora. Extended families were setting up their own little communities away from the pressures and corruptions of settlement life. They were going 'home'.

I was on my way to Eddie. I had no idea what my reception would be. I had brought him an enormous bowie knife with scabbard and belt, and a skirt and new billycan for his wife, Winkicha. I had also brought the customary load of fresh meat.

By the time I got to his wilcha it was dark. He and Winkicha were sitting on the ground behind the corrugated-iron windbreak, surrounded by old blankets and mangy dogs, cooking a hunk of roo over their fire. Eddie was naked and smeared in ash.

'*Nyuntu palya*, Eddie?' He leaped up, peered through those milky-blind eyes into the darkness, then dashed out from behind the windbreak. He squinted up into my face for a second to make sure it was really me, then grabbed my breasts and gave them a vigorous and heartfelt shake. '*Laarrrrraaa!*' he said. 'Raaaapie!'

The next morning, early, people began gathering at Eddie's camp. Old women came up to me, stroking my chest, indicating they wanted to paint me up for a ceremony. I had forgotten almost all my Pitjantjatjara but I knew that this big a welcome was...odd. Did Eddie seem nervous, or have I inserted that into my memory? He was certainly very proud of the bowie knife and passed it around for everyone to see. A younger man who could speak a little English said: 'That proper good knife that one. You proper good wife, eh.'

Anyone who enters an Aboriginal community for any length of

time will be placed in a family category. You will be daughter, sister, daughter-in-law, mother, auntie and so on, and your relationship to everyone in the community will thus be formalized. I knew I would be claimed by Eddie as a valuable resource, useful not just for the bowie knives I might provide, but as a conduit to the white world—that bewildering cornucopia of Toyota trucks, government money, white advisers and bureaucrats. I suppose I had assumed Eddie would make me his daughter, though I had never given this more than a cursory thought. But wife? What did this astonishing bit of news portend? What was expected of me?

That evening I went to visit the whitefellas—a nurse and doctor living in a caravan—hoping to avoid the problem. Eddie's son (and therefore my 'son'), Lance, who was about five years my junior, escorted me. He showed me where I was to camp that night—a crumbling cement plinth surrounded by broken glass, plastic bags and a razor-wired cyclone fence. It stood next to a suppurating ablution block and near to Eddie's wilcha. The fence was to protect me from the dogs. I stayed with the whitefellas until late at night, then quietly made my way back to my swag.

The Aboriginal community was long asleep by now. But Eddie was standing by the fence with his dogs. My heart lurched into my throat. We whispered in Pitjantjatjara: 'Are you OK?'

'Yes, I'm OK. Are you OK?'

'Yes, I'm OK.' But he looked uneasy. Then I thought I understood. He must have boasted that during our journey together we had been lovers. And now he had to save face. We touched each other on the shoulder and started laughing in a suppressed sort of way. I brought him across to my swag. We sat there for a short time in affectionate and amused silence, the dogs slumped against us, and then he went back to his wilcha.

At dawn he woke me up, shaking me gently by the shoulder and grinning down into my face. 'Raaapie, Raaapie.' He had brought a chunk of cold, bloody, fly-encrusted meat and some damper. I put the billy on the fire and made tea. For the rest of that morning we sat on the cement plinth, under the shade of corrugated iron, sanded by a hot, gritty wind, receiving guests—old men and women, presumably my relatives.

I gleaned several things from Eddie's conversation. He wanted me to come back the following winter with my camels, a rifle, a new shirt and a jumper for him, and we would go walking into 'country'.

'I can't come back then, Eddie, but I will try to come back the winter after that.'

He laughed. 'But I'll be dead by then.' He lifted his shirt to show me a long scar down the front of his body. Something had been sung into him by an enemy near Perth. He, Eddie, was counter-singing this person, but there was no guarantee whose sorcery would prove the stronger. There was not a shred of anxiety displayed over the possibility of his imminent death. The personality known as Eddie would disappear, but the essence of the man, that fragment that had been extruded from his country, would return to it.

He expressed what I assumed was fatherly concern over my childlessness. '*Tsc tsc, nyaltajarra* [poor thing], Raaapie.' He surveyed my body, and then patted me on the stomach, breasts and thighs. No question about it now—this was erotic intent. There was nothing awkward about his approach. It was frank and straightforward. And full of tenderness. I was floored by it.

Later that afternoon, I found out from the medical team that Eddie had had an operation to remove a stomach tumour. The prognosis was about five years, they thought.

I went for a long walk by myself up into the hills. I had been so concerned with simply managing this weird event that I hadn't had time to think through my own responses to it. I perched on a rock and surveyed the land below. Plains of yellow grasses like wheatfields swept up to the foot of rocky chocolate-brown ranges, covered at the foot by pale-green spinifex and silvery bushes which gradually gave way to bare outcroppings at the top. Small washaways sheltered a filigree of trees, and here and there, a single, flame-coloured sand dune rose out of the yellow. Eagles, kites and crows carved up wind currents in a perennially cobalt sky. The space was empty of people yet saturated with human meaning. Just as paintings can gain in value until they become priceless, this place was so old that it had become timeless. As so often before in that landscape, I felt as if I belonged somewhere, that I was home.

In the years since Eddie and I travelled together, I had entered and taken up residence in many and various worlds, in many and various countries. I had never consciously articulated what drove me to do this—the desire to see things through others' eyes; to go beyond the confines of my prejudices and habits—but these impulses had undeniably given my life its shape. I had not just studied, but had tried to participate in other ways of life, not in order to bring them within the already existing boundaries of my own, but to break through those boundaries. But these explorations had left me oddly dislocated. I had learned that each world had its own coherence and validity. Each was logical to itself, a whole. And that meant that I no longer felt firmly fastened inside *any* version of the world. I was a stranger, now, wherever I was, with no reliable centre from which to judge or compare elsewhere.

It is as extraordinary to me now as it was terrifying to me then, that, while sitting on that rock, I seriously considered staying with Eddie. All it would take was a tiny act, as simple as opening a door. I was as close to immersion in another universe as that. Just opening a door, and stepping through. What, in ordinary life, was unthinkable—entering into a psychological and physical intimacy with an eighty-year-old traditional Aboriginal man—was not just thinkable, it was effortlessly doable, once you understood that there was no such thing as ordinary life. There was only the habit of sticking with what one knows—a version of how-things-really-are, which is as arbitrary, strange and illusory as anyone else's. Why not 'marry' Eddie? Why not?

I felt the appalling ease of it, the seduction of it, as vertigo; as if the fabric of the world had unravelled and I was falling through it. But a self-preserving cowardice acted as a parachute. I would most certainly not step through that door. Apart from anything else, there would be no way back. I left Wingelina the following day, with relief, yet in a state of intense and bewildering grief.

A few years later, when I was living in India, I received a formal letter from the community notifying me that Eddie had died.

It wasn't until 1999 that I felt ready to go back. I intended to drive down from the Alice to Wingelina, where Eddie was buried, past Ayers Rock, following my own tracks. Again, I had no idea what my reception would be. Would the family be angry that I hadn't come sooner? Would they care at all?

In the ten years I had been away, Aborigines had undergone something of a transformation in the national psyche. Previously, they had been on their way to extinction because social Darwinism said we were better than them. Now they had become—at least for the purposes of commerce, eco-tourism, international art markets and the spiritually destitute, that is to say, outside the realities of politics—better than us.

All down the Alice mall there was a barrage of photographs and advertisements suggesting that here, contact with 'natural man' could be bought. (A visitor could, for a certain sum, spend a morning out bush, hunting and gathering with bona fide blackfellas, though later she might bump into those same blackfellas buying sweets and grog at a supermarket.) Dot-dots in nauseating profusion covered everything—shopfronts, didgeridoos, tea towels, T-shirts, and, of course, the canvases that now sold for thousands of pounds.

Plus ça change.

And yet, there were the drunks in the Todd river bed, Aborigines in bandages, Aborigines cadging from tourists.

Plus c'est la même chose.

As always, those old friends who worked for Aboriginal organizations were on the verge of burnout. As always there was only one conversation in town—Aborigines—and although it was an endlessly fascinating one, I didn't feel I had much to contribute. I hadn't been involved in the day-to-day political struggles that defined life for my friends here. But it was pretty clear that very little had turned out as anyone had expected or hoped.

No one had believed the situation for Aborigines in Australia could get worse, but in many ways it had. There were patches of coherence and success, but they quickly faded. Did this mean that the liberal policies of the past twenty years had paved a way to hell, or did it mean that there had not yet been enough time for those policies to work? Had welfare crippled Aboriginal self-respect, or had too little money been thrown at their problems? These were not debates it was easy to have publicly—the old fear that admitting anomalies and failures only gave ammunition to 'the Right' effectively shut everyone up—though they certainly went on privately.

The Seventies had been a romantic and idealistic time. Now relations between town Aborigines and the do-gooders were more complicated, less innocent. Black bosses sometimes treated their white workers with a contempt and hostility that would be tolerated nowhere else. And where there is money and power to be gained, there will always be nepotism and corruption.

It was, therefore, in a somewhat disheartened state that I set out for Eddie's country, three days' drive away. On the way I called in at the outstation I had spotted from the plane over a decade before. It was all but abandoned—a straggle of people lived there, among them just one adolescent boy without companions. He stood outside the group, the epitome of hopelessness, uselessness and desolation. He had shot himself a few months before but the bullet had missed his heart. No one seemed to know what to do with him, perhaps even how to think about him. Suicide was apparently unknown in traditional Aboriginal society. Now there was an epidemic amongst the young—hangings, shootings, self-mutilations.

Previously boys would have been removed from their families and placed under the tutelage of older men, who would guide them through a series of initiations, gradually introducing them into the masculine 'mysteries'. Only when this education had been successfully completed would they be allowed to marry. All these structures have now collapsed.

I reached the settlement late on the third evening. It had grown—more tin houses, more rubbish, more rusted cars, abandoned Toyota trucks, dogs snuffling at used nappies, groups of staggering teenagers sniffing petrol, some boys playing basketball on a weedy court, their caps turned backwards, Harlem-style.

I found Lance, my son, the following morning. He was wearing the red headband of a fully initiated man, and he looked more like Eddie than ever. He invited me to his outstation, twenty miles away from the settlement, close to one of his Dreaming sites. His dogs jumped in the back of his truck, then we picked up his wife Linda, various other relatives and children and more dogs and headed for the hills.

The outstation consisted of a tin house with two rooms joined by a roofed cement veranda. Along one side of the cement platform there was a sink; inside the rooms, blankets and dogs; a loo and shower out the back. Stretching away from the house in all directions: desert, marked by one corrugated dirt track and a line of low hills formed by ancestral sisters as they danced their way across Australia.

My companions barely spoke English; only a few words of Pitjantjatjara floated up from the mud of my memory. Awkward silences punctuated the efforts to communicate on both sides. But what was genuine and palpable was their pleasure at my arrival, and my pleasure in being with them.

I had brought the customary gift of meat, but Lance went out to shoot some game—two bush turkeys—the very best he could find. The shyness passed, and we settled down to serious talk. He told me of a new mining venture trying to 'get in' down here; of the crooked black bureaucrats out to line their own pockets. He told me that a lot of Aborigines from the city were coming home to find the families they had been 'stolen' from. He mimed something knitting together. He told me that the problem in remote places like this was still poverty. Owning land was all very well, but if there was no work, no industry, what was the point of it. The old people were dying, and with them the old certainties. Young people were not so interested in ceremonial life. They fell into the twilight zone between the world of their elders and the world of European Australia. The traditional systems of sharing were breaking down. What money there was down here was absorbed by ten per cent of the families, while the others starved—an unheard-of state of affairs in the old days.

That night a sleeping place was cleared for me on the veranda. Linda washed down the cement floor with a broom, then the sink, then our tin cups with the same broom. I was covered in red sand because all afternoon I had been helping Lance plant fruit trees around the house. A fire was lit on the cement, and we all crowded around it, smoke stinging our eyes. First course was a tin of beef stew. The old man opposite me poured honey on slices of white bread, loaded beef stew on top and passed it over. As I ate, the dogs stared at my mouth, waiting for handouts. When I threw something, they snapped it in mid air, not six inches from my face. The bush turkeys, cooking all afternoon in the ground outside, were ready. The old lady next to me blew snot out of her nose with her hand, then with the same hand passed me the turkey leg. Few would understand how privileged I felt to be with these people who had managed to survive the apocalypse with their humanity, their generosity and capacity for laughter intact.

The next day we went to visit Eddie's grave. It had been Christianized by his grandchildren—plastic flowers and a plaque which read:

> MANTJAKURA EDDY. HE WAS A CHRISTIAN MAN
> HE ALWAYS CARRIED HIS BIBLE
> SO CARRY YOUR BIBLES WHERE
> EVER YOU GO

It was an odd epitaph for a man who had needed no gods because nothing he had been or done in his life could have affected the inevitability of his return to the spirit of place. But Eddie's world was ending, and no one could say yet what might evolve out of it.

A strange intimacy had existed between us, but it was across such a vast divide that we could never have come close to answering the questions we posed each other: who are you, how do I make sense of you, how can I accommodate what you know? But with Lance and his generation, the respect, amity and compassion were grounded in something closer to familiarity.

When we all piled back in the truck, I told Lance that a couple of weeks before I'd received the news of Eddie's death, I had dreamed of him for the first time I could remember.

'Oh yeah,' he said, without a twitch of surprise, 'that was 'im.'

□

GRANTA

TRUE HISTORY OF THE KELLY GANG, FIRST PART

Peter Carey

Ned Kelly, 10 November 1880, the day before he was hanged AUSTRALIAN HIGH COMMISSION

Ned Kelly was the last and greatest of Australia's bushrangers, or rural outlaws, and still the country's most legendary hero. He was captured after the police laid siege to the township of Glenrowan, in up-country Victoria, in June 1880, and hanged in Melbourne later the same year. The following account of his early life, in his own words, is taken from a long autobiographical manuscript recently discovered in Melbourne; stained and dog-eared papers, each filled with the same distinctive hand, and divided into thirteen parcels, of which the story of his life until the age of twelve comprises the first.

I lost my own father at 12 yrs. of age and know what it is to be raised on lies and silences my dear daughter you are presently too young to understand a word I write but as this history is for you and will contain no single lie may I burn in hell if I speak false.

God willing I shall live to see you read these words to witness your astonishment and see your dark eyes widen and your jaw drop when you finally comprehend the injustice we poor Irish suffered in this present age. How queer and foreign it must seem to you and all the coarse words and cruelty which I now relate are far away in ancient time.

Your grandfather were a quiet and secret man he had been ripped from his home in Tipperary and transported to the prisons of Van Diemen's Land I do not know what was done to him he never spoke of it. When they had finished with their tortures they set him free and he crossed the sea to the colony of Victoria. He were by this time 30 yr. of age red headed and freckled with his eyes always slitted against the sun. My da had sworn an oath to evermore avoid the attentions of the law so when he saw the streets of Melbourne was crawling with policemen worse than flies he walked 28 mi. to the township of Donnybrook and then or soon thereafter he seen my mother. Ellen Quinn were 18 yr. old she were dark haired and slender the prettiest figure on a horse he ever saw but your grandma was like a snare laid out by God for Red Kelly. She were a Quinn and the police would never leave the Quinns alone.

My first memory is of Mother breaking eggs into a bowl and crying that Jimmy Quinn my 15 yr. old uncle were arrested by the traps. I don't know where my daddy were that day nor my older sister Annie. I were 3 yr. old. While my mother cried I scraped the sweet yellow batter onto a spoon and ate it the roof were leaking above the camp oven each drop hissing as it hit.

My mother tipped the cake onto the muslin cloth and knotted it. Your auntie Maggie were a baby so my mother wrapped her also then she carried both cake and baby out into the rain. I had no choice but follow up the hill how could I forget them puddles the colour of mustard the rain like needles in my eyes.

We arrived at the Beveridge Police Camp drenched to the bone and doubtless stank of poverty a strong odour about us like wet dogs and for this or other reasons we was excluded from the Sergeant's room. I remember sitting with my chilblained hands wedged beneath the door I could feel the lovely warmth of the fire on my fingertips. Yet when we was finally permitted entry all my attention were taken not by the blazing fire but by a huge red jowled creature the Englishman who sat behind the desk. I knew not his name only that he were the most powerful man I ever saw and he might destroy my mother if he so desired.

Approach says he as if he was an altar.

My mother approached and I hurried beside her. She told the Englishman she had baked a cake for his prisoner Quinn and would be most obliged to deliver it because her husband were absent and she had butter to churn and pigs to feed.

No cake shall go to the prisoner said the trap I could smell his foreign spicy smell he had a handlebar moustache and his scalp were shining through his hair.

Said he No cake shall go to the prisoner without me inspecting it first and he waved his big soft white hand thus indicating my mother should place her basket on his desk. He untied the muslin his fingernails so clean they looked like they was washed in lye and to this day I can see them livid instruments as they broke my mother's cake apart.

'Tis not poverty I hate the most
Nor the eternal grovelling
But the insults that grow on it
Which not even leeches can cure

Your grandma was never a coward but on this occasion she understood she must hold her tongue and so she wrapped the warm crumbs in the cloth and walked out into the rain. I cried out to her but she did not hear so I followed her skirts across the muddy yard. At first I thought it an outhouse on whose door I found her hammering it come as a shock to realize my young uncle were locked inside. For the great offence of duffing a bullock with cancer of the eye he were interred in this earth floored slab hut which could not have measured more than 6 ft. x 6 ft. and here my mother were forced to kneel in the mud and push the broken cake under the door the gap v. narrow perhaps 2 in. not sufficient for the purpose.

She cried God help us Jimmy what did we ever do to them that they should torture us like this?

My mother never wept but weep she did and I rushed and clung to her and kissed her but still she could not feel that I were there. Tears poured down her handsome face as she forced the muddy mess of cake and muslin underneath the door.

She cried I would kill the b-----ds if I were a man God help me. She used many rough expressions I will not write them here. It were eff this and ess that and she would blow their adjectival brains out.

These was frightening sentiments for a boy to hear his mamma speak but I did not know how set she were until 2 nights later when my father returned home and she said the exact same things again to him.

You don't know what you're talking about said he.

You are a coward she cried. I blocked my ears and buried my face into my floursack pillow but she would not give up and neither would my father turn against the law. I wish I had known my parents when they truly loved each other.

My mother had one idea about my father and the police the opposite. She thought him Michael Meek. They knew him as a graduate of Van Diemen's Land and a criminal by birth and trade and marriage they was constantly examining the brands on our stock or sifting through our flour for signs of larceny but they never found nothing except mouse manure they must of had a mighty craving for the taste.

Nor was your grandmother as unfriendly towards the police as you would expect if solely instructed by her testimony she might of wished to murder them but would not mind a little drink and joke before she done the deed. There was one Sergeant his name O'Neil my mother seemed to like him better than the rest. I am talking now of a later time I must of been 9 yr. of age our father were away contracting and our small hut was crowded with children all sleeping between the maze of patchwork curtains Mother hung to make up for the lack of walls. It were like living in a cupboard full of dresses. Into this shadowy world Sgt O'Neil did come with queer white hair which he were always combing like a girl before a dance he were v. friendly to us children and on the night in question he brung me the gift of a pencil. At school we used the slates but I never touched a pencil and was most excited to smell the sweet pine and graphite as the Sergeant sharpened his gift he were very fatherly toward me and set me at one end of the table with a sheet of paper.

I set to work to cover my paper with the letters of the alphabet. My mother sat at the other end of the table with the Sgt and when he produced his silver flask I paid no more attention than I did to Annie & Jem & Maggie & Dan. After I made each letter as a capital I set to do the smaller ones such were my concentration that when my mother spoke her voice seemed very far away.

Get out of my house.

I looked up to discover Sergeant O'Neil with his hand to his cheek I suppose she must of slapped him for his countenance were turned v. red.

Get out my mother shrieked she had the Irish temper we was accustomed to it.

Ellen you calm yourself you know I never meant nothing in the least improper.

Eff off my mother cried.

The policeman's voice took a sterner character. Ellen said he you must not use such language to a police officer.

That were a red rag to my mother she uncoiled herself from her seat. You effing mongrel she cried her voice louder again. You wouldnt say that if my husband were not gone shearing.

I will issue one more warning Mrs Kelly.

At this my mother snatched up the Sergeant's teacup and threw the contents onto the earthen floor. Arrest me she cried arrest me you coward.

Jem were 5 yr. old sitting on the floor playing knuckles but when the brandy splashed beside him he let the bones lie quiet. Of a different disposition I begun to move towards my mother.

Did you hear your mother call me a coward old chap?

I would not betray her I walked round the table and stood next to her. Said he You was busy writing Ned?

I took my mother's hand and she put her arm around my shoulder.

You are a scholar aint it he asked me.

I said I were.

Then you must know about the history of cowards. I were confused I shook my head.

Next O'Neil was bouncing to his feet and showing the full hard stretch of his policeman's boots said he let me educate you young man. No said my mother her manner now completely changed. Please no.

A moment earlier O'Neil had a stiff and worried air but now there was a dainty sort of prance about him. Oh yes said he all children should know their history indeed it is quite essential.

My mother wrenched her hand from mine and reached out but the Ulsterman ducked behind the first set of curtains and emerged to prowl in and out and around our family he even patted little Dan upon his silky head. My mother were afraid her face was pale and frozen.

Please Kevin.

But O'Neil was telling us his story we had to quiet to listen to him he had the gift. It were a story of a man from Tipperary named only A Certain Man or This Person Who I Will Not Name. He said A Certain Man had a grudge against a farmer for lawfully evicting his tenant and This Person etc. conspired with his mates to kill the farmer.

I'm sorry said my mother I already apologized.

Sgt O'Neil made a mocking bow continuing his story without relent telling how This Certain Man did 1st write a threatening letter to the landlord. When the landlord ignored the letter and evicted the tenant This Certain Man called a SELECT MEETING of his allies to a chapel in the dead of night where they drank whiskey from the

Holy Goblet and swore upon the Holy Book then he said to them Brothers for we are all brothers sworn upon all thats blessed and Holy. Brothers are you ready in the name of God to fulfil your oaths? They said they was they swore it and when they done their blasphemy they descended upon the farmer's house with pikes and faggots burning.

Sergeant O'Neil seemed much affected by his own story his voice grew loud he said the farmer's children screamed for mercy at the windows but the men set their home alight and those who escaped they piked to death there was mothers and babes in arms the Sgt would not spare us either he painted the outrage in every detail we children were all silent open mouthed not only at the horror of the crime but also the arrest of the Guilty Parties and the treachery of This Certain Man who betrayed all he had drawn into his conspiracy. The accomplices was hanged by the neck until dead and the Ulsterman let us imagine how this might be he did not conceal the particulars.

What happened then he asked though we could not speak nor did we wish to hear.

This Certain Man kept his life he were transported to Van Diemen's Land. And with that Sergeant O'Neil strode out our door into the night.

Mother said nothing further she did not move not even when we heard the policeman's mare cantering along the dark road up the hill to Beveridge I asked her what was meant by This Certain Man and she give me such a clip across the ears I never asked again. In time I understood it were my own father that was referred to.

The memory of the policeman's words lay inside me like the egg of a liver fluke and while I went about my growing up this slander wormed deeper and deeper into my heart and there grew fat.

Sergeant O'Neil had filled my boy's imagination with thoughts that would breed like maggots on a summer day you would think his victory complete but he begun to increase his harassment of my father rousing him from bed when he were drunk or fast asleep he also needled and teased me whenever he seen me in the street.

He would mock the way I dressed my lack of shoes and coats.

I were 11 yr. old all knees and elbows and shy of any comment I couldnt walk past the Police Camp with my friends without him calling out some insult. I pretended to be amused for I would not give him the satisfaction of seeing blood.

It was during Sgt O'Neil's hateful reign that we heard Mr Russell of Foster Downs Station was to sell off a great mob of bullocks and cows in calf also a famous bull he was said to have brought from England for 500 quid. It were a much bigger event than we was accustomed to in Beveridge just a straggly village on a difficult hill reviled by all the bullockies between Melbourne and the Murray River. 1/2 way up the hill were a pub and blacksmith and portable lockup then further west a Catholic school. That hill were too much effort even for the bitter winds which turned around and come howling back towards our hut below. West of the road the water were salt. Our side had good water but it were still known as Pleurisy Plains. No one ever come to Beveridge for their health.

The sale changed all that and suddenly there was squatters and stock agents come to visit even a veterinarian from Melbourne all these strangers set up camp beside the swamp between our place and the hill. There was gaffing & flash talk & grog drinking & galloping up & down the Melbourne road it were good as a circus to us boys to hang about the boggy crossing and see the fancy riding. Day by day Jem and me run the long way to school to see what new tents were set up at the swamp. We was on tenterhooks awaiting the beasts but it were not until dusk on the day before the Auction we heard that particular mournful bellowing on the wind it were a mob of cattle being driven over a track they did not know.

I told Jem I was going to meet them.

Me too.

We wasnt finished tending to the pigs and chooks we did not care our feet was bare the ground were hard and rocky though we was used to it and run right through the Indian corn. Said Jem We'll be whipped.

I don't care.

I don't care neither.

We had just gained the swamp bulrushes when the beasts come into view flooding down the smooth green hill of Beveridge like a breaking wave it were the gleaming wealth of all the nations pouring down towards us and the water. Cor look at them blacks said Jem.

Of the 7 stockmen 5 was blackfellows they rode ahead of the coming storm with flash red scarves round their necks and elastic sided boots upon their feet. Said Jem Look at them boots.

Damn them I said. Yes damn them said Jem we was raised to think the blacks the lowest of the low but they had boots not us and we damned and double damned them as we run. Soon we gained the rutted ruined Melbourne road where we passed Patchy Moran he were 16 yr. old rawboned and lanky but we was faster any day.

Wait you little b----rs.

But we wouldnt wait for Patchy or no one else splashing through Boggy Crossing to the splintery top rail of the yard. Moran made no comment on our victory but lit himself a cigarette and the leftover beard of tobacco fell in glowing cinders to the earth. Look at them effing niggers.

We already seen them.

I heard the rattle of a bridle and turned to see my father's tormentor had ridden up behind us Sgt O'Neil had his stirrup leathers so long the iron could be held only with the tip of the toes it were the English fashion. His horse was 17 hands he thought himself high and mighty but if you had give any of us boys a pony we would of left him in the dust.

Patchy Moran said Look at them niggers Sergeant did you see their adjectival boots how much would that cost do you reckon Sir boots like that?

O'Neil did not answer but leaned forward in his saddle looking down at me beneath the visor of his shako his eyes as watery as a jar of gin. Ah young Kelly he said.

Hello Sergeant said I so accustomed to his teasing that I thought Moran's remark about the blackfellows boots would lead to comments about my own bare feet. Said I thats a mighty bull they got by Jove we heard he was worth 500 quid.

Said O'Neil I just saw your father. I knew from his lazy drawl he had something worse than shoes to hurt me with. He said I just seen Red Kelly galloping across Horan's paddocks dressed like a woman can you picture that now?

I couldnt see the policeman's expression in the failing light but he spoke so very conversationally. Patchy Moran laughed but stopped midbreath I looked towards poor little Jem he sat on the rail staring grimly at the ground his brow furrowed in a torture of confusion and my friends gone v. quiet around me.

Pull the other one Sergeant.

Your father was seen by Mr McClusky and Mr Willett and myself he was wearing a dress with roses on its hem can you ever imagine such a thing?

Not me but you can Sergeant its the very thing you just done.

You watch your lip young fellow do you hear? When your father saw us he galloped away down the north face of Big Hill. He can ride I grant him that but do you know why he would go that way?

No.

Oh said the Sergeant he was off to be serviced by his husband I suppose.

I leapt upon his high armoured boot I tried to twist him off his saddle but he only laughed and swung his horse around so I was almost crushed against the fence.

Thus were the great day destroyed. I told Patchy Moran I did not come to see a nigger show Jem said he did not want to see one neither. We walked home together through the dark. We did not say much but was very melancholic. She'll strop us won't she Ned?

No she won't.

But of course our mother had the razor strop laid out ready on the table she hit my hand 3 times and Jem once. We never told her what O'Neil had said.

I doubt I had the courage to repeat O'Neil's slander to my father but I were anyway denied the opportunity for he had departed once again to shear the fat merino sheep for Mr Henry Buckley of Gnawarra Station. As it were spring he should of been engaged on his own land but couldnt afford it and on the way to Gnawarra he nearly died.

A vicious Sydney black by the name of Warragul had gotten a mob together made of the remnants of different tribes my father had done nothing against Warragul but when he arrived at the Murray

River near Barnawantha a shower of spears sailed out of the bush and struck his donkey dead beneath him. My father dragged his carbine from its saddle holster and by careful use of his remaining powder were able to keep Warragul's mob at bay until dark. Then he retreated into an abandoned hut he barricaded the door and windows and so imagined himself safe but in the early hours of the morning he woke.

The roof were on fire and the hut surrounded by shouting savages.

He used the last of his powder to shoot into the faces of blackfellows who was peering through the gaps between the logs but when the powder were gone he had nothing more to look forward to than death and begun to say his prayers while the blacks thrust their spears through the gaps. The roof were already burning falling in lumps when Father paused from praying long enough to realize the spears was only entering from the front. He removed the barricade from the rear window and with the blacks keeping watch on one side of his funeral pyre he made his way out the downwind side thereafter hiding in a hollow log for 2 days before he were discovered by Mr Henry Buckley himself and thus finally delivered to Gnawarra.

At the time my father had been battling for his very life Sergeant O'Neil's slander spread about the Catholic school the source of this contagion being Patchy Moran I cautioned him.

You say that one more time I'll whip you.

Patchy Moran were a good foot taller his voice broken like a man. Said he You are an adjectival tinker you can't give me orders.

And with that he punched me in the temple so I fell.

Regaining my feet I faced him again he hit me hard enough to push the pudding out of me. I were bent over wheezing to get my wind back he called out I were a sissy and the son of a sissy. He seemed a giant all hair and pimples I thought he soon would kill me but I closed with him on the barren ground beneath the peppercorn tree and then by skill or luck I got round his dirty neck and pulled him to the ground. How he hollered to be brung down how he kicked & bucked & twisted rolling me amongst the tree roots and the gravel. I felt a red hot sting on my back and rolled him over. There were a bull ant also fastened to his pimply neck.

I wouldnt let him go not even when I felt a second bite myself I hope you may live your life without a bull ant bite for it is worse than any wasp or bee. Patchy howled in my arms cursing and pleading but I held his shoulders to the earth as he thrashed and drove his tormentors into greater fury still.

Take it back.

He bawled the snot run down his lip

Take it back.

He said he would not take it back but in the end he couldnt tolerate the pain he cried D--- you d--- your eyes I take it back. Brother Hearn heard his blasphemies so did 16 other scholars standing by the schoolhouse door observing us. No one said nothing they stood v. quiet and watched Patchy Moran rip off his shirt and britches the girls all saw his private skin.

I were soon ill from my great number of bites but no one said no more about my father from that time.

I thought my problems over and I once again imagined there were never a better place on earth than where I lived at Pleurisy Plains. I could not conceive a better soil or prettier view or trees that did not grow crooked in the winds. I were often in the swamp it were a world entire with eels and bird eggs and tiger snakes we tried to race them along the Melbourne road. Then one mild and dewy morning I went out to find some worms and discovered my younger sister Maggie seated on a cairn of them brown pitted rocks the ancient volcanoes had throwed around the plains of Beveridge. Our father often had us busy tidying the earth in this manner. This particular pile of rocks was in a thistle patch near our back door and Maggie were using it as a throne while she squeezed milk from the thistles onto her warts. She asked would I please squeeze some on a difficult place behind her elbow.

I were very fond of Maggie she were always my favourite sister as true and steady as a red gum plank. As I set down my worms and dripped the white sap over her warts she warned she had found something I would not like.

What?

You'll have to move them rocks.

I already moved them once.

You better do it again.

There were no more than 8 rocks Maggie helped me roll them to one side and I discovered the freshly broken earth beneath.

Its something dead.

It aint nothing dead.

From down amongst the thistles she produced an old gooseneck shovel with a broken handle.

I took it from her hand and dug until I uncovered something hard and black it were 3 ft. x 2 ft. It were also deep so I levered and jemmied and soon dragged a battered tin trunk out to the light of day. It were inside that trunk I found the thing I wish I never saw.

It were a woman's dress v. soiled along the hem the roses was exactly as Sgt O'Neil had said. There was also masks made of red paint and feather I hardly seen them it were the dress that made my stomach knot a mighty anger come upon me.

I heard our sister Annie calling and I whispered I would kill Maggie if ever she mentioned what we seen. Her dark little eyes welled up with tears.

Annie were demanding I bring firewood she come down the path in a mighty fret with her thin shoulders hunched forward and her hands upon her hips. If youse don't come now you'll get no adjectival dinner.

I split the wood all right but then carried it back to the thistle patch and made a fireplace from the rocks.

What are you doing? You can't do that you know it aint permitted.

Just the same she give me the matches I asked for. She were a worrywart she retreated back to the doorway while I burned the horrid contents of the trunk. By the time she come back I were poking the last bits of dress into the flames.

She asked me what I were destroying but all us children had suffered from O'Neil's story and she knew the answer to her question well enough.

Said Annie You better bury that trunk. Her face were pinched her mouth set with worry she were only 9 yr. old but she must of already saw her future it were written on her face for all to see.

A 2nd time she ordered me to hide the trunk so I dragged it

down the yard and shoved it under the lower rail of the horse yard.

You can't do that.

I pulled the trunk through all the manure into the middle of the yard.

You'll get the strop said she.

I never doubted it would be worse than that and when our father come ambling up the track 3 days later I awaited my thrashing it were as sure as eggs turn into chickens.

At 1st he didnt see the trunk he were surveying his crop of Indian corn doubtless pleased he had not been speared or burned and had money in his pocket. But finally he saw his broken secret lying in the air and while the little children all run around crying for him to dismount he stared silently down at the blackened trunk his eyes small inside their puffy lids.

Where's your ma?

Grandma took ill she's gone to Wallan.

My father dismounted and then carried his saddle and bags into the hut I were waiting by the door to get my punishment but he never even looked at me. After a little while he gone up the pub.

I lost my own father from a secret he might as well been snatched by a roiling river fallen from a ravine I lost him from my heart so long I cannot even now properly make the place for him that he deserves. Forever after I unearthed his trunk I pictured him with his broad red beard his strong arms his freckled skin all his manly features buttoned up inside that cursed dress.

Up to that point I had been his shadow never losing a chance to be with him. In the bush he taught the knots I use to tie my blanket to my saddle D's also the way I stand to use a carpenter's plane and the trick of catching fish with a bush-fly and a strip of greenhide these things are like the dark marks made in the rings of great trees locked forever in my daily self.

I don't know if my mother realized what were hidden in the trunk she never said nothing and it were left to lie in the middle of the dusty yard and when it rained the horses drank from it.

A rich man driving his buggy past our home might see the tin trunk in the yard and the pumpkins growing on the skillion roof but he would never imagine all my father's issue the great number of us packed behind the curtains breathing the same air snoring farting blind and deaf to each other as a newborn litter.

I had long taught myself to be deaf to my parent's private business but after digging up that trunk I would stay awake at night listening to my mother and my father talking.

I learned not a thing about the dress I discovered it were land my parents whispered about and in particular the Duffy Land Act of 1862 it gave a man or widow the right to select a block between 50 and 640 acres for £1 per acre part payable on selection the rest over 8 yr. My mother were for it but my father were against it he said the great Charles Gavan Duffy was a well intentioned idiot leading poor men into debt and lifelong labour. He were correct as it happened but when my mother abused my da for cowardice the terrible turmoil in my heart were somehow soothed. Only a simpleton she said would try to farm 20 acres like my da were doing. I thought yes you must be a mighty fool.

This debate about the Land Act were life or death and my mother enlisted her family who was presently our neighbours but in the midst of buying land far away in the North East.

The Quinns was purchasing 1,000 acres at Glenmore on the King River they was Irish and therefore drunk with land and fancy horses all the old hardships soon to be forgotten. The Quinn women come visiting with soda bread and surveyor's maps the men was tall and reckless they cursed and sang they fought anyone they did not like and rode thoroughbreds they could not afford to buy. My uncle Jimmy Quinn were a man by now there were a dreadful wildness in his eyes like a horse that has been tortured. The Quinns would of tossed my father down the well if they had seen the dress but they chivvied and joked and finally prevailed upon him to sell everything he owned in Beveridge he got a total of £80.

But when my da finally had the cash put in his hand the thought of giving the govt. so large a sum were more than he could bear and when the new owners arrived to take possession he borrowed a cart and shifted us to rented land on the outskirts of the township of Avenel. So while my mother's brothers and sisters went on to farm 1,000 virgin acres at Glenmore my father transported us 60 mi. to a district of English snobs and there to my mother's great outrage he slowly pissed away the 80 quid on rent and booze. I were his flesh and he must of felt me draw further away but he were proud and did not try to win me back.

The question of our lost opportunity were now always present my mother could not leave it alone my father would sit solid in his chair and quietly rub the belly of his big black cat. I am thinking now of one night in particular when he broke his silence.

Your family arent bad fellows said he at last.

If you're planning to speak ill of them you can stop right there.

Oh I aint got nothing against them personal.

Of course not they was always good to you.

I'm sure the land will do the job. Them rocks aint nothing but the land can't touch this land Ellen.

And us with no meat but the adjectival possums.

We aint got beef its true.

Not even mutton.

But do you notice we aint got no police? Now thats an interesting thing I wonder why that is do you imagine your family is as lucky up at Glenmore?

Oh no not this again.

Well you must agree the Quinns attract the traps as surely as rabbit guts will bring the flies.

My mother shrieked a plate or cup were dashed against the wall.

Well Ellen said he I know you're very low about your farm but I would rather die than go to prison.

You great galoot no one wants to put you in prison.

So you say.

No one she cried her voice rising. Are you mad?

And why was the traps always visiting us do you imagine?

You have been a free man 15 yr. they don't want you back again.

The Quinns bring attention its the truth.

Oh you adjectival worm.

My mother were now sobbing Maggie also I could hear her little rabbit noises on the far side of the curtain. Then my mother said my father would rather his children starve than take a risk and beside me Jem pulled his pillow tight across his ears.

The land were very good at Avenel but there were a drought and nothing flourished there but misery I were the oldest son I thought it time to earn my place.

There were no dam or spring upon our property each day I took the cows to water them at Hughes Creek. In a good year it would of made a pretty picture but in the drought that creek were no more than a chain of sandy waterholes. It were across this dry river bed that Mr Murray's heifer calf come calling out my name I were very hungry when I heard her and knew what I must do. I had never killed nothing bigger than a rooster but when I saw the long line of the heifer's crop above the blackberries I knew I could not be afraid of nothing. Her eye were a little wild but she was a poll Hereford and very sleek. I later heard that Mr Murray had made a great investment on her and poddied her with corn and hay which must be true for there were no feed in any of his paddocks and although he owned 500 acres his stock was out grazing on the road sides finding what nourishment they could. I did not care I bailed her up and led her down the creek into a thick stand of wattles with a clearing in the centre. She did not like the rope around her neck she fought and bucked and would of done herself a damage had I not bound her hind legs and tied them to a wattle trunk. She began to bellow terribly. Soon she were trussed up like a Christmas chook but I had no pity nor did I have a knife. I ran up through the scrub to fetch one from the hut. Inside my mother were occupied trying to plug the spaces between the slabs with clay and straw so I took the carving knife from beneath her very nose she never even noticed.

Said she Theres one of Murray's beasts caught down the creek.

You must be mistaken.

I can hear it bellowing from here.

I said I would attend to it and let her know.

Within the year I would of learned to kill a beast very smart and clean and have its hide off and drying in the sun before you could say Jack Robertson but on this 1st occasion I failed to find the artery. I'm sure you know I have spilt human blood when there were no other choice at that time I were no more guilty than a soldier in a war. But if there was a law against the murder of a beast I would plead guilty and you would be correct to put the black cap on your head for I killed my little heifer badly and am sorry for it still. By the time she fell her neck was a sea of laceration I will never forget the terror in her eyes.

And this is how my ma found me with the poor dead creature at my feet and my hair and shirt soaked with blood and gore.

We have beef I said we'll feast on her.

But my words was bolder than my upset heart and I were very pleased she relieved me of the bloody knife I didnt know what next to do having not the faintest idea of how to butcher the heifer and yet not wanting the privilege to go elsewhere. My mother took my gory hand and led me across the dusty paddock to the hut and after tying up the dogs she ministered to me with soap and water all the time berating me and saying I were a very bad boy and she was angry with me etc. etc. but this were for the benefit of the other children who was listening at the door and watching through the chinks between the logs. My ma cleaned me so very gentle with the washer I knew she must be pleased.

Of course Annie could be relied upon to tell my father what I had done before he even got the saddle off his horse. He had been delivering butter to people with English names a job that always put him out of temper so when Annie showed him the dead beast he come inside to give me a hiding with his belt. There is a mark on my leg I carry to this day. When it were dark he took a lantern down by the creek and skinned and butchered my beast and carried the 4 quarters back across the paddock one at a time and then burned the head and hung the hide and cut out the MM brand so none could accuse us of stealing Murray's heifer. He salted down what meat would fit into a barrel and the rest he ordered my mother to cook at once.

All through this Annie would not speak to me even Maggie kept her distance but very late that night we had a mighty feast of beef and I noticed it were not just my excited brothers who ate their fill.

2 days later I were sent home from school at lunch time to collect my homework which I had forgot again I found a strange bay mare tethered beneath our peppercorn tree it had VR embroidered on the saddlecloth in silver. I knew it were the police. I entered the hut and my father were sitting in his usual chair watching a lanky

fair haired Constable spreading out the heifer's hide across our table.

Come on John said Constable Doxcy putting his hand right through the hole where the brand had been. John we know whats missing here.

As you can see said my father I slaughtered a cow and made a greenhide whip.

Ah you made a whip.

Correct my father said but did not protest or struggle against the accusation.

So be a good fellow will you John and bring me the whip.

My father did not say nothing he did not move he stared at the Constable with puffy eyes.

Perhaps you never made a whip at all.

Oh I must of lost it.

Must of lost it.

I'll bring it up to you soon as I find it.

More likely it were the brand John. Did you cut out Mr Murray's brand?

No I made a whip.

Did you ever hear of Act 7 and Act 8 George IV No 29?

I don't know.

It is a law John it says that if you duff another fellow's heifer then you're going to go to adjectival gaol and you can bring me any adjectival whip you like but unless it can fill this hole exactly John you're going in the adjectival lockup. We don't like Irish thieves in Avenel.

I can't bear prison my father spoke as plainly as a man who don't like Brussels sprouts.

Well thats a shame said Doxcy as he moved towards him.

I done it I said I thrust myself forward.

I put my hand on Doxcy's hard black shoulder belt and he rested his hand upon my arm.

You're a good boy Jim said he.

I'm Ned I done it.

The policeman asked my father is this so?

But my father would say nothing he were like some creature drugged by spiders.

I turned back to Doxcy demanding he arrest me and he laughed ruffling my hair and smiling a foolish sentimental smile.

Pack up your things John he said to my father you can bring a blanket and a pannikin and spoon.

I done it I said the brand were MM I done it with the carving knife.

Shutup my father says his eyes now alive and angry. Shut your gob go back to school.

Thus were Father taken from me handcuffed to the stirrup iron of Doxcy's mare.

In the days before our father were imprisoned we Kelly children would walk to school along the creek but now we took a new path through the police paddock where the lockup stood. Apart from this stockade the paddock had no feature other than a dreary mound of clay which marked the grave of Doxcy's mare. Even this miserable sight my father were denied for there was not one window in them heavy walls. At 1st we would shout out to him but never got any answer and finally we all give up excepting Jem who run his hands along the frost cold walls and pat the prison like a dog.

I dreamed about my father every night he come to sit on the end of my bed and stare at me his eyes silent and puffy his face were lacerated by a thousand knife cuts.

I were so v. guilty I could never of admitted that life without my father had become in many ways more pleasant. Only when his big old buck cat went missing did I frankly tell my ma I were pleased to see it gone.

Do not misunderstand me our lives was far harder for his absence. The landlord provided no decent fences so the mother and her children was obliged to build a dog leg fence 2 mi. long to save our cows from impounding. In any case our stock would still escape the fines was 5/- for a cow 3/- for a pig. This we could ill afford. Our mother were expecting another baby she were always weary yet more tender than before. At night she would gather us about her and tell us stories and poems she never done that when my da were away shearing or contracting but now we discovered this treasure she had committed to her memory. She knew the stories of Conchobor and

Dedriu and Medb the tale of Cuchulainn I still see him stepping into his war chariot it bristles with points of iron and narrow blades with hooks and hard prongs and straps and loops and cords.

The southerly wind blew right through the hut and it were so bitter it made your head ache though it aint the cold I remember but the light of the tallow candle it were golden on my mother's cheeks it shone in her great dark eyes bright and fierce as a native cat to defend her fatherless brood. In the stories she told us of the old country there was many such women they was queens they was hot blooded not careful they would fight a fight and take a king into their marriage bed. They would of been called Irish rubbish in Avenel.

Our mother grew bigger. We boys laboured beside her in the garden it were a good loam soil and we was set to improve it further. That 1st winter we had parsnips and potatoes only. We had to sell the wagon and 2 horses but kept our small herd of dairy cows. We produced 2 lb. of butter per day but rarely had anything except lard for our own bread. Jem and I tramped into town and back delivering the butter on foot walking right past our father's lockup not calling out to him no more. Each day I waited for the night to fall who can imagine from where happiness will come?

On the 5th of August 1865 I come home in the loud dripping dark. It had been raining already for a week the creek were a river roaring so I did not hear Mother's cries until I were at the door. I picked up a shovel and inside I discovered her lying on the earthen floor. When she saw me she sat up and explained she was beginning to have her baby. The handywoman were already gone to Hobb's Creek for another birth so my mother had sent Maggie to borrow the Morgans horse and ride to fetch old Dr May. That were 2 hr. previous and now the pain was very bad and my mother feared Maggie had been thrown off the horse or drowned crossing the creek.

Annie were the oldest but of a nervous disposition she had chosen this occasion to have the gastric fits. So while my mother laboured Annie vomited into a bowl beside her. I helped Mother onto her bed which were made from 2 thick saplings set into the wall and a piece of jute bag suspended between the shafts. Thinking her darling Maggie dead she cried continually. Jem were just 7 yr. and Dan were only 4 yr. they was both disturbed to see their mother in such distress.

In the hours that followed she could find no comfort or relent finally directing me to place a quilt over the table which she climbed upon at the same time instructing us all to go back behind our curtains. Dan begun bawling in earnest the table were revealed to be too short and my mother could not lie down as she had planned. Little Jem tried to help and were shouted at for his trouble. Mother instructed me to come and hold her hand then squatted on the table it had one loose leg my father had not attended to. The light were very poor just the one tallow light burning but I could see my mother's pain and were vexed I could do nothing to please her. She asked for water but would not let me go to fetch it. She cursed me for a fool and my father for abandoning her. All the while we expected the doctor but there were no sound from outside not even a mopoke nothing save a steady rain on the bark roof and the thumping of flotsam in the flooding waters of Hughes Creek.

All through the endless night I stood at her side and with every hour her cries and curses got wilder in the end Dan and Jem just fell asleep.

Around 4 o'clock Mother got herself once more onto the table and I thought the baby were finally coming but she swore at me and would not let me look. I heard a high thin wail like a lamb and knew my sister were arrived but she told me keep my back turned and find her best scissors in her tin box and then to put them in the flame of the fire. I done as ordered.

I heard her shifting on her table she gave a little cry of pain then she spoke more tenderly. All right come on here and see the little girl.

My mother sat on the table holding your Aunty Grace to me. She were a little foal a calf her eyes were wide her newborn skin glistening white and bloody nothing bad had ever touched her.

Cut says Mother cut.

Where I asked.

Cut she said and I saw the pearly cord going from her stomach down to the dark I shut my eyes and cut and it were just as the old scissors crunched into the flesh that Maggie led Dr May into our hut and there he saw a 11 yr. old Irish boy assisting at his sister's birth. He seen the earthen floor the soot black scissors the frightened children peering out from behind the curtained beds and all this he would feel free to gossip about so every child at Avenel School would soon get the false idea I seen my mother's naked bottom.

After the old drunk checked my sister with his instrument he handed her to me and attended to my mother. Dont drop her lad said he it were not likely I held our precious baby in my arms she were bright and light her eyes so clear and untroubled. She looked me frankly in the face and I loved her as if she were my very own.

By the time he finished doctoring to my mother it were dawn a luminous grey light filled the little hut and all the world seemed clear and new. I were happy then.

Said she Go tell him now.

I'll go later.

Go now.

But I did not wish to leave my new sister with her soft downy black hair and her white white skin how it glowed like a sepulchre inside that earth floored hut. Go tell your da he has a little girl.

So as the doctor ambled his groggy way along the track I cut across through the wet winter grass. There were a low mist lying across the police paddock lapping the edges of my father's solitary gaol. I approached the logs they was always damp and stained green with moss and mildew they give off a bad smell like dog s--- in the rain.

You got a girl I yelled.

The magpies was carolling the lories screeching and fighting in the gums but from the walls of the lockup come no sound at all.

Her name is Grace.

No answer the prison were silent as the grave but then I seen a movement from the corner of my eye it were my father's big buck cat standing on the mound where the mare were buried. The cat looked at me directly with its yellow eyes and then he arched his back and swished his tail once more as if I was no more than a robin or a finch. I threw a stone at him and went home to see my sister.

Soon all the scholars at Avenel School heard of my role at the birth. They never dared venture nothing to me but Eliza Mutton said something to Annie it made her most distressed. Them scholars was all proddies they knew nothing about us save Ned Kelly couldnt spell he had no boots Maggie Kelly had warts Annie Kelly's dress were darned and fretted over like an old man's sock. They knew our pater were in the logs and when we come to school each day they learned from Mr Irving that all micks was a notch beneath the cattle.

Irving were a little cock with a big head and narrow shoulders his eyes alight with finer feelings which he did not wish to share with me. It took the whole year until September before he would appoint me ink monitor by then he had no other choice for everybody with an English name had taken a turn. I cannot now remember why I desired such a prize only that I wanted it a great deal. When my time came at last I vowed to be the best monitor that were ever born. Each morning I were 1st to school lining up the chipped white china ink wells upon the tank stand then I washed and returned them to their hole in every desk.

Monday mornings I were permitted to also make the ink climbing up on Mr Irving's chair and taking down the McCracken's powder from the upper shelf it had a very pungent smell like violets and gall. I measured 4 Tblspn. with every pt. of tank water it were not a demanding task but required I get to school by 8 o'clock.

It were on account of this I saw Dick Shelton drowning.

In my desire to avoid the lockup I had walked to school along Hughes Creek which were very swollen from the spring rains all sorts of rubbish piled up in the current 1/2 burned tree trunks broken branches fenceposts a drowned calf with the water rushing across its empty eye. From the opposite bank I seen a boy edging out into the water. At the time I thought he had a fishing rod but later I learned he were using a pole to pick up the new straw hat that were swept into the flood and caught up in a jam. He stepped into the creek the black water drove up his legs he were no more than 8 yr. old.

I hollered go back but he never heard above the thunder of the creek. There were a bed of twigs like a lyrebird mound he tried to jump onto. Then he were gone.

Never one to wait I were swimming in the flooded creek before I knew it the water so fast and cold it would take your breath like a pooka steals your very soul. It were v. rough sweeping me violently down into a wide pool you would not credit the power of it. I glimpsed the boy's white face young Dick Shelton knew himself a goner and no more for this world. I got his arm but we was washed on down together more under than above the flood.

50 yd. down the creek has a dog leg where the proddies swim in summer. The pair of us was driven close to the bank against an old river red gum 1/2 submerged in flood. It were slippery as a pig but I were able to gain sufficient purchase to drag his drenched and soapy body back from that other world where he had imagined himself consigned.

Though the little chap were 1/2 drowned I got him upon my back he were crying and vomiting and agitating a great deal. He wore boots but my own feet was bare as usual I set off straight through the bush towards The Royal Mail Hotel where I knew his father were the licensee. It were a sharp and rocky bit of ground I chose.

The yardman at the Mail were a failed selector named Shaky White he were burying night soil in the scrub when he seen us coming and he started hollering Missus Missus Jesus Christ.

An upstairs window in the pub flew open a woman screamed a moment later Mrs Shelton were running down the yard towards her son but even in her great emotion she never ignored the Catholic boy and I were taken into her hotel and given a hot bath in a large white tub. I had never seen a bathtub until that day it were a blessed miracle to lay in that long smooth porcelain with all the steaming water brought to me by Shaky in 10 buckets I never saw so much water used to wash.

Then Mrs Shelton brought her older son's clothes to wear while mine was laundered they was soft and had a very pleasant smell. I would of given anything to keep them but Mrs Shelton didnt think of making that offer instead she put her plump arm around my shoulder and led me down stairs saying I were an angel sent by God.

In the dining room I discovered a merry fire and a man in a 3 pce. suit doing great damage to a plate of eggs and bacon but apart from him the room were empty. Mrs Shelton sat me at a table near the fire it were set with shining silver knives & forks & cruets & salt & pepper & a sugar bowl with a curved spoon. I knew my mother would have liked it very much.

Mrs Shelton asked Would I prefer cocoa I said yes she asked

Would I like a breakfast and presented me with a menu. I never seen such a thing before but soon I got the gist of it and used it well. I had begun the day with bread and dripping now I was ordering lamb chops and bacon and kidney it were very tasty. There were carpet on the floor I can see the pattern of the red roses to this day. Mrs Shelton wore a bright yellow dress and a gold bangle on her wrist she wept and smiled and stared at me all the time I ate she said I were the best and bravest boy in the whole world.

Mr Shelton had been in Seymour overnight but soon arrived in his wagon and rushed into the dining room in his muddy gumboots and oilskin coat. He tried to give me 1/2 a crown but I wouldnt hear of such a thing.

Mr Shelton were tall and broad with long side whiskers and his thin straight mouth would of looked mean were his eyes not so bright and brimming.

Is there nothing you wish for boy?

Nothing.

It were not true I would of liked a dress for my mother but I didnt know how much one would cost.

Very well said he then let me shake your hand.

I took his hand but confess that I were not nearly so noble as my speech suggested. I walked to school in my nice borrowed clothes and a pair of shining pinching boots I were so disappointed I were sick at heart.

The following morning a buckboard drew up at the schoolhouse Mr Irving were always fearful of inspectors he were suddenly as nervous as a quail.

Wipe clean your slates he commanded while trying to make some order of his pigpen desk. He were fast with multiplication but very queer and jerky in this crisis and now it didnt help him that his head were big he still couldnt reckon where to hide his fretsaw.

To Caroline Doxcy he said Go to the window see if it is a gentleman with a case. Smartly smartly Caroline.

He has a parcel.

Yes but does he have a satchel?

Oh Sir it is only Dicky Shelton's father.

Mr Irving were a king amongst children and didnt like visitors to his castle so he was out the door before the publican could enter. We could hear their voices clearly.

Damn it Irving roared Mr Shelton I'll do what I adjectival like.

The door banged against the wall and Esau Shelton burst inside with the odour of stale hops and raisin wine they was his constant friends.

Ah children cried he granting us a rare sight of his teeth.

Mr Irving come following behind rubbing his big pale hands together and telling us unhappily that we must listen to Mr Shelton.

Now look here little children said Mr Shelton and he placed his brown paper parcel amongst the litter on the teacher's desk. My son Dick nearly drowned yesterday. Did you know that? No? My Dick would be in heaven now were it not for someone in this very room.

The scholars now began to crane their necks and look enquiringly around and Annie seemed she might die folding her hands in her lap and staring ahead with glassy gaze. Jem were 7 yr. and so copied what his older sister done but my barrel chested Maggie never feared it were she who raised her hand.

It were my big brother Ned.

The blood rushed to my face.

Correct said Mr Shelton v. solemn please come and stand up here Ned Kelly.

I knew he were going to give me the brown paper parcel I had no doubt it contained the respectable clothes I always wanted. As I rose I caught the eye of Caroline Doxcy she smiled at me the 1st time ever. I put my shoulders back and walked up to Mr Irving's platform.

Mr Shelton bade me face the class then shut my eyes there were the crinkling of the paper the smell of camphor and the smooth feel of silk against my cheek.

I thought thats women's stuff it were a dress to give my mother.

Open your eyes Ned Kelly.

I done as ordered and saw his little slit of mouth all twisted in a grin and then Eliza Mutton and George Mutton and Caroline Doxcy and the Sheltons and Mr Irving staring at me with his wild bright eyes. I looked down at my person and seen not my bare feet my darned pullover my patched pants but a 7 ft. sash. It were peacock green embroidered with gold TO EDWARD KELLY IN GRATITUDE FOR HIS COURAGE FROM THE SHELTON FAMILY. At the very hour I stood before the scholars in my sash the decapitated head of the bushranger Morgan were being carried down the public highway—Benalla—Violet Town—Euroa—Avenel—perhaps it would be better had I known the true cruel nature of the world but I would not give up my ignorance even if I could. The Protestants of Avenel had seen the goodness in an Irish boy it were a mighty moment in my early life.

If these events made a big impression on my own young mind they made an even bigger one on Esau Shelton. What phantoms haunted his top paddock I have no way of knowing but it is very clear he could not stop dwelling on how his son were nearly dead and the more time that passed the more he felt the agony. He had been previously known as a tight lipped b----r not suited to his profession but now dear Jesus he could not be shutup and must offer endless accounts of young Dick's rescue to every bullocky selector or shearer who come to prop up his long bar. He never considered the embarrassment his emotions might be causing others it were his own peace of mind he sought.

Not many nights after I brung the sash home to my mother I were woken by the low growling of our kangaroo dogs and then detected the faint odours of stale hops.

Then come the most distinctive whisper from the night Mrs Kelly Mrs Kelly might I trouble you?

My mother replied with that hiss so particular to the mothers of young babes. What is it you want Mr Shelton?

But what is it you want Mrs Kelly?

My mother stayed silent but I could hear Mr Shelton scraping the mud off his boots as if he were intent on entering regardless.

What are you thinking Mrs Kelly?

What am I thinking? And any of her children would of recognized the dangerous rise and hook on its last word. Mr Shelton she said I'm lying here wondering who might be adjectival fool enough to wake my baby.

Beg pardon Mrs Kelly I'll come back tomorrow.

I don't want you back tomorrow Mr Shelton. She rose from her bed and knocked the pegs from the door and I watched through the curtain as the big smelly man shambled to the table and begun to noisily arrange his pipe and tobacco amongst our dirty dishes. He appeared pretty much a wreck as far as I could judge.

Mother wearily pulled her possum skin around her shoulders and waited impatiently for her guest to speak he was tongue-tied and required a v. loud impatient sigh to get him rolling again.

Mrs Kelly said he at last your boy has given me back my son.

We know that Mr Shelton just tell me what is bothering you.

Its the sash he admitted.

I thought please Jesus don't talk about the sash I valued that reward more than anything I ever owned but my mother had taken a shocking set against it on account of her opinion the Sheltons should have offered money.

The sash?

I'm thinking.

Go on Mr Shelton she encouraged.

Frankly it just don't seem sufficient.

There were a very long silence.

Would you like a cup of tea Mr Shelton?

No Mrs Kelly there is nothing you can offer me.

Some oatcake?

I just ate.

Would you take a brandy to settle your digestion?

Mrs Kelly you're a woman who lost her husband just like I nearly lost my son.

Dont cry Mr Shelton they aint neither of them exactly dead.

Thats it Mrs Kelly that is what my wife has pointed out to me. I have the power to bring Mr Kelly back to you.

Though I couldnt see my mother's face I did see her back shiver like a cat with ringworm.

How do you mean?

Mr Kelly is in the lockup you'll forgive me mentioning it.

It is a private subject.

I made an enquiry of Constable Doxcy.

That aint your business Mr Shelton.

You'll forgive me he says it is a matter of £25.

But my mother did not want her husband back. Oh no she cried I will not let you.

But I must Mrs Kelly I am bound to it.

Mr Shelton it is a lovely sash you give our Ned but if you don't watch out you'll spoil him. He's a good boy but very headstrong and don't need no encouragement to take more risks he's lucky he didnt drown himself.

But surely you aint saying you wish his father left in gaol?

No cried my mother I'm saying you shouldnt make a fuss of my boy.

But you would not object to your husband being freed?

Dear Jesus cried my mother what sort of woman do you think I am?

What else could she say? One week later her husband walked back into her life. We was seated round the table eating tea when he come and stood behind me. I twisted in my seat but didnt know whether to rise or what to say.

Get out of my adjectival chair.

I squeezed down the long bench and my father took his place he rested his freckled forearms on the table and asked my mother the baby's name. I could not take my eyes off the arms all puffy white and sweaty like cheese wrapped up too long in summer.

Grace as you know.

How would I know?

I sent Ned to tell you.

Again my father turned his eyes on me and I felt he were looking into my heart at all the sins I committed against him and he pushed his stew away telling my mother to give him what money she had hidden. I thought she would say no but she emptied her sock and give him all she had and my father walked back out into the night. We was all very quiet after he were gone.

You may think it strange that a man can survive transportation and the horrors of Van Diemen's Land and then be destroyed in a country lockup but we cannot credit the tortures our parents suffered in Van Diemen's Land—Port Macquarie—Toongabbie—Norfolk Island—Emu Plains. Avenel lockup were the final straw for your grandfather he did not speak more than a dozen words to me from that day until his death.

Once he worked with us putting in the oats but he no longer liked the light of day and mostly remained inside the hut. By late spring the following year he were so bloated you could hardly see his eyes was lost and lonely and angry in the middle of his swollen face. We moved around him as if he were a pit too deep to fall into. Dr May come and told us he had dropsy and we paid a great deal of money for his medicine but there were no improvement and our father lay on his crib he could hardly raise his head to sip the rum.

Mother and I now did all the ploughing we seeded 20 acres but it were too late in the season. One day at noon it were a hot December day the sky were blue and the magpies carolling my mother returned to the hut then come straight back out to fetch me.

Come she said come now.

We entered the hut together our bare feet caked with soil our hats already in our hands and there we saw our poor da lying dead upon the kitchen table he were bulging with all the poisons of the empire his skin grey and shining in the gloom.

I were 12 yr. and 3 wk. old that day and if my feet were callused one inch thick and my hands hard and my labourer's knees cut and scabbed and stained with dirt no soap could reach yet did I not still have a heart and were this not he who give me life now all dead and ruined?

Father son of my heart are you dead from me are you dead from me my father? □

GRANTA

THE NEW HIEROGLYPHICS

Les Murray

In the World language, sometimes called
Airport Road, a thinks balloon with a gondola
under it is a symbol for *speculation.*

Thumbs down to ear and tongue:
World can be written and read, even painted
but not spoken. People use their own words.

Latin letters are in it for names, for e.g.
OK and H_2SO_4, for musical notes,
but mostly it's diagrams: skirt-figure, trousered figure

have escaped their toilet doors. *I* (that is, *saya*,
ego, *watashi wa*) am two eyes without pupils;
those aren't seen when you look out through them.

You has both pupils, *we* has one, and one blank.
Good is thumbs up, thumb and finger zipping lips
is *confidential*. *Evil* is three-cornered snake eyes.

The effort is always to make the symbols obvious:
the bolt of *electricity*, winged stethoscope of course
for *flying doctor*. Pram under fire? *Soviet film industry*.

Pictographs also shouldn't be too culture-bound:
a heart circled and crossed out surely isn't.
For *red*, betel spit lost out to ace of diamonds.

Black is the ace of spades. The king of spades
reads *Union boss*, the two is *feeble effort*.
If is the shorthand Libra sign, the scales.

Spare literal pictures render most nouns and verbs
and computers can draw them faster than Pharaoh's scribes.
A bordello prospectus is as explicit as the action,

but everywhere there's sunflower talk, i.e.
metaphor, as we've seen. A figure riding a skyhook
bearing food in one hand is the pictograph for *grace*,

two animals in a book read *Nature*, two books
inside an animal, *instinct*. Rice in bowl with chopsticks
denotes *food*. Figure 1 lying prone equals *other*.

Most emotions are mini-faces, and the speech
balloon is ubiquitous. A bull inside one is dialect
for placards inside one. Sun and moon together

inside one is *poetry*. Sun and moon over palette,
over shoes etc. are all art forms—but above
a cracked heart and champagne glass? Riddle that

and you're starting to think in World, whose grammar
is Chinese-terse and fluid. Who needs the square-
equals-diamond book, the *dictionary*, to know figures

led by strings to their genitals mean *fashion*?
just as a skirt beneath a circle means *demure*
or a similar circle shouldering two arrows is *macho*.

All peoples are at times cat in water with this language
but it does promote international bird on shoulder.
This foretaste now lays its knife and fork parallel.

□

GRANTA

GROWING UP

David Moore

PHOTOGRAPHS INTRODUCED
BY DAVID MALOUF

David Moore was born in 1927 and grew up beside Sydney Harbour. He served his apprenticeship in the Sydney studio of Max Dupain, then Australia's greatest photographer, but soon began to take pictures which, in his own words, were far removed from 'the artificiality and applied gloss' of advertising photography. His earliest documentary pictures were of the streets, slums and wharves of Sydney. In the Fifties and Sixties he worked outside Australia, producing photostories for the best and most demanding international magazines—*National Geographic*, *Life*, *Sports Illustrated*. The photographs on the following pages are chosen from his own favourite selection of fifty out of the thousands of images he has made for magazines, for picture books and for his own pleasure: landscapes, cityscapes, people at work and at play, portraits of the famous, studies of architectural detail, or sections of a bridge or a motorway in construction in which his eye finds the elements of contemporary sculpture.

Australia is an island. Its first white inhabitants were seagoing island-dwellers who settled round its coastline and looked to the sea as a gateway of exit and entrance. In my childhood, as in David Moore's, the ports of call on the P. & O. and Orient routes to England told us not how far off the rest of the world was, but—in terms of feeling, at least—how close. The arrival and departure of the great liners in Sydney Harbour were events of an almost mystical significance, and this Moore catches in images that are full of the poetry of such occasions: the festivity of farewell, with one of Moore's mysterious figures looming up dark in the foreground against the shimmering cascade of thousands of streamers that are just about to break; and the anxiety of arrival, with a group of migrants at the ship rails, all eyes—curious, resigned, hopeful, with one woman's hand thrust up to dramatize the image with an open palm, all light.

Again and again Moore goes back to celebrate the harbour in its many forms: southbound traffic on a winter morning in 1947, with the great arch of the bridge unusually foreshortened under one of Sydney's 'dramatic' skies; fifty years later the Glebe Island Bridge with a full moon between its spars. Grandest of all is the great open expanse of the harbour seen from 16,000 feet up and looking westward into the sun, all its bays and branches brimming with quicksilver light, and

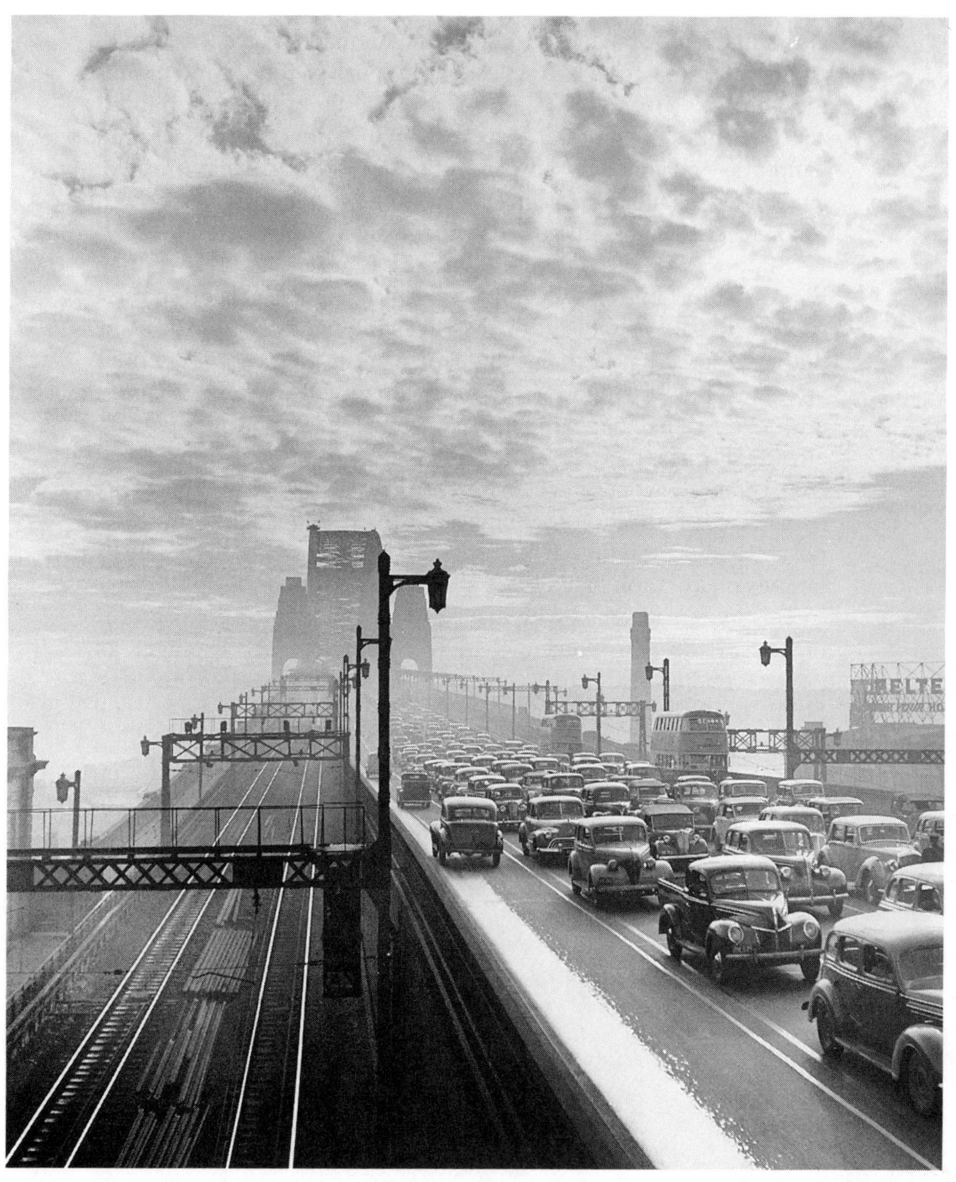

Sydney Harbour Bridge, 1947

in the midst of it the bridge, its single span made fragile by distance and doubled in hard-edged reflection. In other pictures, Moore turns the bridge's ironwork into abstract sculpture—he himself acknowledges a debt to Robert Klippel, doyen of Australian sculptors—to remind us how gigantic the bridge is, what a feat of intricate yet monumental engineering. Moore's father was an architect; concrete, steel and stone structures have always intrigued him.

In his 1948 photograph of Surry Hills Street the effect is of an Expressionist film. The telegraph pole in the middle ground forms a giant cross and at the end of the street the figure of a man, made tiny by distance, appears in silhouette against the sky, a mysterious arrival on the scene; and in the foreground, half hidden in shadow, a watcher, a small boy whose gaze adds another point of view to an already disturbing occasion.

There is a wonderful generosity in these pictures, the generosity of interest, of affection for things and for people as they are, with no straining after moral or political significance. Even his justly famous photograph of a Sydney slum ('Redfern Interior, 1949', page 112) is more concerned with expressing the individual presence, the dignity of the two women, than with making them examples of poverty or injustice; and in 'Martin Place, Sydney, 1949' the vast facade of the bank, towering above the figures below, in the forceful lyricism of its Ionic columns and the play of light across them, has too much soaring beauty, is too fully an image of human aspiration and achievement, to be a symbol of economic oppression or inhuman power.

DAVID MALOUF

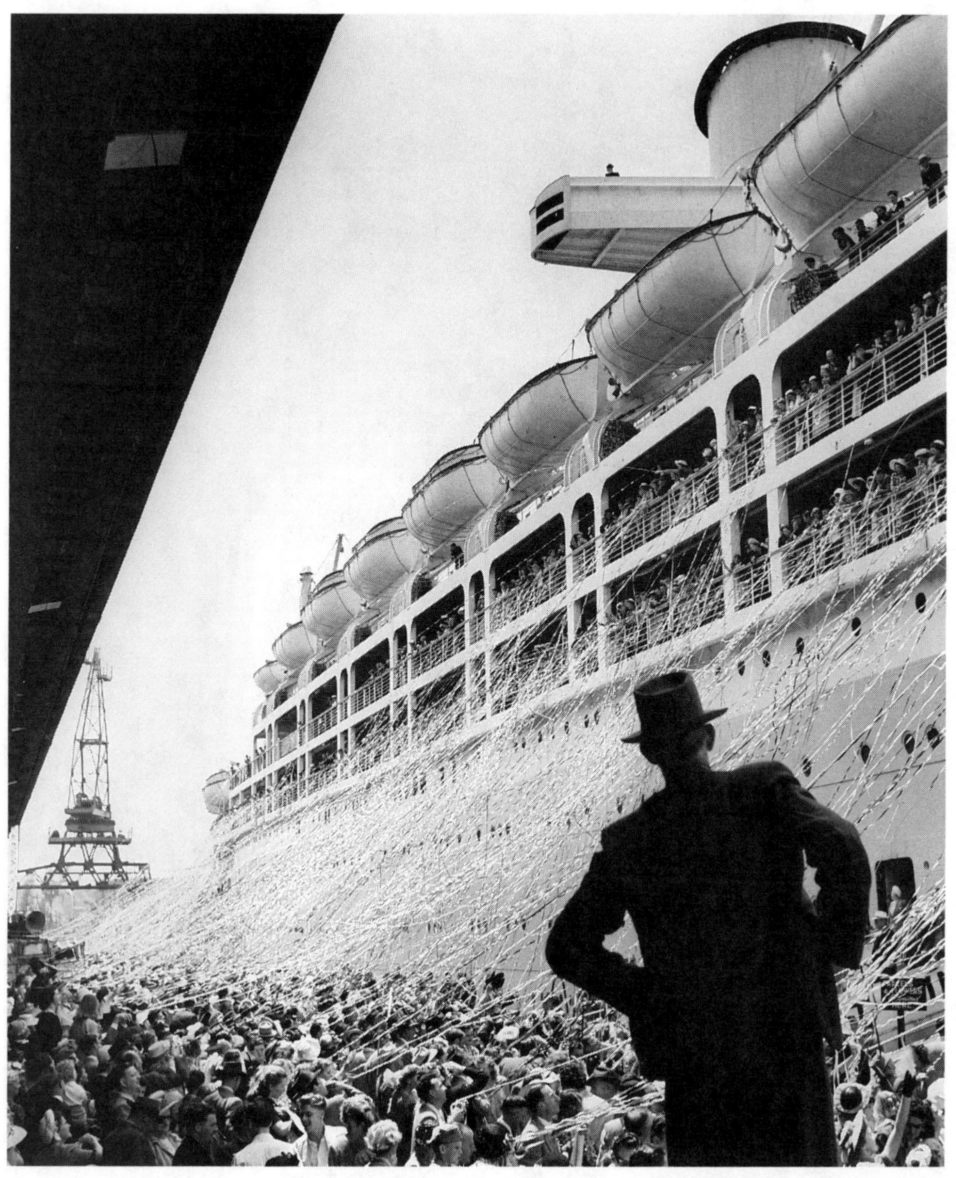

The 'Orcades' departing from Pyrmont, c 1948

Surry Hills Street, Sydney, 1948

Left: Martin Place, Sydney, 1949

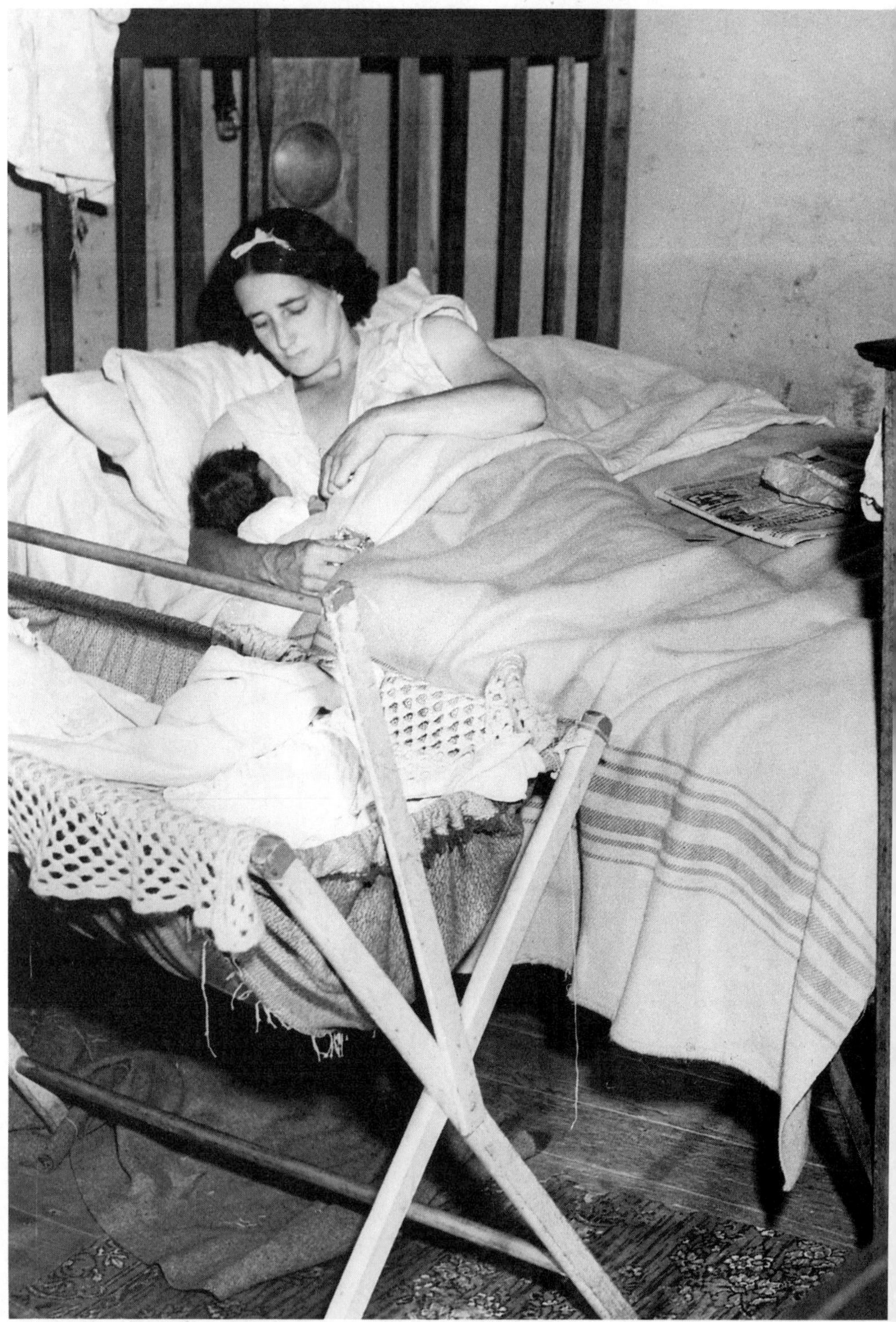

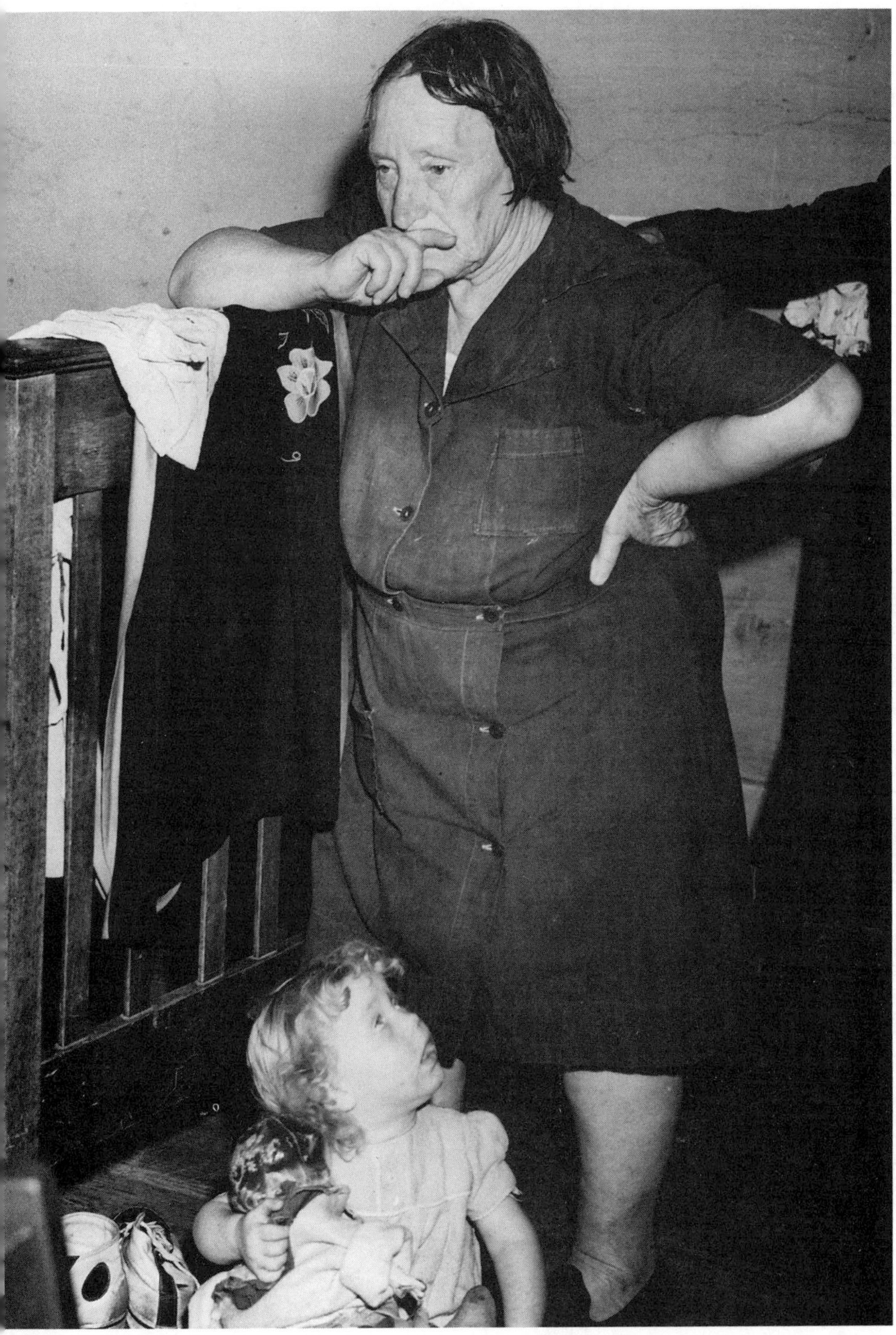

Bar at Betoota Races, Queensland, 1961

Pitjantjatjara children, South Australia, 1963

Outback children, South Australia, 1963

Billy tea, Mern Merna station, South Australia, 1963

Newcastle steelworks, New South Wales, 1963

Peters
PIES
CLAREMONT
SUBIACO

Bar billiards, Lancelin, Western Australia, 1963

Sydney Harbour from 16,000 feet, 1966; previous page: arriving in Sydney, 1966

Sydney Opera House under construction, 1966

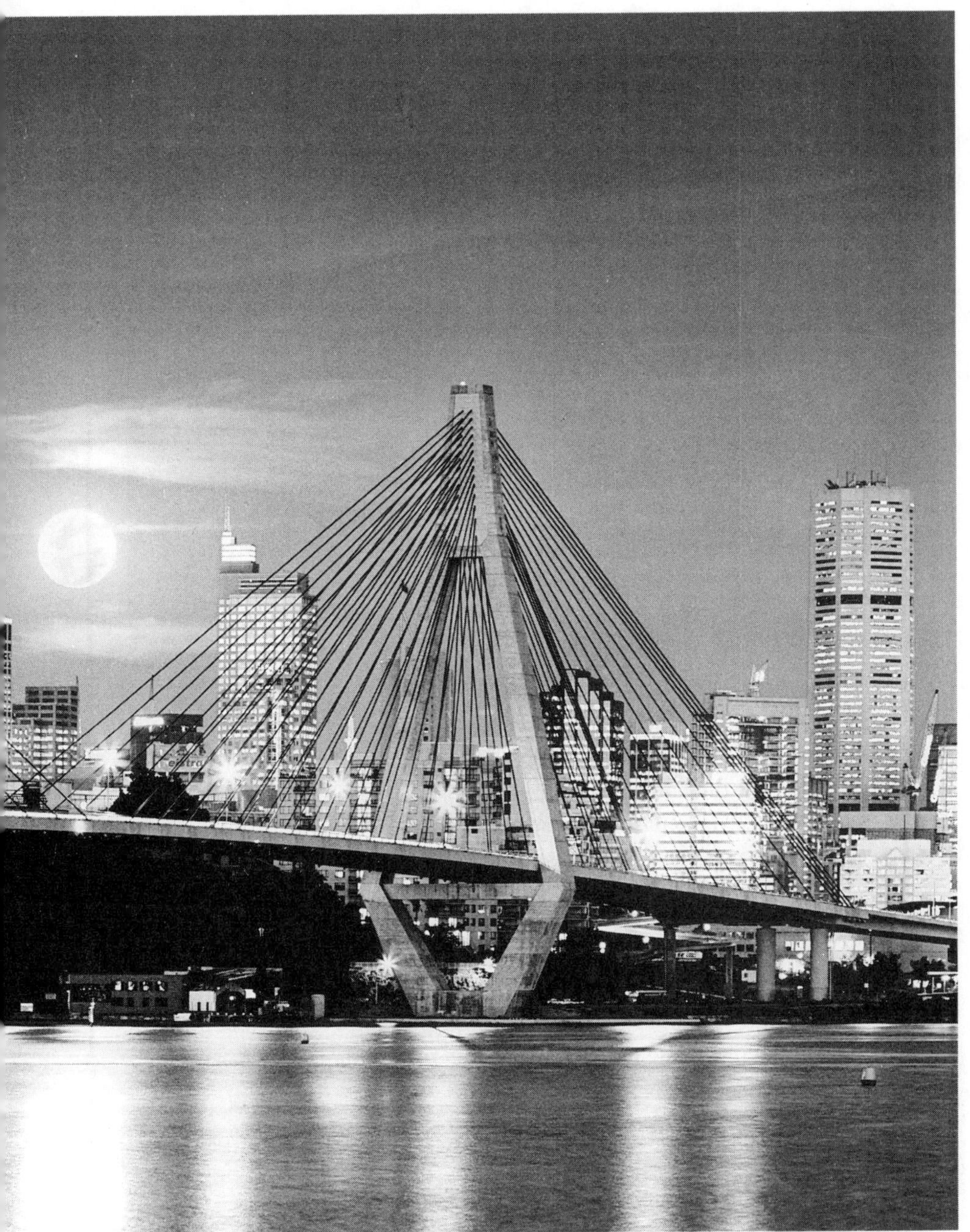

Glebe Island Bridge, Sydney, 1997

GRANTA

POBBY AND DINGAN

Ben Rice

'The secret of an opal's colour lies not
in its substance but in its absences.'

Australian Geographic

Lightning Ridge GRAHAME MCCONNELL/AUSTRALIAN GEOGRAPHIC

One

Kellyanne crawled into my bedroom through the car door. Her face was puffy and pale and fuzzed-over. She just came in and said: 'Ashmol! Pobby and Dingan are maybe-dead.' That's how she said it.

'Good,' I said. 'Perhaps you'll grow up now and stop being such a fruit-loop.'

Tears started sliding down her face. But I wasn't feeling any sympathy, and neither would you if you'd grown up with Pobby and Dingan.

'Pobby and Dingan aren't dead,' I said, hiding my anger in a swig from my can of Mello Yello. 'They never existed. Things that never existed can't be dead. Right?'

Kellyanne glared at me through tears the way she did the time I slammed the door of the ute in Dingan's face or the time I walked over to where Pobby was supposed to be sitting and punched the air and kicked the air in the head to show Kellyanne that Pobby was a figment of her imaginings. I don't know how many times I had sat at the dinner table saying: 'Mum, why do you have to set places for Pobby and Dingan? They aren't even real.' She put food out for them too. She said they were quieter and better behaved than me and deserved the grub.

'They ain't exactly good conversationists, but,' I would say.

And at other times when Kellyanne held out Pobby and Dingan were real I would just sit there saying: 'Are not. Are not. Are not,' until she got bored of saying: 'Are. Are. Are,' and went running out screaming with her hands over her ears.

And many times I've wanted to kill Pobby and Dingan, I don't mind saying it.

My dad would come back from the opal mines covered in dust, his beard like the back-end of a dog that's shat all over its tail. He would be saying: 'Ashmol, I sensed it today! Tomorrow we'll be on opal, son, and we'll be bloody millionaires! I can feel those bewdies in the drive just sitting there staring at me. Checking me out. Waiting. They're red-on-blacks, Ashmol, I'll bet you anything! And there's rumours going that Lucky Jes has taken out a million-dollar stone and a fossilized mammoth tooth with sun-flash in it. We're close, boy. Close. There's something in that earth with the name Williamson on it.'

His excitement always caught a hold of me. I would get a tingle down my neck and I would sit there with my ears pricking up like a hound's, my tongue hanging out, watching my dad's eyes darting around in his head. They were strange eyes—blue and green and with a flicker of gold in them. 'Eyes like opals,' my mum once said with a sigh, 'only a little easier to find.'

Well, while Dad was pacing around the yard brushing himself off a bit and swigging from a stubby of VB, Kellyanne would say: 'Dad, be careful! You almost trod on Pobby with your fat feet! Watch what you're doing!' And Dad would be too excited to do anything but say: 'Aw, sorry princess. Did I tread on your fairy-friends?' That was Dad. Me and him never took Pobby and Dingan seriously one bit.

But there were others who did. The older softer folks in Lightning Ridge had sort of taken to Pobby and Dingan. They had totally given up throwing Kellyanne funny looks and teasing her about them. Now when she walked down Opal Street, the old-timers would stop and say: 'G-day Kellyanne, g-day Pobby, and how's Miss Dingan doin' today?' It made you want to be sick all over the place. Lightning Ridge was full of flaming crackpots as far as I could see. It was like the sun had burned out their brains. I was as much a rockhound as the next kid, but I wasn't crazy enough to talk to imaginary friends, I'll tell you that for nothing. But one time Ronnie Hope let Kellyanne enter Dingan in for the Opal Princess competition because Kellyanne had a cold. I'm not kidding. And the judges voted Dingan third place, and Nils O'Reiordan from the newspaper came and took photographs of Kellyanne with her arm around Dingan's invisible shoulder, and made out he was asking Dingan questions and everything. It was embarrassing. When the newspaper came out there was a picture of Kellyanne wearing a little silver crown over her long blonde hair, and underneath there was this sentence saying: *Two Opal Princesses—Kellyanne Williamson (aged eight) and her invisible friend Dingan who won third prize in this year's Opal Princess competition.* Plus every time we went to Khan's, Mrs Schwartz would hand my sister three lollies and say: 'There you go, Kellyanne. One for you, one for Pobby and one for Dingan. They look like they're both doing good.' Everybody knew everybody in Lightning Ridge. And some people even knew nobody as well, it seemed. Pobby and Dingan fat in to the little town just fine.

'Find anything today?' Mum said one night when she'd got back from her job on the checkout at Khan's and me and Dad were relaxing after a hard afternoon's work out at the claim.

'Potch. Nothing special.'

'Nothing?'

I could see Kellyanne through the window over Dad's shoulder. She was sitting out back on a pile of stones, talking to Pobby and Dingan, her mouth moving up and down, her hands waving around like she was explaining something to them. But all she was really talking to was the night and a few galahs. And if she was honest she would have admitted it there and then. But not Kellyanne.

'Where's my little girl?' Dad asked.

'Outside, playing with some friends,' my mum said, fixing my Dad a look straight between the eyes.

'Pobby and Dingan?'

'Yup.'

My dad sighed a little. 'Jesus! That girl's round the twist,' he said.

'No she isn't,' said my mum, 'She's just different.'

'She's a fruit-loop,' I said.

'I kind of wish they were real friends, Mum,' Dad said. 'She don't seem to get on with the other kids around here too much.'

'What d'you expect?' said my mum, raising her voice and putting her hands on her hips as usual: 'What d'you bloody expect when you drag your family to a place like this? What d'you bloody expect to happen when you bring up an intelligent girl like Kellyanne in a place full of holes and criminals and freaks?'

'I still say Kellyanne could do with some real-live mates,' went on my dad, as if he was talking to someone inside his beer.

Mum had stomped off into the kitchen. 'Maybe they are real!' she shouted back at him after rattling a few plates together, 'Ever thought about that, ye of little bloody imagination?'

My dad pulled a face. 'Who? Pobby and Dingan? Ha!' He drained his beer can, stood it up on the floor and then stamped on it until it was a disc of metal. He threw me a wink as if to say: 'Here comes the next wave of the attack, Ashmol!' And it came.

'Damn, Rex! You make me so bloody angry. Honestly! You haven't found any opal in two years! Not a glimpse of it. And opal's real enough for you. You don't stop dreaming about it and talking in your sleep to it like a lover! Well, as far as I'm concerned, Rex Williamson, your bloody opal doesn't exist either!'

But that was a stupid thing for Mum to say, because the shops were full of opal and there were pictures of it everywhere and everybody was talking about it and the Japanese buyers forked out a whole heap of dollars for it. That's a fact. I saw them doing it with my own eyes out at Hawk's Nest.

Well, after my mum said this stuff about opal and after she'd done her usual piece about there being no money left in the tin under the bed, Dad sulked around a bit and kicked a few rocks around out in the yard. But then suddenly the door swung open and he came in full of energy like a new man and with a strange smile on his face. And what did he do? He started asking Kellyanne about Pobby and Dingan and how their days had been and what they were doing tomorrow. And he had never done that before in his life, ever. But he did it in a voice so you weren't too sure if he was joking around or not. Kellyanne was studying his face carefully, trying to work him out for herself. And so was I. And so was Mum. And then Dad asked Kellyanne if he could run Pobby and Dingan a bath. And he asked straight-faced and honest-sounding and Kellyanne eventually said yes, that was all right, but only she was allowed to dry them after it.

I said: 'Dad, what the hell are you doing? You know all that Pobby and Dingan stuff's just horseshit! She'll never grow out of it if you talk like that!'

And Dad answered, looking at his feet: 'No, Ashmol. I think I've been unfair on Pobby and Dingan. I think that they do exist after all! I just haven't, like, recognized it until now.'

He smiled and disappeared into the bathroom to run the taps while Kellyanne stood there glowing with pride and flashing me a smile from the doorway. It made me feel sick. I looked at Mum, but she had a contented grin on her face and started setting about making tea and cookies. I sat at the table feeling like someone marooned me on a desert island.

Well, I don't like thinking about it, but from that moment on my Dad became a total dag. When he got up in the morning and woke up Kellyanne for school he would wake up Pobby and Dingan too. Yes, he would. He started talking to them like they were real people. And he wasted all kinds of money on buying them birthday presents—good money that could have gone into a new generator if you ask me. Oh, yes, Dad had himself some fun by going along with the Pobby and Dingan thing. One time he took Kellyanne, Pobby and Dingan out to the Bore Baths in the ute. When I ran out to join them with my towel around my shoulders, my dad said, 'Sorry, son. Can't take you today, Ashmol. Not enough room with Pobby and Dingan in here.' He waved out of the window with a big smile on his face and drove off thinking he was a funny kind of bloke. Sometimes Mum would ask him to come and help with the washing up. But no! Dad was helping Pobby and Dingan get dressed or helping them with their homework. Kellyanne loved it. But Mum went a bit strange. I don't think she could decide if she was angry or pleased that Dad had become mates with Pobby and Dingan. And I think even Kellyanne began to realize pretty soon that Dad was only doing it to get back at Mum or something. He wasn't a very subtle sort of bloke, my dad, when it came down to it. He drank too much for a start and spent too much time underground in the dark.

Two

When Dad left for the claim one morning he volunteered to take Pobby and Dingan with him to get some exercise while Kellyanne was at school. He was trying to separate her from them, I suppose, now I think about it. Kellyanne's teachers, you see, had complained that she wasn't concentrating in class and was always talking to herself and hugging the air.

Well, I got to admit it was a funny sight seeing my dad heading out holding hands with two invisible people. Kellyanne watched him, making sure he helped them up into the driving seat. Dad started the ute up and waved out of the window and made out he was fastening Pobby and Dingan's seat belts.

'Don't worry, princess!' he shouted. 'I'll look after them while you're at school and make sure they don't get up to no mischief. Won't I, Pobby? Won't I, Dingan?'

I was getting a bit worried. My dad was turning into a poof. And the neighbours were talking about him walking alone and talking to himself and things like that. They said he was even drunker than normal.

That same night Mum still wasn't back from work and Dad had swallowed a few beers too many shall we say. He was singing 'Heartbreak Hotel', and doing a sort of Elvis dance. I knew he had forgotten to bring back Pobby and Dingan from the claim, but I didn't say nothing. I wanted to see what Kellyanne would have to say about it, so I just sat there playing on my Super Mario with its flat batteries, hoping Kellyanne would come in from the kitchen and get all ratty. Dad started talking about how he had stopped by at the puddling dam to do a bit of agitating. I said: 'Do your Elvis dance again, Dad, it's really cool.' Of course it wasn't cool at all, but I wanted to keep him from thinking about his day. He might have remembered about Pobby and Dingan in the nick of time. Luckily he didn't and Kellyanne came rushing in from the kitchen where she was having a go at cooking yellow-belly from Mum's instructions.

'Dad. Where's Pobby and Dingan? Where are they?' she cried, all anxious.

'Now you're in for it, Dad,' I said. 'Better make something up quick.'

Dad's face suddenly flushed all kinds of colours. He swivelled around and spilt some beer on the floor. 'Hi, princess! Relax now, darl'. Pobby and Dingan's right here sittin' on the couch next to Ashmol.'

Kellyanne looked over at the couch. 'No they're not, Dad,' she said. 'They hate Ashmol. Where are they really?'

'Oh no, that's it,' said my dad, 'I forgot. They're out back watering the plants.'

Kellyanne ran outside. She came back looking pale. 'Dad, you forgot all about Pobby and Dingan, didn't you? You've lost them, haven't you?'

'No, princess,' said my dad, 'Calm down, sweetheart. They were in the truck with me when I came back.'

'I don't believe you,' said Kellyanne, tears growing out of her eyes. 'I want you to take me out to the claim to look for them right now.' That was my sister! She was mad as a cut snake.

'Christ, Kellyanne!' I said. 'Grow up, girl!'

Dad looked a bit desperate. 'Aw, princess, come on. Are you sure your little friends aren't here?'

'Positive,' said Kellyanne.

And so Dad couldn't do nothing except take Kellyanne out to the claim called Wyoming where he had his drives.

'You come too, Ashmol,' Dad said.

'No thanks,' I said, folding my arms across my chest. 'Count me out. No bloody way is Ashmol Williamson going looking for two non-existent things.'

But in the end I went along all the same, making sure I did lots of tutting and shaking my head. When we arrived at the claim the two of them walked around calling out: 'Pobby! Dingan! P-P-P-Pobbbbby! Where are you?' I sat firm on a mullock heap next to a citrus and opened up a can of Mello Yello. I knew what my dad was thinking. He was thinking that any minute now Kellyanne was going to imagine she had found her imaginary friends and start beaming all over her face. But she didn't. She kept calling out and looking real worried. She ran around the four corners of the claim looking from side to side. Pobby and Dingan were nowhere to be seen, she said. And who was going to argue with her? Dad wasn't. And I was having shit-all to do with it.

They looked behind the mullock heaps and they looked in the old Millard caravan where we used to live when we first came out to the Ridge, and they looked behind the mining machinery and behind a clump of leopard gums. And I'll bet all the time my dad was thinking: 'I must be going hokey cokey. If the other miners could see me now!' Dad knew pretty darn well, you see, that only Kellyanne was going to find Pobby and Dingan. He would just have to wait until she did. Or maybe he was secretly hoping that this was Kellyanne's little way of putting her imaginary friends behind her for good. Anyway, he kept throwing desperate glances my way and shouting over: 'Come on Ashmol, lend a frigging hand, will you?' But I wasn't budging. And so Dad sat down by the hoist where the blower was curled up like a big snake and just called out: 'Pobby! Dingan! Listen, you two! I'm sorry I didn't look after you proper!

I'm sorry I left you out here! I've got some lollies in my pocket if you want some!' That was a fat lie. He never had any lollies.

Well in the last hour before dark Dad pulled himself off his backside and looked real hard. You had to hand it to him. He got down on his knees and crawled around in the dirt. He rummaged through piles of rocks. He looked behind trees, in front of trees, up trees and down trees. He crossed over on to the next claim which was owned by Old Sid the Grouch. He shouldn't've. But he did. He searched like he was mad and there was sweat or tears slipping down his cheeks. He worked harder than he ever mined in his life, I reckon. And it was hard to believe he was searching for Nothing. Diddly-squat. Stuff-All. And then there was a piece of very bad timing.

Old Sid who had the claim next to my dad's and lived out there on a camp made of pieces of corrugated iron, came running out from behind a weeping wilga tree and stood by the starpicket at the corner of our claim. He had his arms folded. He had a big grey moustache, and he wore this kind of stupid beanie hat that made him look even meaner and stupider than he was. And believe me that was stupid. The rumour was he ate frill-neck lizards on toast for breakfast.

Old Sid was watching my dad pacing up and down, swearing and calling out: 'Pobby! Dingan!' Sid couldn't make head or tail of what was going on. All he could see was my dad down on his knees and leaning over his mineshaft. He thought my dad was ratting his claim and stealing all his opal. He shouted out: 'What's up, Rex Williamson? Hey! Rex! What is it? You lost something?'

My dad turned around startled. He was totally off his guard. He began to go red and get all embarrassed and then he started trying to make up some sort of story about looking for his watch, but then he changed it halfway into a lost-cat story. It all went a bit wrong. My dad wasn't much good at lying.

'You been drinking, Rex?'

I walked up to Sid to put things straight.

'My dad ain't been drinking nothing, Mr Sid,' I said. 'You see, my sister's got two imaginary friends called Pobby and Dingan—maybe you've heard of them—and my dad lost them out on the claim. And we're here looking for them. Sounds strange, I know—but there you go, that's the truth of it.'

Sid looked totally baffled and pretty angry. He said: 'Now don't you go making excuses for your daddy, Ashmol Williamson! You may be a clever kid, but your old man's been ratting my claim, ain't he? Some of us miners have been suspecting him for some time. But now here's the proof of it! And you're just trying to stick up for him, ain't you?'

My dad stumbled over. He was all shook up. He said: 'Now look here, Sid. I ain't been ratting nothing. I ain't no thief. I'm looking for my daughter's imaginary friends and you'd better bloody well believe it, mate!'

But Sid wasn't having any of it. 'You can talk about invisible people as much as you like, Rex Williamson,' he said, 'but when I saw you on my claim this evening, sniffing around for my opal, the first thing I did was call the police, and, as a matter of fact, here they are right now!'

The noise of a car drove into our ears and suddenly a four-wheel-drive police jeep came wobbling down the creamy-red track which leads to our claim. It pulled over by the old Millard caravan and out came two policemen. Big fellas with hats and badges and shit. I was getting a bit worried. Kellyanne was still looking around the claim for Pobby and Dingan, and Dad had started shouting about how dare Old Sid call him a ratter, he who'd worked honestly for God knows how long, and been a pretty good sort of bloke all round. And then I went up to one of the police blokes and told him the truth of the matter about Pobby and Dingan and what my dad was doing on Old Sid's claim. But I hadn't got too far when there was this noise of scuffling and a grunt, and I turned around to see that my dad had lost his cool and snotted Old Sid one in the nose. Well, after that the police were on my dad in a flash, and they had him in handcuffs and everything. Kellyanne came running over in a panic, saying: 'Leave my dad alone! Leave him alone!' But Dad was bundled into the car and driven away in a flash. And it was us who were left alone. And then Kellyanne sat down on the mullock and broke down in sobs, for I reckon it was a bit too much to cope with losing two imaginary friends and one real dad in an afternoon.

So I said, 'Kellyanne, come on, we'd better get home. Pobby and Dingan will come back tonight on their own and Dad will be fine as soon as this is sorted out and he tells them what he was doing on Sid's land. Come on, we'll walk back and tell Mum and get the bad bits over and done with.'

But Kellyanne didn't stop looking worried. She legged it over to the mineshaft and stepped over the tape which was around the top of the hole to stop people going down. She got down on all fours and peeked over the edge. And she called out Pobby and Dingan's names down the mineshaft. There was no reply of course. She stayed there on all fours looking down that mineshaft for half an hour.

'This just isn't like them,' she said. 'This is not like them at all.'

While she was doing this I walked over to Old Sid who was still watery-eyed with pain and holding on to his nose and mooching around his claim checking to see if all his opal dirt was still there. I said: 'You've made a big mistake here, Old Sid. We Williamsons were just looking for my sister's imaginary friends. We ain't no ratters.'

Old Sid said something about our family needing our heads inspected, and how my poor mother was too much of a Pom for this place, and how he felt sorry for us that our dad was a ratter, and how the rumour was my dad had come to the Ridge in the first place to hide away from the law. And I felt so angry I walked right away, pulled Kellyanne up by the arm and marched her home. It took an hour and a half, and all the way Kellyanne was whining about how she'd lost Pobby and Dingan, and how she wouldn't be able to sleep or eat until she found them, and how if they'd been here they could have saved Dad and none of this would have happened. Her worried little face was covered in white dust so she looked like a little ghost.

Well, it was pitch-dark when we got back to our home, and my mum had already heard what had happened from the police, and she sent us to bed and said not to worry because everything would be sorted out in the morning. But I never saw her looking so angry and panicky and unsorted out in her life. And her bedroom light stayed on all night, I swear.

And that night at around twelve was when Kellyanne crawled into my bedroom through the old Dodge door that Dad had fixed up for me to make going to bed more interesting. She was puffy and pale and said: 'Ashmol, Pobby and Dingan are maybe-dead.' And she just sat there in her pyjamas all tearful and hurt. But I was half thinking of Dad and if he was in prison and how the whole thing was Pobby and Dingan's fault. And then I tried to get my head round how it could be their fault if they didn't even exist.

And I fell asleep thinking about that.

Three

When I woke up the next day, Mum told me how Dad had been in prison overnight but he was being released and sent home until there was a trial or something which would prove that Dad hadn't been ratting Old Sid's claim. Mum was pretty frantic with worry though, and she said Dad would have to keep a low profile in the Ridge and stay at home a while until the whole thing had blown over and he'd got his respect back amongst all the miners and stuff. Ratting, you see, is the same thing as murder in Lightning Ridge—only a bit worse.

We waited for him to come home and played us a game of chess to help pass the time and calm each other down. I got Mum in checkmate after fifteen moves. No one can beat me at chess, and I reckon one day I'll be a bloody grandmaster or something. But I have to admit that this time Mum wasn't concentrating too well and so she made it pretty easy for my bishops and knights to do the business. The problem was that Mum kept gazing out of the window with a dazed look about her, and I was pretty sure she wasn't just thinking about Dad, but she was also Pommy-sick again and thinking about Granny Pom and the other Pommy friends she left behind her in England all those years ago.

Anyway, when Dad came in he gave us all a hug and said that the prison was like a motel except that the beds were hard and the bars weren't the sort that served beer. He said not to worry because he was going to sort out this whole mess good and proper. But he didn't know how. And Mum told him he'd better not try and sort out anything but just keep his head down and keep out of trouble until the trial and all that shit. And then he asked if Pobby and Dingan had come back. I shook my head. 'Kellyanne thinks they are maybe-dead,' I said.

'She's still very upset,' said my mum. 'You shouldn't have been so careless, Rex, you really shouldn't.'

'I shouldn't have done a lot of things,' said my dad, letting out a long sigh. But he was pleased to be back. And he was glad, I think, of all the attention we were giving him. I even went and got him a stubby of beer and sat there asking him things about prisons. And then we talked about opal all day until it got dark and until there was suddenly this god-awful shriek and Mum came rushing in from near the front door saying: 'Oh, my Lord! God! Help! Get water! Get water fast!' She ran into the kitchen and started filling up a bucket from the sink.

We rushed out front and what hit me first was a smoky smell like the smell of a cigar. And then, when I peered out into the dark, I could see grey figures moving up into the sky quite awesomely. Dancing. But my dad whispered: 'Jesus! They've set our fence on fire!' And then I twigged that those figures were swirls of smoke, and some of the stakes were actually flaming at the tops. The light from the flame danced against the walls of our little house and showed up big dark lines. They were letters sprayed on with an aerosol can or something, and they said:

BURN THE RATTERS

Mum threw her bucket of water over the fence post while I ran in to fill up some more and Dad just stood gaping at the words on the wall beside the living room window. He was there when I came back, still staring, not saying a word. And then he disappeared around the back of our house for paint. When the flames were out I went in and told Kellyanne what had happened. But she just hid under her blanket and said nothing.

Four

About this time Kellyanne started getting really sick. I can't explain it and neither could anybody else. She just lay in bed saying she was very very tired and worried because Pobby and Dingan hadn't come back, and how she couldn't be sure if they were dead or not. They might still be wandering around over the opal fields all lost and frightened, and there were wild pigs out there and snakes and all kinds. It made her puke just to think about it. Well, Pobby and Dingan had got us into enough shit as it was, thank you very much, and I felt angry with them. Pretty goddam angry for spoiling our family name. And I thought Kellyanne was faking at first, pretending to be ill like she pretended to have friends. But then I heard her puking in the dunny. She was sick. She really was.

She wouldn't eat anything. Mum called Jack the Quack and he came and sat on Kellyanne's bed and did some stethoscope stuff. He told my mum that Kellyanne was suffering from a nervous illness, a kind of depression, and that she had a fever. He tried to persuade her to eat a little of something. But she wouldn't. He said that if this kept up we would have to take her to hospital and force-feed her. I told Jack about everything that had happened with Pobby and Dingan but he just smiled and frowned and smiled again and used the words 'syndrome' and 'clinical' and 'psychological' a lot. There was something funny about the way he was behaving, too. Sort of nervousish. And when he said Kellyanne would be better off in hospital, I reckoned he said that because he didn't trust my folks to look after her. When Mum asked him to stay for dinner he made some excuse about going line dancing and scuttled away like a goanna.

My dad started to look pale, too. He said: 'No one's taking my princess to no stupid hospital,' over and over again. 'The Williamsons can look after each other just fine. We don't need no charity or help from nobody!' Late at night he would pace up and down shaking his head, saying: 'You're right, Mum. This is all my fault. Maybe we should never have come out to the Ridge in the first place. She's a sensitive kid. Too precious for this place. She gets bullied at school, don't she?' That was my dad. He started to get all emotional, and cracked open tinny after tinny of VB. And then he cried. It was like the beer was going in his mouth and coming out of his eyes.

Well, Mum and Dad didn't dare tell Kellyanne to stop this once and for all, or to explain to her straight that Pobby and Dingan were only in her imagination and she'd better switch the bloody thing off. They'd done it once before, you see, and Kellyanne went a little bit crazy and started screaming so hard the whole town thought they was being air-raided by nuclear missiles from France. They knew better than to tell my sis that she was being stupid. Kellyanne didn't handle that kind of criticism too well.

So now Kellyanne just lay in bed, her face peeking over the sheet.

She slept or just lay whimpering. That's all that she did for a week: cried, slept and occasionally sipped water. She got so thin that it didn't look like there was any kind of body there at all.

Well, all this started to rattle my mind, and at night I wouldn't go to sleep I would just clamber up on to my bunk and sit thinking. I figured this was the end of the world because we were all going crazy. Pobby and Dingan were messing up my family and they weren't even here. And they also weren't even anywhere. And although I thought my sister was nuts, I didn't like to see her pale and weak like this. And I wanted my dad to cheer up and go off to his mining again, and I wanted my mother to stop worrying and being homesick, and I wanted the Williamson family name to shine and sparkle and be all right.

And I knew flaming well that the answers to all these problems lay with Pobby and Dingan themselves.

And then I figured out something else. I didn't like to admit it, but it seemed to me the only way to make Kellyanne better would be to find Pobby and Dingan. That's what I decided. But how do you go looking for imaginary friends? I stayed awake all night trying to get my head around the problem. I reckoned that the first thing would be to have as many people as possible looking for them, or pretending to look, so that at least Kellyanne knew people cared, that they believed in her imaginary friends and wanted to help out. See, I'd remembered that Kellyanne was always most happy when people asked questions about Pobby and Dingan. Usually that made a smile crawl over her face. And it seemed to me if a lot of people were asking questions about them then she would get better fast. I also knew darn well that there were quite a few people in the Ridge who loved Kellyanne to bits even though they were a little unsure about the rest of us Williamsons, and there were some who almost believed in Pobby and Dingan or who were real nice and understanding about it. And I had it in the back of my mind that if those people believed in imaginary friends and all that shit, or if they knew how real those friends were for Kellyanne, then they'd believe that my dad really had been looking for them out at the mine and not ratting Old Sid's claim.

The two problems seemed to go together somehow.

So this is what I did. The next day I went around town calling in at the shops telling people why Kellyanne was sick. I even went to The Wild Dingo, and to The Digger's Rest where the toughest miners drink. I said: 'Howdy, I'm Ashmol Williamson, and I've come to tell you my dad's no ratter and my sister's sick cos she's lost her imaginary friends.' Well, there was a silence and then one of those miners came up to me, grabbed my collar, and held me up by it so that my feet came off the ground. He looked at me so close I could smell his stinking breath and said: 'Listen here, kid. You go back and tell your daddy, if he ever shows his face in here again *he's* gonna be the imaginary one. Understand? Imaginary! Geddit? Dead!' Well, I was just about to shit myself when a bunch of other miners came over and said to the bloke, 'Put the kid down, mate. Rex Williamson is a friend of mine and those kids of his are good kids.' Well, this bastard threw me on the floor and said: 'You wanna watch who your friends are!' to the men, and then walked out. The group of miners picked me up, brushed me down and asked if I was OK. I told them yes, but I was a little bit worried about my sister Kellyanne because she was really sick and might get taken away to hospital, and how I was gonna try and lick clean my dad's name until it shone red on black.

I had me a busy day, allrightee. I went to the Bowling Club to tell the pokie players and also to the Wallangalla Motel where there was some line-dancing practice going on. You should've seen me. I tried to go up to people on the dance floor and get them to stop dancing and listen to me, but they were too busy doing their moves to the music and I kept getting caught up between people's arms and legs and shit. In the end I just grabbed the microphone and shouted: 'Ladies and gents! Sorry to interrupt your dancing, but my name's Ashmol Williamson, and my sister is sick and we need to help her find her imaginary friends tomorrow!' There was this nasty high-pitched screech from the microphone, like it didn't exactly enjoy what I'd said, and then everyone, about fifty people in all, stopped dancing and turned around, looked at me all at once and started mumbling to themselves. And I swear I heard people say my dad's name and whisper the word 'ratter' to each other. Well, I explained into the microphone in a shaky voice about my sister and Pobby and Dingan and our family's troubles. And then I suddenly ran out of things to say and felt a bit weird with all those lines of people looking at me, so I just ran out and got back on my bike and pedalled off wobbly-legged.

I went almost every-bloody-where. I went to the Automobile Graveyard. I went out to the camps at Old Chum and The Two Mile. And some people whispered to each other about Dad and some didn't. And some folks thought I was nuts. And some were nuts themselves, anyway, so it didn't make no difference. I even went and told the tourists out at The Big Opal. They patted me on the head and smiled and whispered to each other in funny languages. One big American man filmed me with his video camera and told me to say something cute into it so he could show his friends back home. But then I realized I was wasting time, and Kellyanne was sick, and my dad was getting called a ratter, and these tourists wouldn't really give a shit, but.

I went out to the town hall where some of the black kids were practising a traditional Korobo-something dance with their teacher in funny outfits and didgeridoos and drums and shit. I stood there for a while and watched them and had a good laugh at how dumb they looked. And then one of them started running straight at me with a spear and told me he was going to shove it up my ass unless I durried-off out of the hall. But their teacher stopped him and honked on her didgeridoo and told him to shut up and listen. And then I told them about Kellyanne and her sickness, and I asked them if maybe they could do a dance to conjure up Pobby and Dingan some time tomorrow. And the teacher said they would certainly think about it if they had time, and then she started spinning some bullshit about how her ancestors thought opals were dangerous and contained evil spirits, and how maybe my family was paying the price for worshipping it so much and digging horrible holes in beautiful Aboriginal land.

Well, I'd had enough of hearing this goddam hooey, as my dad called it, and so I shot off and cycled out on the dirt roads around about a couple of hundred more camps on my old Chopper bike telling people about Kellyanne and how she was ill because of losing her imaginary friends. It was a hot day, and hard work, and so I made sure I was tanked up with Mello Yello to stop my mouth getting dry from all that yakking I was doing. When I told people what had happened to my sis, some of them looked at me like I was a total fruit-loop. But a lot of them already knew about Pobby and Dingan because they had kids who went to the same school as Kellyanne out at Walgett and they had seen her talking to them on the old school bus. One older girl out at the caravan park came up to me and said: 'Are you Kellyanne Williamson's brother? My mum says you Williamsons are stupid people and your dad's a drunk ratter and so you better go away or I'll punch you the way I punched your sister that time at the swimming pool.' I gave her the finger and pedalled off fast cos she was too big for me. But she called after me: 'The only friends you Williamsons have are imaginary ones! Just you remember that, Ashmol Williamson!'

But some people were real nice about it all. On one of the camps a woman gave me a Mello Yello and a cake and asked me how my mum was doing. She said: 'The sooner they get your pretty little sister to hospital the better.' I answered: 'Yup. But it's more complicated than that, Mrs Wallace. See, Kellyanne's sick-with-worry sick; she ain't hospital-sick sick.' I met this kid who knew as much about Pobby and Dingan as I did. He said he didn't like Kellyanne too much but he thought Pobby and Dingan were all right. He said he had a better imaginary friend than Kellyanne. It was a giant green ninja platypus called Eric. He didn't talk to it, but.

I stayed out till dark explaining to all these Lightning Ridge families how they had to make a big show of looking for Pobby and Dingan so that Kellyanne could see that people really cared about them. And I did some explaining about what had happened to my dad and what a mix-up there had been. And how Pobby and Dingan weren't real but Kellyanne thought they were and that's what counts, and how my dad wasn't a ratter but people thought he was and that's what counts, too. I went around putting up signs I had made saying:

LOST! HELP!
KELLYANNE WILLIAMSON'S IMAGINARY FRIENDS POBBY AND DINGAN.
DESCRIPTION: IMAGINARY. QUIET.
REWARD IF FOUND.

And I put on the address of our house and tacked the notices up on telephone poles and fence posts and walls. When I cycled home I watched people looking at the notice, and I saw some of them had been graffitied over with the word *Ratter*, but I also noticed that a lot of them hadn't been and that a lot of folks were smiling and laughing. Well, that was a good sign. I went to bed that night pretty full of myself for having had a good shot at least at clearing my family name and standing up for everybody. And I hadn't got beaten up or anything, either—which was good.

Well, Kellyanne wasn't getting any better and she wasn't saying anything except muttering the names of Pobby and Dingan, and Mum and Dad were spending all their time by her bedside taking her temperature and telling her everything was going to be all right and making her soup which she never ate. And Dad was still pacing up and down clutching at this letter from the hospital which said Kellyanne had to go there immediately, and that they needed to do some tests. My folks, I reckon, were beginning to think hospital was the only way out.

That night I heard Mum and Dad shouting at each other in their bedroom. And I only caught a few words because it sounded like they was shouting with bits of cake in their mouths or through balaclavas or something. But I heard Mum say she was tired of Lightning Ridge and how she was homesick for England and Granny Pom and fed up of working at the checkout at Khan's and not being able to look after her family for herself. And then I heard my dad shouting something about Her Royal Highness, and he kept repeating a man's name, but I can't remember what it was exactly. Probably some bloke who'd called Dad a ratter again and got him all upset and irritable.

Five

The next day, I got up early, gobbled my breakfast, attached bits of cardboard on to my spokes with clothes pegs and rode into town in third gear sounding like a motorbike. There were no streams of trucks driving out early in the morning, and no sounds of the drilling rigs going at all. It seemed like the whole town had stopped mining or something. Then, just as I was going down Opal Street, I saw that there were people crouched down on the roadside looking under bushes and cars and over fences and everything. When they saw me riding by on my souped-up bike, some of the people saluted me like I was some sort of general and shouted out: 'Young Ashmol! Go tell Kellyanne we're searching as hard as we can!' I almost fell off my bike with surprise. The first part of my plan had worked. People were actually looking for Pobby and Dingan, they really were! I pedalled home like a maniac to tell my family.

When Dad heard what I'd gone and done he patted me on the head and said: 'Good thinking, son.' I told him it was important that Kellyanne saw what was taking place and Dad managed to persuade Kellyanne to get out of bed. He lifted her up in her sheet and took her out to the ute. Mum drove because Dad still wasn't comfortable about going out and being seen by people yet.

I sat in the back watching everything. I made Mum pull over so Kellyanne could see the special signs I had put up on the fences and gates and trees. She smiled a little when she saw them. I said: 'Sorry, Kellyanne. I didn't know how to describe them proper. I mean, what do they look like?' And Kellyanne whispered that they didn't look like anything in particular, but Dingan had a lovely opal in her belly button, a beautiful stone with rolling flash in it, only you had to be a certain kind of person to see it. And Pobby had a limp in his right leg.

There were lines of people all over the dirt roads, and people out with their dogs, and as we pulled up alongside them, they came up to the ute window and said: 'Hey, Kellyanne, we've been looking for six hours now and we're not giving up until we find Pobby and Dingan. So don't worry your pretty head about it.' My sis smiled weakly. One boy asked her: 'Do Dobby and Pingan speak Australian?'

'No,' said Kellyanne. 'They speak English quietly. And they like to whistle. But you have to be a certain kind of person to hear them.' It was the first time Kellyanne had done this much speaking for a long while and it brought a look of hope into my mum's face.

Well, everywhere we drove we saw a few people out and about hunting or pretending to hunt around the trees. I saw some of the line-dancers had a banner saying POBBY AND DINGAN SEARCH PARTY. One big black bloke was standing on a mullock heap looking through a pair of binoculars. I recognized he was the man who brought Kellyanne home one time when his son kicked her in the shin and pulled her long hair when they were playing out behind the service station. Dad called him 'the good coon' because he was dead-crazy about opals and one time I'd seen him doing a traditional mating dance at the wet T-shirt competition. When we drove up in the ute he came over and poked his head through the window on Kellyanne's side and did a big grin and said: 'Don' worry girl. I'll find Pobby and Dingan in a flash for ya. I ain't Lightning Dreaming for nothing, you hear me?'

Well, I think Kellyanne was pretty amazed by all this, because her eyes were wide open. She turned and whispered to me: 'Are all these people looking for Pobby and Dingan?'

'That's right,' I said. 'Even the Abos.'

Kellyanne didn't say anything after that. We drove her back home and she went to sleep a little peacefully. But when Jack the Quack came around later in the evening my mum was in floods of tears. I knew then that he must have told her my little sis was really very ill and that my plan to make her feel better had failed. I went and hid in my room feeling like there was a rock in my throat.

My dad went walkabout that night. I heard him leaving. He was sniffing and sobbing and breathing heavy like a kettle.

Six

I woke up in the middle of the night all restless and got out of bed. A light was on in the living room and my mum was sitting on the floor with her back towards me and her chin on her knee. I tiptoed up to her. She had something rectangular in her hand. 'What you looking at, Mum?' I asked.

She jumped up and said: 'Hey, Ashmol! Not sleepy?' I noticed she had put the thing she was holding behind her back.

'What were you looking at, Mum?' I said.

Colour went rolling across her cheeks. 'Oh. It's just a photograph, Ashmol.'

My mum paused for a while, and then handed me the photograph and knelt back down on the floor. I sat down opposite her, cross-legged. The photograph was of four people standing in a line with their arms around each other. Two blokes and two women. Behind them was a sort of a hill with trees on it and the side of a building. And the hill was covered with purple dots. The sky was a mixture of blue patches and very bulging sorts of grey clouds. But the most amazing thing was the purple dots.

'What are those?' I asked, pointing at the dots.

'Bluebells,' said Mum. 'It's a photograph taken in England, Ashmol.'

'And who're those fellas in the line?' I asked, scanning over the faces. The girls were very pretty and the blokes looked smart and rich and totally into themselves. And the blokes had expensive black suits and sharp noses, and the sheilas had flowers in their hair and pale skin and dresses like they wear at the Opal Princess competition.

'That's me, Ashmol,' said my mum, in a whisper. 'Aged nineteen. In Granny Pom's paddock before the Castleford Ball.'

'What?' I said. 'Which one?' And I looked again at the photo and saw her immediately. But she looked so different it was amazing. Much sparklier and cleaner in the photograph. Slimmer and with more hair but not as pretty as now, that's for sure. And then I noticed one of the blokes in the photo was holding his face very close to my mum's. And his hand was on her bare shoulder.

'Who's that bloke?'

'Which one?'

'That one.' I pointed to the man in the photograph with the side parting and the hand.

'Peter Sidebottom.'

'Peter what?'

'Peter Juvenal Whiteway Sidebottom.' My mum paused and did her long-look-out-of-the-window thing. 'He was my boyfriend before I met your father, as a matter of fact,' she said.

'Oh,' I said, a bit embarrassed and not sure what to say next. 'Did he know the Queen?'

My mum laughed. 'You're a funny boy, Ashmol! What do you mean: Did he know the Queen?'

'Well, he looks sort of rich,' I said, 'and like he might know the royal family or go to the same shops or go bowling with them or something.'

'No. He didn't know the Queen,' said my mum. 'But you're right. He was rich. Well, his parents were, anyway. Now he's left England and gone to live in America.'

'I bet that Sidebottom's a total dag,' I said. 'And I bet he's not half as happy as we are here at the Ridge.'

'Are you happy here at the Ridge, Ashmol?' my mum asked, not taking her eyes off herself and Peter Sidebottom in the photo.

'You betcha,' I said, forcing out a big smile. 'And you want to know why? Because here there's always something to dream about, and some huge opal waiting to be found, like another Fire Bird or a Christmas Beetle or a Southern Princess or an Aurora Australis.'

'Well, yes, I suppose that's true,' said my mum a little sadly.

'And I reckon Dad is going to find something really special pretty soon,' I went on. 'Because he may not have been first in line when the money got handed out, and he may have rocks in his head, and he may have the rough end of the pineapple at the moment, but he's a pretty amazing kind of a dad all in all.'

Well, then I stood up and walked back towards the door, but before I went out I said: 'One thing's for sure, I'm bloody glad I ain't called Ashmol Juvenile Sidebottom.' I went out and closed the door behind me. I heard my mum call after me: 'Goodnight, Ashmol Williamson! See you in the morning, hey?'

Seven

The next day people came up to our camp saying they had found Pobby and Dingan. When I made my plan I hadn't reckoned people would actually claim they had found the imaginary friends and come for their reward. I hadn't even got a reward to reward them with because I hadn't thought that far ahead. I always just sort of thought Kellyanne would find them by herself when she realized other people were taking an interest, like. But no. At nine o'clock in the morning Fat Walt who owned the house-made-completely-from-bottles came out and knocked on the door calling out: 'Hey, Little Kellyanne Williamson! I got yer Pobby and Dingan right here wi' me!' He strode in holding his arms outstretched like he was carrying a bundle of dirty washing or something. I looked at him with a doubtful expression, knowing it wasn't going to work. 'Found them out at Coocoran, I did,' he said.

I led Fat Walt through to Kellyanne's bedroom. I said: 'Kellyanne! Fat Walt's here! Says he's found Pobby and Dingan.'

Kellyanne opened her eyes and I helped her sit up.

Walt came though into the bedroom. 'Here they are, Kellyanne,' said Fat Walt, 'they're asleep. I found them out at Coocoran. They was shooting roos and they must've dozed off under a tree.'

Kellyanne closed her eyes again and pulled up the covers. 'Stop pretending,' she said. 'You haven't got Pobby and Dingan there, anyone can see that. Pobby and Dingan don't sleep and they don't shoot roos. They're pacifists. You've got nothing in your arms but thin air and you know it.'

Walt looked defeated. He said something like: 'Well, have it your way then, you little Williamson brat!' and walked straight out. I felt sort of sorry for him all in all.

An hour later the legendary Domingo the castle-builder came in all excited, mopping his forehead with a cloth. His hands were blistered from all that lugging of rocks and castle-building he had been doing and he wore a pair of boots and blue socks pulled up to his knees. He yelled, 'Hey, you fellas! You'll never guess what I found roaming around the dungeon in my castle, all lost and bewildered? Yup—your friends Pobby and Dingan. They said they'd walked for six hours back from some opal fields. Well, you can relax now, mate, because old Domingo has found them and I've come to claim my reward. They're back at the castle waiting to be collected.'

'What did they say when you found them?' asked Kellyanne in her weak little croaky voice.

Domingo thought carefully and scratched at his chin, and said:

'Hmmm...well, they said they were very relieved and they wanted to see their friend Kellyanne Williamson and have a big meal of steak and chips because they were bloody starving.'

'No they didn't,' said Kellyanne. 'Pobby and Dingan only eat Violet Crumbles and Cherry Ripes and lollies.'

Domingo looked a bit desperate. 'Maybe they've outgrown them now,' he said. You had to give him points for quick thinking. But Kellyanne wasn't having any of it. She rolled over in her bed saying, 'I wish people would stop making up such stupid stories about finding Pobby and Dingan. This whole town is going crazy. They should go back to their mines. I need to get some more sleep.'

I led Domingo out of the house saying I was real sorry and

thanks for trying at least, and he sloped off back to his half-built castle shrugging his shoulders and kicking at the dirt saying, 'Seems to me she doesn't want to find them at all.' I was worried he was also thinking: 'Reckon Rex Willamson's a ratter.' But anyway he went off to work on his turrets and to wait for his dream princess to arrive on her flying horse.

All in all about ten people in total came that day claiming they had found Pobby and Dingan. One old lady turned up with a little jar saying she had caught them in it. Ken from the chemist's came in all stooped over saying he was giving Dingan a piggyback. He made out he had found her with a broken leg. He said he hadn't found Pobby yet, but would go back to the same place he found Dingan and have a scout around. Joe Lucas, who won the log-throwing competition the year before last, reckoned he had found Pobby and Dingan drunk in his grandpa's wine cellar. He spent about twenty minutes doing this conversation thing in front of Kellyanne to try and make her laugh. He pretended to be trying to keep Pobby and Dingan under control and cracked lots of good jokes. A girl called Venus turned up with her Alsatian saying her dog had sniffed out the imaginary friends. Even the little boy with the Eric the platypus came along claiming that his own imaginary friend had found my sister's friends. He reckoned it was only possible for imaginary friends to be found by other imaginary friends. He did the best job of all of them. But at the end of the day Eric and he were sent away with their tails between their legs. Kellyanne said that there was no way Pobby and Dingan would come back with a giant ninja platypus because giant ninja platypuses don't exist. Anyone knows that.

Eight

Well, for a day or so all this action perked up Kellyanne a bit. It perked Lightning Ridge up too, I reckon. People around here like to get a hold of weird things, and they got so involved with the idea of Pobby and Dingan and my sister Kellyanne that they seemed to forget about Dad and Old Sid for a while. And no one had tried to burn down our fence recently either. But even though everyone was giving her plenty of attention, Kellyanne still wasn't eating. She really thought Pobby and Dingan had died now and all she could talk about was bringing their bodies back so that she could pay her last respects. She said she'd feel plenty better if she could just be with their dead bodies. But bodies still need finding. I was getting a bit impatient with all this and so I said: 'Kellyanne, you're worrying Mum and Dad sick. Everyone's trying to help, but you know damn well that you're the only one that's ever going to find Pobby and Dingan or Pobby and Dingan's dead bodies or whatever. Now for shit-sake, either find them or forget about them so you can get better and we can go back to normal!' Kellyanne looked like she was thinking this one over and over and over. Eventually my sister said: 'Ashmol. Listen! Please can you go out one more time to Wyoming and go down the mine. I've have a hunch about it. A sort of a feeling.'

'You want me to go down the mine looking for Pobby and Dingan?'

'Please. And go at night because people won't be able to see you, and you won't get into trouble.'

'You think they'll be there?'

'Like I said. I've got a hunch.' She put her head on the pillow and pulled the blanket up. 'Maybe they got lost in the drives and their bodies are still lying there in the dark all rotting and starved.'

'Supposing I go,' I said, 'How will I know it's them? I can't see Pobby and Dingan like you can. Never could.'

Kellyanne didn't answer. She had fallen asleep, and her arm was thin and deathly-looking. There were rings under her eyes and her face was the colour of shin-cracker.

Nine

So that night I got dressed into warm clothes and took a sausage from the fridge and put it in my pocket. I could hear Mum and Dad talking in their room in murmurs. I also got a ball of string out of the garage, and then I crept out of our little house and tiptoed over to where I keep my bike lying down in the dirt. I pushed it out of the drive so it didn't clank too much. And then I tied my little pocket torch to the handlebars with a bootlace and started the long journey out to the Wyoming claim. My heart was beating so hard it was like someone was pedalling inside of me.

When I was half the way out I stopped and asked myself what

the hell I was doing going looking in the middle of the night for two dead people who didn't exist. It seemed like a pretty stupid thing for a kid to be doing. I almost made up my mind to turn around and go back, pretending I'd found the corpses of Pobby and Dingan straight away. But I knew Kellyanne wouldn't believe me. So I decided just to go and have a look down the mineshaft, and hang out there for an hour or so, so at least I could say I'd been down and done my best. I thought Kellyanne would appreciate that. And she'd think I'd come a long way since the days when I used to punch the air where Pobby and Dingan were supposed to be. And I didn't want her to die thinking I was the kind of Ashmol who didn't believe anything.

It was so quiet that I could hear the blood in my head creeping around and my teeth chattering together. Plus—there was this huge sky with stars peppered all over it, and I remembered Dad telling me that for each star in the sky there was an opal in the earth. And that opals are hidden from view because they are even prettier than stars and the sight of a whole lot of them at once would just break people's hearts. And I also remembered him telling me that all this land, where Lightning Ridge is now, was once covered by sea water and how all kinds of sea creatures had been found fossilized in the rock. I felt a shiver go down my spine just thinking about how strange this was, that a sea was once here where now there is nothing but hot dry land. And suddenly I thought how maybe, if this amazing thing was true, then why couldn't it just be possible that Pobby and Dingan were true, too. But then I told myself: 'Jesus, mate, you're losing your marbles, you fruit-loop. Snap out of it.' And that made me bike a little faster towards my dad's opal claim.

When I got there I undid my torch and turned it off. I laid down my Chopper and tiptoed off carefully because I was worried that Old Sid might wake up and think I was ratting his claim. See, ever since my dad snotted him in the face for calling him a ratter, everyone knew that Sid stayed up late with a candle burning in his caravan, eating his frill-neck lizards and holding a gun out of his window. And I also knew he had bought a guard dog which was why I'd put a sausage in my pocket.

Sure enough Sid's dog ran out barking like hell. He was attached to Sid's caravan by a rope. I threw him the sausage quickly and crept over to our mine, taking care not to trip over the starpicket or fall down any holes that had been left uncovered. I heard that dog slobbering in the dark. When I got to the main mineshaft I heard my dad saying in my mind: 'Always put your lid on when you go underground, kiddo!'—and so I tiptoed over to our old caravan and took out a yellow mining helmet from underneath it. And that made me feel a little better. Then I tied my torch to my belt by the bootlace.

The mineshaft was narrow and dark. I lowered myself down on to the ladder. There was only enough room on each rung for my toes and so I had to grip extra hard on to the sides with my hands as I climbed down backwards in case I lost some footing. Normally my dad came down with a cord and a light-bulb thing that's attached to the generator, but all I had was my little one-battery torch which didn't let off too much light.

One foot after the other I went down, trying not to think about how I would end up if I fell. After every five steps I took a breather to make sure I was still alive and on the ladder and not at the bottom in a heap. And the further I went down the more I felt like I was in some throat being swallowed by some monster.

Well, pretty soon my foot was on the bottom rung and I was standing on the floor of the ballroom. It still felt like I was on the ladder because I could feel where the rungs had been pressing into my feet.

I didn't want to get too lost and so I remembered a story Kellyanne had told me from her *Book of Heroes and Legends* about a Greek bloke who went into an opal mine to kill a giant huntsman spider, and how he took a ball of wool so he could follow it back out and not get lost in the drives. And that's why I'd packed a ball of string and I tied it to the bottom rung of the ladder and went off down the drive. I was concentrating so damn hard on what I was doing that I nearly forgot why I had come in the first place.

I set off across the ballroom flashing my torch around and being careful not to walk into any props. Then I picked the drive on the left, ducking my head the whole time, even though I didn't need to by a long shot. I kept walking, unravelling the string as I went, and keeping an ear out for the slide of a snake.

Well, I knew those drives pretty well, but after a bit I found a new part I hadn't ever been in before. There was a strange monkey in the left wall. And a monkey isn't a thing that swings through the trees but the word we miners use for a sort of a hole. And I figured it must be where Dad had been jackhammering recently because he had left his pick there. Well, there was a smell of some kind which I'd never smelt here before. I reckoned it might just be the smell you get at night down an opal drive because I'd never been out in one at night like this. Anyway, I went through the monkey and as far as I could go down along the new drive.

Well, right in this corner I waved the torch around until I suddenly saw something pretty unusual. There was a massive heap of rubble in the corner. It wasn't just opal dirt and tailings. It seemed like the whole part of the roof had collapsed and fallen in like a big mushroom. The first thing I thought was: 'Shit, that means some more of the roof might fall down on top of me.' The last thing my family needed now was a squashed Ashmol. Then I suddenly had this peculiar kind of mind-flash. I said to myself: 'Hey Ashmol, what if Pobby and Dingan got caught under the pile of rock?' And then I listened carefully and sort of convinced myself that I could hear a little moaning and breathing. And then I, Ashmol Williamson, found myself calling their names. I really did. 'Pobby! Dingan! Don't worry, Ashmol is here! Kellyanne's brother! I'm here to rescue you.' And then I remembered that Kellyanne was convinced that Pobby and Dingan were dead, and that meant they probably were. And so I took off the stones more slowly and didn't hurry so much. But I was so excited I could have filled up a bucket with my sweat and sent it up on the hoist.

I set about on hands and knees taking off rocks and moving them to one side until I got to the floor. And there right in front of me was the wrapper of a Violet Crumble chocolate bar. And it was just great to see something a little familiar with those good old words written on it way down there in the middle of nowhere. But then suddenly my eye caught hold of something flashing up at me. Something sitting there in the dark. A sort of greeny-red glint. I headed straight for it. It was a nobby the size of a yo-yo, and when I shone my torch on it I could see there was a bit of colour there. My heart beat the world record for the pole vault. I brushed the dirt off as best I could and then I licked the nobby. It was opal. It was definitely. Just like in the books. Green. Red. Black. All of them together. And it was strangely warm like it had already been in someone's hand or close to someone's skin. I sat there for a while, my heart doing a backflip, thinking: shit, we Williamsons are going to be rich bastards. I rolled it around and licked the dirt off again to make it shine. And I reckoned the opalized bit was as bright as a star and the size of a coin, or a belly button, and that gave me the idea. Yes, this was Dingan's belly button, that's what it was. This was Pobby and Dingan who got trapped under the roof of the drive where it fell in. And the smell I smelt earlier was death. And the last thing they ate before they died was a Violet Crumble. Everything sort of fat together perfectly.

I put the nobby in my shoe and my torch in my mouth and took up the bodies of Pobby and Dingan in my arms. They were heavier than I'd thought. Much, much heavier. I made my way back along the drive towards the foot of the ladder, the torch moving along the browny-red walls. I found myself groaning and muttering as I dragged Pobby and Dingan back. There was something heavy about the air, too, if you know what I mean.

At the foot of the ladder I paused and lay Pobby and Dingan down remembering that there was no way a little bloke like me was going to get them up to the top all by myself. So I lay them both down and took off my coat and draped it over them. As I climbed up the ladder I kept looking back down over my shoulder to make sure the corpses were still at the bottom. And then I got back on my Chopper and pedalled back home. I was colder than any cold thing a bloke could think of.

Ten

In the morning I walked into Kellyanne's room to tell her what had happened. Everything smelt a bit of sick. I shook Kellyanne on the shoulder and said: 'Wake up, Sis. I've got to show you something. Wake up!' Kellyanne's eyelids fluttered and her eye peeped out. She looked like she didn't have much life left in her. I felt sort of desperate. It was going to be me against death. Me on my own. I'd seen Fat Walt and Domingo and Joe Lucas and all those others fail. I knew this was my last chance and so I took a real deep breath.

'I did what you said, Kellyanne—I went down the mine last night—and guess what—the roof had collapsed in one of the drives—Pobby and Dingan got caught under it—I know it because I found the opal that Dingan wore in her belly button—they was lying all bruised in the mine—they was—they was dead—but they looked peaceful like—they was lying together holding hands—and they was still a little warm and everything.'

Well, tears started coming out of my eyes, maybe cos I was tired a bit, but also because I was damn worried that Kellyanne wasn't going to believe a word of what I was saying. I thought too that if I stopped talking she would suddenly turn and say: 'That wasn't Pobby and Dingan,' so I just sort of spouted everything out in a big blabber. 'They had their eyes closed, Kellyanne—in Pobby's hand was a Violet Crumble wrapper.' I waved the wrapper around while I was talking to try and get her attention. 'You can see for yourself, Sis—I left the bodies laid out at the claim under my coat—because I couldn't lift them—see—and if you come with me I'll show you—but you gotta believe me—they were there—I lifted off the rocks and I could smell them—no kidding—the roof came down on top of them—there were no props or pillars—it came down and squashed them—honest—I dragged them back to the ladder—but I couldn't get 'em up—I really couldn't.'

'Can I see the opal?' Kellyanne said after a while.

I took off my shoe and held out the opal in the palm of my hand which was shaking like a fish. I suddenly got really worried because I thought: 'This opal doesn't look like nothing anyone would put in their belly button.' It was too big.

But Kellyanne sat up suddenly and put her arms around my neck and said: 'Ashmol! You've found the bodies. You've found Pobby and Dingan! This is it! This is the stone that Dingan wore in her belly button!'

I was all unplugged and relieved and excited. This huge smile had taken hold of Kellyanne's face. It was like a big rock had been lifted off her. I suddenly thought: 'Great! It's all over! Now Kellyanne will get better and everything's going to be fine.'

But Kellyanne looked at me and her face went serious, and she said: 'Now all you've got to do, Ashmol, is arrange the funeral.'

'What?' I thought for a minute she was talking about her own funeral.

'You can pay for it with the belly button,' she said. 'That's what Dingan would have wanted. That's what she always said. "When I die," she said, "pay for my funeral with my belly-button stone."'

'How much does a funeral cost?'

'A fortune, I think,' Kellyanne replied. 'But the opal should just about cover it.'

My heart sank when I heard this. I never knew death was so expensive. I had reckoned on buying a new house and getting my mum an air ticket for a holiday in England, and plenty of other things with the money from that opal.

'I'll only do it if you get better and stop worrying the hell out of Mum and Dad,' I said all firm. 'And only if you promise not to go dying because then I'll have another funeral to arrange and that's going to be a real chore.'

'I promise,' said Kellyanne. 'Thanks, Ashmol. And now you promise me something too. Promise you won't tell Mum and Dad about finding Dingan's opal.'

'OK. OK.'

'And that you won't go showing it to anyone except the funeral director.'

'I promise.'

'And don't go trying to get any money for it. This isn't your opal, and it's not Dad's opal either, Ashmol. This is Dingan's belly button. It isn't some ordinary stone you can go making a heap of money from.'

I thought about this long and hard, and what a shame it was that I was going to be giving away my first red-on-black. And then I said: 'I promise not to go making any money on it.' And then I left the room, almost worn out with promising.

Eleven

So the next day, after Mum and Dad had gone off with Kellyanne to take her to the hospital, I walked out on the road that goes past the golf course and out to the cemetery. I walked past the sign which says LIGHTNING RIDGE POPULATION—? And the question mark is there cos of all the people who pass through to mine, find nothing and give up and go back home. And because of all the folks out hidden at their mines in the bush. And all the criminals and that who don't care to register themselves down on the electoral roll. My mum said she reckoned there were around eight thousand and fifty-three plus Pobby and Dingan that's eight thousand and fifty-five residents out at the Ridge altogether. But now Pobby and Dingan were dead I guess it was back to eight thousand and fifty-three.

And as I walked I turned Dingan's belly button around in my fingers. I had been so busy I hadn't had a hell of a lot of time to look at it. It was pretty incredible. It was mixture of black and greens and when you turned it in your fingers a flash of red went through it from side to side. And it was wrapped up cosy in a duvet of white and brown rock. It had good luck written all over it, that's for sure. And it was warm from the Lightning Ridge sun.

I finally got to the cemetery and I had a good look around. I'd never been there before. It's a small quiet place, not far at all from some mines and about the size of two mining claims strung together. If you look hard you can see the tops of drilling rigs peeking over the trees like dinosaurs or skeletons of giraffes. Well, you could tell which ones of the dead people had struck opal and which hadn't, because some of the signs were cut out of stone and marble, and some were just two bits of rotting wood crossed over. Kellyanne was right. Death looked like it was just too expensive for some people. Plus, it was weird thinking of all those dead people under the ground, especially when you thought about how a lot of the dead folks had spent their lives working under the ground as well. Many of the signs said KILLED IN MINING ACCIDENT.

I noticed that Bob the Swede had a bit of space next to his grave. Room enough for two more, I thought, if old Fred budged over a bit. There was graves for little kids who died young as well. They were under piles of earth like the mullock piles out at the claims. And then I suddenly felt very sad about Kellyanne and I was thinking what it might be like if she had to be buried out here in a sad little grave with a few plastic flowers, and all because of a couple of imaginary friends who died out in my dad's drives. But I told myself to stop thinking like this, and that it was OK now because I'd managed by some fluke to find the bodies. She'd get better once she'd mourned at the funeral I was going to buy with Dingan's belly-button stone. There were tears in my eyes, though. Maybe it was just because I had to get rid of my first opal. Anyway, I think it was only the second time I ever had them in my whole life.

Twelve

I knocked on the door of Mr Dan Dunkley the funeral director. A voice said: 'Come in.' I turned the handle of his door and entered.

Mr Dan was a fat man with too many chins for his own good. His office was spick and span and he was sitting at his desk with his cheek in his flabby white hand. Behind him he had a grinding wheel going and a couple of dibbers and dob-sticks laid out on a tray next to a bottle of methylated spirits and a Little Dixie Combination Assembly. On his forehead Mr Dan had those weird glasses for looking at opals. Like most people out at the Ridge who don't have the guts to mine, he did a bit of cutting and buying and selling on the side to keep him ticking over when not enough people were kicking the bucket.

Mr Dan looked up at me. He didn't know who I was, unlike most people, and my guess is he wasn't too sociable and only got to know people when they had croaked it. I said: 'My name is Ashmol Williamson and I have come to talk graves.'

Mr Dan took off his specs and did a frown and lit up his pipe. After a while he muttered: 'School project?'

'No, Sir,' I said. 'You may have heard about my sister Kellyanne Williamson? She's dying.'

Well, I figured he was bound to catch on when I told him Kellyanne's name. He probably had her coffin all ready and made up out back. Sure enough a bit of a nod came up on his face.

'Reason she's dying is she lost two of her friends a while back. And she's sad,' I said.

'Oh,' said Mr Dan. 'I didn't know that. All I know about you Williamsons is that your daddy's in a spot of trouble.'

I walked over and bunked myself up on to Mr Dunkley's desk and sat there like a cat, looking at him. 'These friends of my sister,' I said, 'They went missing. They were gone a few days and nobody could find them.'

Mr Dan suddenly looked interested. 'I didn't know any of this.'

'Well, you're the only one who doesn't,' I said. 'See, that's the reason you ain't had too many people coming in with opals to sell recently. Everybody's not mining any more. They're out looking for Pobby and Dingan all day long. Nobody's working.'

'Are you sure you ain't making this up, kid?'

'Positive,' I said, all cool and confident and smart.

Mr Dan walked over and switched off the cutting wheel on his Assembly.

'Well, boy, what do you want me to do? Go looking for two kids down a hole? Happens all the time, little fella. Kids don't take any notice of where they're going cos they got their heads in the clouds, and then they trip up and fall. Wham! Splat!' Mr Dan wopped his hand down hard on his desk.

There was a silence, and then I looked at him and said: 'There's no point in going looking for them, Mr Dan, I don't want you to do that. The thing is these two friends of my sister's, they are sort of imaginary anyway. They don't exist. They're invisible. And besides, I've found them, or found their bodies at any rate. They're both dead.'

Mr Dan almost choked on his pipe. He sighed and said: 'Listen kid...Ashley...whatever you're called, I'm a busy bloke. Now hop it.'

'I noticed there is a space next to Bob the Swede in the cemetery,' I said, refusing to budge.

Mr Dan took the glasses off his forehead. 'You been playin' around in my cemetery, kid?'

I didn't see how he could claim it was his cemetery. The dead owned it. It was their claim. Or else they were ratting it under his nose.

'I wanna buy that bit of space for a grave for my sister's friends Pobby and Dingan,' I told Mr Dan. 'You see I don't think my sis is going to get better until she sees them buried once and for all.'

'You can't bury imaginary people,' said Mr Dan. 'There's nothing to bury.'

'Believe what you want, Mr Dan,' I answered. 'Just let me buy the claim. Let me have a space in the cemetery.'

'What you offering?'

'Opal.'

I took off my right shoe and fished out Dingan's belly button. I had chipped off all the dirt and polished it up with a cloth so it looked better than ever. So beautiful and sparkling. My fingers didn't like handing it over. Mr Dan Dunkley took it in his big hand and held it under his little light. I was all twitchy and I never took my eyes off it once.

'Fuck me dead!' he said. 'Where d'you get this, kid? You rat this? You better not have ratted this. Where d'you get it?' I never saw anyone put on his opal glasses so quick.

'Noodling.'

'You found this noodling?'

'Yup. Noodling on a mullock heap at my dad's claim.'

'This don't look like no opal some kid found noodling on his dad's mullock heap. I reckon you ratted it from Old Sid.'

I started getting a bit pissed at this. I suppose I was beginning to feel like Kellyanne and Dad. It wasn't too brilliant having folks not believing what you were saying all the time.

'I bloody well did not,' I said.

'This is a valuable stone. This is worth a lot of money, kid,' said Mr Dan.

'Is it worth as much as a grave and a couple of coffins?' I asked him.

Mr Dan sharpened up his eyes and looked me up and down. He leaned closer over his desk.

'Just about,' he said in a whisper. 'Your daddy know about this, son?'

'Nope. And I don't want him to. Because if he knew about it, Mr Dan, then he'd go crazy with excitement and then he wouldn't let me buy Pobby and Dingan a grave with it, and then Kellyanne wouldn't get any better.'

'Anybody else know?'

'Nobody 'cept Kellyanne.'

Dan Dunkley held the stone under the light again and twisted it around so the red flash streaked across it. I could see those colours coming out beautiful and I knew I was on to a winner.

'OK, son. You got a deal,' said Mr Dan. 'I'll let you have the grave for the stone.'

'Great!' I said. 'And I want you to arrange the funeral for Pobby and Dingan too, Mr Dan,' I said. 'And make it realistic. My sis won't get better if it's not realistic. You better make it like a funeral for two normal kids and make them coffins and everything and read some Bible stuff. Make it on Sunday at eleven.'

'I'll talk to the preacher,' said Mr Dan, not taking his eyes off Dingan's belly-button stone. 'And you'd better talk to him too. He's gonna think I'm doolally or something.'

Thirteen

I walked out of Dan Dunkley's house a little dazed. I was pleased I'd got a space for Pobby and Dingan in the cemetery, but I had a hollow, aching feeling behind my ribs which wouldn't go away. I couldn't believe an opal had passed through my hands so quick. An opal I had found on my lonesome on the Williamsons claim at Wyoming. I felt like I was living in a dream or something. Everything was moving so fast.

The preacher was a small weedy man drinking beer from a green bottle on the stump of a sandalwood tree around the back of his poky white church. I told him what was what. After a long pause he looked at me and said: 'OK, I'll do it, young Ashmol. Now you'd better give me some hard facts about these imaginary friends so I can make a speech.'

I thought about it long and hard. Eventually I said: 'Well, Vicar, they was quiet and they always went around together. And they liked chewing lollies and Violet Crumbles and Cherry Ripes.'

The preacher noted these things down in his pad. He repeated the words 'Violet Crumbles' and 'Cherry Ripes'.

'And they used to go and bathe at the Bore Baths with Kellyanne.'

And then I reeled off a sort of list of all the things I had learned about Pobby and Dingan, including:

Pobby was a boy and the oldest by a year.

Dingan was the pretty one. Real pretty. And smart as a fox.

And Pobby had a kind of limp, and when Kellyanne was late for anything she always said Pobby slowed her up and that's why because she had to wait for him.

And Dingan had an opal in her belly button.

And Dingan was a pacifist, because every time I stamped on her or punched her air and said: 'If Dingan is real why doesn't she hit back?' Kellyanne would say: 'Cos Dingan is a pacifist, stupid.'

And they talked English or whistled to make themselves understood.

And you had to be a certain kind of person to hear them.

The preacher had stopped writing and was staring into space. 'Thanks, Ashmol,' he said, 'that's plenty of information. Now take care of your sister and I'll see you on Sunday.'

'Will Pobby and Dingan go to heaven or hell, Vicar?' I asked before I went. I was sort of testing him out to see if he'd take Kellyanne's friends seriously.

The preacher thought long and hard about this and said: 'What do you think?'

'Heaven,' I said firmly, 'so long as there's Violet Crumbles there.'

'I think you're right,' said the preacher and took another swig out of his green bottle. As I rode off on my bike, he shouted: 'I shall be praying for your father, Ashmol Williamson!'

'Do what you want, Vicar!' I called back, 'just come up with the goods.'

I zoomed off down the road thinking about heaven. It was like the ballroom of an opal mine, full of people with lamps on their heads. And everyone was singing Elvis Presley songs and gouging and swinging picks.

Fourteen

Before I got home I stopped off at Humph's Moozeum which is a place full of amazing junk. Humph's Moozeum is just down from the half-built castle which the bloke Domingo who I told you about was building single-handed out there in the middle of nowhere. That's Lightning Ridge for you. People go all weird on you all the time because it's so hot.

Humph has spent his whole life collecting weird things. Well, I liked to stop by and talk to him sometimes, and when I was sad it was a good place to go to cheer yourself up and get your mind on something else. There is a whole load of outhouses and old buses and cars and bits of mining machinery, and bush fridges, and there is a whole assortment of objects, old pictures, bones, bottles, books, machinery, sewing machines. There's a car up a tree and Humph even has the arm of one of his miner-friends pickled in a jar. He is getting some bloke's leg pickled too. He has a chunk of old Turkish Delight from Gallipoli and a bent-neck putter and a bottle of vodka which he says a band called The Rolling Stones gave him. He's a clever old bugger, Humph. You never know if what he is saying is true.

One of the sections of the Moozeum is underground, and that's where I found old Humph sitting at the little bar he has in the corner. He was wearing a big floppy hat. 'Ah, Ashmol,' he said. 'Any news of Pobby and Dingan yet? Bit like looking for a needle in a haystack, I reckon.'

'Yeah, I found them,' I told him proudly. 'They were both dead.'

Old Humph didn't know whether to say: 'Good,' or: 'That's too bad,' and so he grunted and held up something to show me. I trundled over and stood looking. I was pretty impressed. It was a framed invitation to the funeral of Princess Diana. And the writing was done in really fancy silver lettering and there was a royal stamp on it and everything. 'You got invited to the funeral of Princess Diana?' I asked with my eyes wide open.

'Did I hell!' said Humph, fairly splitting his sides with laughter. 'This little bewdy I cut out of a magazine and stuck down on a piece of card… Don't tell anyone, mind. The tourists love it.'

'Could you do me some invitations for Pobby and Dingan's funeral?' I asked.

'Having a funeral are you?'

I nodded. 'I reckon Kellyanne won't get better until we bury the dead bodies and show them some last respect.'

Humph nodded solemnly. 'I wouldn't have minded having their dead bodies in my Moozeum,' he said. 'I haven't got any dead imaginary friends yet. 'Bout the only thing I haven't got.'

'Maybe Kellyanne will let you get Pobby's finger pickled and put in a jar,' I suggested.

'Maybe,' said Humph taking a swig of Johnny Walker. 'So how many invitations do you want?'

'I want to invite everyone in Lightning Ridge.'

Humph nodded all thoughtful and scratched the top of his

floppy hat. 'That makes eight thousand and fifty-three by my calculation,' I said.

Fifteen

The day of Dad's trial arrived. I wasn't allowed to go to the magistrates' court so I can't say exactly what happened. I can only imagine it. But the fat and the thin of it was that, after he'd finished punishing someone for breaking and entering and when he'd fined John the Gun and some other blokes for shooting too many roos, Judge McNulty made Dad stand up and tell the little jury about what he was doing out at Old Sid's mine that evening.

Well, this time my dad didn't make up a lost-cat story or make out he was just looking for his contact lenses. No way. He stood up straight and told them that he was out looking for Pobby and Dingan the imaginary friends of his daughter Kellyanne Williamson, and that he was just checking to see if they'd wandered over on to Old Sid's claim. And Mum said Judge McNulty looked all confused like a jigsaw puzzle before you put it together, and that he asked Dad to describe their appearance. I flinched a bit as I imagined my old man stuttering and tongue-twisting as he tried to get to grips with that one. Well, my dad must have handled it pretty well, but, because then McNulty moved straight on and asked whether Dad was on any drugs, and whether Dad thought the imaginary friends really existed, and apparently Dad looked old McNulty and the jury and everybody dead straight with his opal eyes and said that at first he thought they didn't exist, and then he wasn't too sure about it, and now he was positive they did exist after all because he was on trial for ratting because of them and he was a little angry with them for it too.

Judge McNulty rubbed his chin and scratched his head a lot. And then Old Sid, that whiskery bastard—as Mum called him—got up with a bandage over his nose and testified and called my father 'mentally deranged' and lots of other things including a 'low-down piece of roo shit'. And some of Old Sid's miner-mates backed him up and talked a lot about how much my dad would drink and how he was always interested in other people's opal and asking them where they had found it. And that confirmed he was a ratter as far as they could see. And then a policeman said how he saw Dad snotting Sid in the nose, only he didn't say snotting.

Well, according to Mum, the judge fidgeted around and whispered things to people. And then McNulty looked at the little jury and told them that the whole question of Mr Rex Williamson's guilt depended on whether it should be considered a crime to hit someone on the nose when they have called you a ratter and also on whether the jury believed he was really out looking for his daughter's imaginary friends that night. And he told the jury that meant they needed to work out for themselves how real they thought Pobby and Dingan were.

And Mum said you could see the jury mulling it over, and whispering the names Pobby and Dingan and she reckoned that most of them were thinking: 'Since half the town has been out looking for Pobby and Dingan why couldn't it just be possible that the father of Kellyanne Williamson was looking as well?' And then the jury heard from my dad that the funeral of Pobby and Dingan was taking place the next day, organized by his son Ashmol Williamson, and if the judge wanted he and the jury could come along and see how real they had been.

Mum told me that then Judge McNulty did lots of racking of his brains, and sometimes he looked a bit pale, but eventually he decided to break up the court until it was possible to interview Kellyanne. But he only did it after asking Sid about his family. And Sid said he hadn't got any, and that his wife had died twenty years ago. And the Judge asked him if he ever talked to her privately even though she was dead. And Sid said he did sometimes when he was up at the agitator because his wife used to help him sift through opal dirt because she had better eyes than he did. But I don't think Sid realized what was going on, that the sly old Judge McNulty had trapped him into admitting that everybody has an imaginary friend of some kind even if you don't think they have, and that Old Sid himself was a bit on the short-sighted side.

Well, the court was going to come together again when Kellyanne was better, and at the end of the proceedings only about twenty or thirty people were outside the courtroom to throw cabbages and things at my dad and hiss: 'Ratter. Ratter. Ratter. Ratter.' And only one bloke had a banner saying POBBY AND DINGAN WERE RATTERS on it in red paint like blood.

Sixteen

Well, to be honest, all this trial stuff cheered me up no end, and Mum and me got ready for the funeral of Pobby and Dingan the next day with smiles on our faces while Dad went off to fetch Kellyanne from the hospital.

Mum had bought me some new black pants and a black sweatshirt. We went out to the cemetery and decorated the fence with flowers and opened up the gate. And the priest came and talked things through with us, you know, about what the proceedings were. And Mr Dan drove up around eleven o'clock and shuffled around a little awkward in his suit and tie. And then the coffins of Pobby and Dingan turned up and I helped carry them up to the grave.

And then all that was left to do was to wait for people to start arriving. I had some butterflies in my stomach, but. See, I'd been round the whole of Lightning Ridge posting Humph's invitations into everybody's letter boxes. And I was sort of nervous to see how many came and how many tore up the invitations and still called us Williamsons a bunch of frigging fruit-loop lunatics. And I was also nervous because of the reports of Kellyanne and how she was getting worse by the day even though they'd managed to pump some food into her at the hospital. So it seemed pretty much like it was now or never.

I got so afraid that people wouldn't turn up and that I might have to imagine myself a whole town that I got really impatient and an hour before the funeral was due to start I got on my bike again and went pedalling around Lightning Ridge to see if people were getting ready. The place was a sort of deathly quiet. I sat on the step outside The Digger's Rest for half an hour trembling and wanting to go for a piss.

Eventually a few people started stepping out of houses and shops, coughing, or pulling back curtains and doors. And then suddenly, as the sun got hotter in the sky, old buggers, young buggers, men and women and dogs started appearing on the street and walking out towards the cemetery. A couple of them saw me and waved. I got on my bike fast and cycled around the back way, standing up on the pedals to get a good view of the crowd walking along in silence between the gum trees and houses. And I noticed that everyone had like made an effort and got out of their mining clothes and put on their best boardies and singlets.

I got back to the cemetery ahead of the people and I saw them all coming up the road past the balding little golf course like a massive great wave. I stood on Bob the Swede's gravestone and saw that actually there were many more than I'd expected. Thousands of people all coming out towards us. More even than you saw at the goat races, more even than I'd ever seen in my whole life except on the football on TV. And for a moment I was worried that there was something else going on that they were all going to, and that they were going to walk straight past the gate or something and head out of town. But I shouldn't have worried because pretty soon the little cemetery was full of living people, and everyone closed in around the grave and the coffins which had Pobby and Dingan inside. And some people sat on the scorched grass, and some wandered around looking at the other graves. And no one was saying nothing except a few words to each other. But most just gave me a nod and gazed out over the land or fanned themselves down. And Mum and me had made some lemonade and cookies earlier and so we passed cups around and began pouring so that people had something to graze on. But although I was relieved to see all these people turn up at the cemetery for the funeral of Pobby and Dingan, the most important ones hadn't arrived. And that was Kellyanne and Dad.

Kellyanne and Dad. Dad and Kellyanne. They still hadn't come back from the hospital.

It was way past time for the funeral to start and people were starting to do a bit of muttering and all that. Perhaps some folks were beginning to look at each other and at me and Mum and starting to ask each other what the hell they were doing attending the funeral of two figments of a little girl's imagination especially when that girl wasn't even there. But at least the preacher was doing a good job. He was pretty sober and he was still going around welcoming people and saying hello and handing out sheets with some songs printed on them. I reckon he wasn't keen to lose all these people. Because if they stayed it would be the biggest congregation he ever preached to in his life. At one moment he looked up and gave me a thumbs up sign as if to say: 'Don't worry, mate, Kellyanne will be here soon.'

And then suddenly she came. I recognized the sound of the ute as it came in the gate, and there was Dad at the wheel. And everyone turned around and stood watching as he climbed out and walked to the back and began to take out a fold-up wheelchair and assemble it on the grass. I ran down to meet him. Through the back window I could see Kellyanne's pale face. I ran to the back door and opened it and Kellyanne turned and gave me a twitch—because she had no strength for a whole smile. She was as thin as I have ever seen a person get, and Mum came and helped me lift her into the wheelchair which Dad had assembled. And there were tears in Mum's eyes and the funeral hadn't even started. Well, then Mum gave Dad a big hug and a kiss right on the lips and I did a 'Yuck' sign to Kellyanne by sticking my finger down my throat, and together we pushed Kellyanne up the slope through the crowd and up to the grave of Pobby and Dingan. And most people I think were pretty shocked to see my sister looking so sick. And some of them said nice things to her on the way up like 'good on yer, gal' and 'she's a brave one'. And somebody else's mum put flowers on her lap. And then when she got to the top everyone suddenly started clapping and everyone was cheering and people were slapping my dad on the back. It took a fair while for everyone to settle down and listen to the preacher who was now standing up at the front and looking like he wanted to speak.

He shouted out: 'G-day, everybody! And welcome to the funeral of Pobby and Dingan, friends of Kellyanne Williamson and members of the good honest Williamson family!' My dad had a little smile to himself. And then the preacher told us we were going to sing from our song sheets and everyone rustled their papers.

Well, Kellyanne had chosen the songs, and first we sang the Australian national anthem, 'Advance Australia Fair,' and all that, and then Fingers Bill played a Cat Stevens song on his guitar and those who didn't know the words sort of just hummed it, and it went 'Oooh baby it's a wide world', or something like that. Kellyanne had chosen it because it was Pobby and Dingan's favourite song. And it was quite amazing hearing all these people singing together. And I wouldn't say it was too tuneful or anything like that. But it was loud as hell and I reckon the emus out on the Moree road didn't have no trouble hearing it.

Well, then the preacher coughed and took out a piece of paper and said: 'I would now like to say a few words about the deceased.' And this is how his speech went:

> People of Lightning Ridge, G-day. We are together here today to celebrate the lives of Pobby and Dingan. Well, where can I start? Two close mates of Kellyanne Williamson. They have brought much pleasure to our hearts and what a sad loss it is to say our final goodbyes to them—whom many of us never even saw...but only felt. We recall with pleasure Dingan's calm pacifist nature, her opal belly button and her pretty face, and many of us will recall Pobby's limp and his generous heart, and let us give thanks for their lives which...whatever anyone says...they most certainly lived.

Well, people were sniffing and taking out handkerchiefs already. And even some of those real legend, tough miners were weeping on to the backs of their hands, and taking out rags covered in dirt to blow their noses into. The preacher raised his hand and pointed out at the crowd. He turned up the volume on his voice:

> And there are some of you here today who have not believed! You have not believed in the invisible because it does not shine forth from the earth and sell for thousands of dollars! And there are many of you here who have not believed in Pobby and Dingan. But God believes in them. And he believes in you. Yup. He sure believes in everyone here. Oh, yes indeedee. And we are invisible. We are invisible and transparent and shallow and yet God believes in us. And God believes in Pobby and Dingan and he is in every one of those lollies they sucked and was with them on the school bus, and when they played rigaragaroo and when they danced in the lightning, and even, I tell you, when they went missing so tragically out at the Wyoming claim where Kellyanne and her brother Ashmol and their honest dad Rex Williamson went looking for them. God was with Pobby and Dingan and is still with them in heaven. Amen.

Well, thank God the preacher didn't go on for too long after that! He just said some things about Kellyanne and what a brave girl she was and he said I was a plucky kid for sticking up for Pobby and Dingan and fighting for them to have a proper burial. And there was more clapping and my dad slapped me on the back so hard he almost knocked my teeth out. And then the preacher gave himself a more serious look and shouted out something about how if anyone had any reason why Pobby and Dingan should not be buried in the cemetery for them to step forward and say it. And there was a long silence and I held my breath until the preacher said OK, now he'd go on with the burial.

So me and Dad and Mum and a few others got down and lifted the coffins into the grave and Kellyanne watched us silently. And only when we had the coffins all lined up in the dark hole did the preacher say, 'Ashes to ashes and dust to dust,' and tears start glimmering down her face. And then I pushed Kellyanne forward in her wheelchair and she placed in the grave a whole pack of Cherry Ripes and Violet Crumbles, a couple of books and things. And Mum put in some flowers and then we stood in silence while two youngish miners shovelled in some soil like they did when they filled in a mineshaft that wasn't being used any more. And then the coffins were covered and buried. The preacher led a prayer, and after that everybody started walking slowly home sniffing into their sleeves. And I walked out last with my dad resting his hand on my shoulder. And on the way out someone stopped us at the gate. It was Old Sid and he was holding out his fists and swaying in the road and shouting: 'Come on, Rex Williamson! Come and fight me, you fucking ratter! You're not going to get away with this! Turning the whole of the Ridge against me, you piece of shit! You ever come trespassing on my claim again...and I'll...I'll kill...!' But then some kids ran up to him and started shouting: 'Lizard-eater! Lizard-eater! Old Sid is a lizard-eater!' and Sid turned away and we watched them hounding him back up the road as he swiped at them with drunk arms.

Dad and I caught up Mum and Kellyanne on the road. Well, Mum was suddenly smiling and singing out that it was about time we menfolk got back to mining, because she reckoned it wouldn't be too long before we found something. And me and Dad looked at each other and couldn't believe those words came out of her mouth. And as we came up to them, Mum turned the wheelchair around to show us that Kellyanne was smiling too. And Kellyanne Williamson smiled for the rest of her life.

But her life was short. A week later the whole population of Lightning Ridge came out to the cemetery again. My sister Kellyanne Williamson was buried with her imaginary friends in the same grave in the same place where millions of years ago there had been sea and creatures swimming cheerfully around. And she took with her some Violet Crumbles in case Pobby and Dingan had run out.

And although in the end everyone believed that Pobby and Dingan had really lived and were really dead, nobody at the Ridge could quite believe the funeral of Kellyanne Williamson was actually happening. And I, Ashmol, still can't believe that it did. I just can't. I can't believe it at all. Even now, one year later, it feels like she's still totally alive. And I find myself lying awake talking to her all the time. And I talk to her at school and when I am walking down Opal Street, and you will still see today if you go to Lightning Ridge people pause in the middle of doing whatever they are doing to stop and talk to Kellyanne Williamson, just as they still pause to talk to Pobby and Dingan and to opal in their dreams. And the rest of the world thinks we are all total nutters, but they can go and talk to their backsides for all I care. Because they are all just fruit-loops who don't know what it is to believe in something which is hard to see, or to keep looking for something which is totally hard to find. □

GRANTA

THE WEEPING POM

Howard Jacobson

The Weeping Pom

A wildly unfunny joke I'm unable to stop telling:

I'm playing deck quoits on the *Oriana*, steaming from England to Australia. The year is 1965—just. Steaming in the opposite direction is the *Canberra*. We meet somewhere in the middle of the Indian Ocean, passing close enough to take photographs. Hearing voices calling my name, I look up. There on the deck of the *Canberra*, also playing quoits, are Clive James, Barry Humphries, Germaine Greer and Robert Hughes. 'You're going the wrong way,' they cry as one. 'Where it's at is where you've come from.'

It isn't really a joke. More a tic, a repetitive mechanism for dealing with this queer mischance—that I appeared to have chosen to go to Australia when everyone was choosing to leave it. Of course not *everyone*. True, for so many to have answered Gough Whitlam's call in the early Seventies and returned to a land fit for film stars and scribblers, many must originally have left; but they may simply have been the over-ambitious or the easily impressed—those who'd swallowed all they'd read in the colour supplements about existential Paris and swinging London. Whoever they were, they were quickly replaced. Cultures have a wonderful way of repairing their own damage. One genius flies the coop, another miraculously appears. Certainly I noticed no depleted community when I got to Sydney. Manchester was where I'd grown up, and Cambridge where I'd gone to university—so I knew about depleted.

Maybe that's why I go on telling that wildly unfunny joke: because I hold the view that Australia is a more sweetly civilized country than England, but I don't want people to think I've gone soft in the head.

Take, as an example of the civilization I am talking about, Frieda the Tit. Take her as paradigmatic in her own right. And take her as a prototypical creation of the Australian way of life.

She had a keen, slightly foxy face, glacial green Latvian or Lithuanian eyes, and too grand a chest for her own equilibrium; hence the nickname, given to her—and this is important—by other girls. Australians in general love a nickname and Australian women in particular love calling a tit a tit. Or they did. They have become watchful now, along with everybody else; then, though, an unguarded hilarity pervaded the entire social structure. Everything was funny.

Circular Quay, Sydney DAVID MOORE

Lord Chesterfield would not have taken that to be a mark of an advanced civilization; but Lord Chesterfield was limited in his views. It is the highest refinement not to be afraid of broad laughter. The English are supposed to be the rude ones in the seaside picture postcard manner, but to the eyes of a Mancunian just graduated from Cambridge, Sydney University was more an oops-a-daisy holiday camp than an academic institution, and Frieda the Tit was more the McGill cutie on Margate Sands, watching the dog run off with her bikini top, than any English girl I'd encountered.

Think of me as the dog.

I had no business taking Frieda for a beer. There wasn't much of an age difference to speak of—she was maybe nineteen, I was three years older; but I was a lecturer, and she was a student. More than that, I was married. On the other hand, an afternoon beer in Sydney carried no sinister associations. Back home an afternoon beer was possible only if you knew the landlord's daughter or supped among reprobates in a pub on Ilkley Moor, but you could drink, legally and democratically, all day in Sydney. A humane licensing law for the times, even though its concomitants were bars tiled to look and be cleaned like public lavatories, early closing in the evening, and no drinking on a Sunday unless you travelled thirty miles from your official place of abode and were prepared to sign a visitors' book swearing to that effect. Sometimes Sydney seemed the most cosmopolitan of cities—another Rome or Amsterdam with the upward thrust of a Chicago or a Dallas—sometimes, especially on a thirsty Sunday, it felt as promising as a village built in the shadow of a Methodist chapel in South Wales. With Frieda the Tit in tow, I felt I was in Venice during Carnival.

There were plenty of pubs in walking distance of the university, several of them the old 'push' pubs of half a generation before—'push' denoting a very specific Sydney libertarianism, part European Bohemian, part Australian larrikin, an avidity for advanced thought and an avidity for old-fashioned fisticuffs in equal measure. You gathered here, staff and students alike, in packs, took sides, grew emotional, and more often than not lost the plot. I had become wary of these places. As an Englishman fresh out, so to speak, I was pumped for the latest news—what were people reading back there, what were Europeans thinking—but also as an Englishman fresh out, I was an object of scorn, the latest Pom turning up to tell the natives what to think. The hotter the day, the more alcohol went down, and the more alcohol went down, the sooner curiosity as to Europe turned to anger as to me. They were right to be unimpressed. I was young and knew from next to nothing; yet I was enjoying respect in a prestigious job because of the cachet that still attached to being English. Galling—for them. Doubly galling in that these were the ones who had stayed behind to keep the home fires burning and not sailed off to Europe and America on the *Canberra*. If you stayed, the chances were you'd stayed on principle. Enough now with having to go overseas to grow up. You could grow up well enough at home. In which case why the red carpet for yet another foreigner?

If I'd told the truth, that I was bucking the trend and had come to Australia to grow up, they'd have taken me for a smart-arse (but then they did that anyway).

So Frieda and I drove to a more anonymous rough house in Bondi where we could get a sniff off the sea and play bar billiards. That should show you how innocent an outing it was. We drank cold, Irish-sounding Aussie beer—Toohey's, probably—in small glasses (my fault for asking for middies when I meant schooners); talked about the expatriate Latvian or Lithuanian social clubs her brothers belonged to in the western suburbs—secret blood-brotherhood and fencing societies, as far as I could make out, from which her parents expected her eventually to choose a husband; and knocked balls around. Though Frieda was remarkable in her own person, and not a sight to be missed when cueing or celebrating a big score, there was nothing about *us* to excite either attention or envy.

So I had reason to be surprised when a very small and very drunk Australian in plasterer's overalls tapped me on the shoulder, accused me of looking like Jesus Christ, of being a poofter, and of stealing his country's women, and punched me in the face.

I had reason to be surprised in the particular circumstances, but I was already used to the Jesus and poofter charges. Seeing me waiting at a bus stop, Australian drivers would slow down, point, and note with derision, and not always without hatred, my simultaneous resemblance to a sodomite and the Saviour. That was the price you paid for coming to Australia in the Sixties in a beard and long hair by English standards neither excessively Rabbinical nor effeminate. I say 'by English standards' as though those are universals, but timing is everything when it comes to whether people do or do not take kindly to your appearance. Five years earlier I would have thought twice about being seen in Burnley with shoulder-length hair. Conversely, look at how Sydney comports itself now. It was an inconvenience being badgered like this, and sometimes it was frightening, but what stopped me from branding such intolerance as specifically Australian was precisely how English the people who abused me always looked. It wasn't the new migrants from Sicily or Malta who leered at me threateningly from their cars, it was kids of the sort I'd have thought twice about being seen by in Burnley. To this day English people express surprise that I spend as much time in Australia as I do, marvelling I can cope with the 'absence of culture' and the ugly manners of Australians. To which the answer—though I confess I am not always forthcoming with it—is that everything brutal in Australia is British.

And the punch? What punch? I kept finding plaster dust in my clothes for weeks but no sign of a bruise. If one of us was a fairy it wasn't me. But his Anglo-aggression was enough to get us out of the pub and into a Greek milk bar down the street, where we finished our afternoon with Viennese coffee and Danish pastries.

In the middle of our tea, without any warning at all, Frieda suddenly broke down and cried. Big convulsive sobs that shook her entire frame, accompanied by big soupy tears that pitted the cream floating on her coffee. I never found out what specifically she cried about. It may have been the ugly and ineffective scene of an hour before, trouble at home or in her love life. Or she may have been upset by the burden of her nickname. (Who wants to be famous on the strength of a body part?) But it's significant that I never thought to ask what made her cry, and that nobody in the milk bar thought to notice. Of course she cried. She had a delicate nature. She took life hard. And she was Australian.

In Australia everybody cried, grown men no less than young women. What were the bonding materials of Aussie mateship, when all is said and done, but beer, social awkwardness and tears? Stewed in alcohol and emotion, you threw your arms around one another's shoulders, swore an eternal sheila-free loyalty, and wept. Lovely, I thought, after the aloof, chilly comradeship of Cambridge. Alienation was the cause. In this overheated faraway country, in whose aching heart the explorer Charles Sturt once came upon seven Aborigines weeping inconsolably, not a soul was able to escape a consciousness of estrangement—from home, from God, from water, sometimes even from reality. When the Kabbalists spoke of spiritual exile, of how we were all sparks chaotically scattered from the original One Light, they were thinking of Australia. Not because Australians were unhappy did they cry, but because they could make no rational sense of a happiness to which they did not feel themselves entitled. And to be conscious of such an irrationality is to be civilized.

Maybe I am imposing on Australians the confusion I felt. Not framed to be a cheerful or enthusiastic person, I was in a fever of love for the intense smells and colours of Australia, many of them, by the happenstance of migration, southern European. Culturally a child of sin and exodus, I had been transported to another Eden where, not knowing whether to laugh or cry, I did both.

My notion that I was bucking the trend and had left England to grow up in Australia is wisdom after the event. At the time I'd had no real idea where I was going. I don't mean that existentially, for at twenty-two no one has much idea where they're going. I mean I knew nothing of the department or the university: who taught there, what sort of reputation it enjoyed, how good the students were, or how good they expected me to be. What I knew of Sydney itself came from photographs—lifesavers in elasticated shower caps running up and down Bondi Beach unreeling what looked like yards and yards of hosepipe; triangular pleasure boats bobbing on the harbour (as yet undistinguished by any Opera House); and the grand Meccano bridge arcing a forever blue metallic sky. When I tried imagining what it was going to be like living in Sydney I saw tugs coaxing the *Oriana* under the bridge, people cheering at the dock side, lifesavers in elasticated shower caps helping us down the gangplank, and then nothing. But a benign nothing, caused as much by the name Sydney as anything else. Sydney—a quiet, balding Jewish accountant's name, it seemed to me, unlike the forbiddingly aristocratic Melbourne, or the flibbertigibbet Adelaide.

Something of that undemonstrativeness attached to every idea I had of Australia in general. It was a long way to go, but then again not as far, culturally, as a Greek island. The wireless had made it familiar—*Two-Way Family Favourites*, Bill Kerr, slow-talking Test cricketers in baggy green caps who might have been taking the mickey, but then again might not. A domesticated, half joke place. I'm not sure I had any clear sense where it was either, other than 'down under', ha ha, the land you got to if you dug in your garden long enough.

I knew plenty of people who had *nearly* been to Australia. In the gloom of Fifties Britain all our parents considered starting over again somewhere else. My father spoke repeatedly of emigrating to Canada 'where a working man had a better chance of making a go of life.' Canada rather than Australia, because Canada was easier to come home from when things didn't work out. Of those who had gone to Australia, the majority were indeed still there, while the ones who returned seemed bitter about something and wanted only to frighten us with stories of bed-loving cockroaches and snakes the length of coal trains.

A few weeks before we sailed, some friends of friends of friends of my wife's mother punished us first with their slides then with stories about spiders. There had just been a terrible incident in the eastern suburbs of Sydney when a woman at the wheel of a car had seen a tarantula sidling out of her glovebox and in her panic had driven head on into the oncoming traffic. The irony being—wait for this!—that the spider wasn't even venomous. The so-called tarantulas—huntsmen, actually—were as harmless as pussy cats. The really nasty spiders, the true killers, were not the cuddlesome giant hairy ones at all.

'So generally speaking,' my wife Barbara deduced, 'the bigger the spider, the safer you are?'

'Exactly.'

'Except,' I put in, 'when it comes to the heart attack consequent on the cuddle?'

'Exactly.'

How those who had visited Australia loved frightening those who hadn't! I do it myself now. Spiders? It's not spiders you need to worry about, sport. It's the flesh-eating flies! And you can forget about swimming unless you want to find a toxin-loaded jellyfish in your trunks!

Our families didn't come to Southampton to see us off. They weren't prepared to face the melancholy of driving back to Manchester without us. People making the trek to Australia in 1964 weren't exactly vanishing off the edge of the world, but the journey still wasn't the perfunctory thing it is now. In 1964 there remained the possibility that you would succumb to distance, fail of the will or wherewithal to cross the seas a second time, and perforce forget your loved ones. So we made what might have been our final goodbyes at Piccadilly station, my father filming our leaving with the cine camera he had brought us to make a record of our great adventure. Filming us waving from the train and then having to run the length of the platform to lob the camera into my outstretched arms in the final second before we disappeared took from the melancholy of his farewell. On many a night as I lay awake in Sydney, troubled by the heat, fighting off the mosquitoes and listening for the tread of spiders, I would fret that I had not taken the opportunity to shake my father's hand for the last time. An unnecessary perturbation, as it turned out, but distance breeds morbidity. One by one, in the course of what became a three-year exile, I counted off all those I would never put my arms around again, despite the fact that I wasn't in the habit of putting my arms—not sentimentally, anyway—around anybody. But that was one of the many things Australia did for me: it made me a man of feelings. But before it could remake, it had to undo.

Others have written of what it is like to enter Sydney Harbour, the most perfect accommodation of man and nature anywhere. The word *swoon* gets it best. We swooned in a blue haze and swooned towards the bridge, which turned out to be an even grander mechanism than in photographs, somehow wrong where it was—like a giant at a children's tea party—but then again dead right by very virtue of its freakishness, in the way that rainbows are. We didn't, as I had expected, sail under it. Instead we took a sudden hard left into Circular Quay and parked there. It is something I have never failed to find wonderful, no matter how many times I have been back to Sydney, the way the big ships sidle into the very heart of the city and then dock in what is the equivalent of Oxford Circus. Before the Opera House, two sights would fill your heart to bursting whenever and wherever you glimpsed them: the marvellous arc of the bridge and the painted funnels of the liners. You could be out shopping just about anywhere in Sydney, you would look up and you would see those funnels jostling with city tower blocks, and it was all you could do to stop yourself weeping, so melancholy and so exhilarating were their associations.

Today, though, liners are in the cruise not the exile business. People no longer cheer them in and wave them off, except ironically. But on that blazing January afternoon we arrived to a reception almost as emotional as our leave-taking from Southampton had been three and a half weeks before. Tears, streamers and 'Rule Britannia' saw us off and now tears, streamers and 'Waltzing Matilda' welcomed us in. I say 'us' but of course the tears were for returnees, or for friends and relations coming to start what my father had always wanted—a new life. We were more orphaned than that. No one in Sydney loved us. But we were met anyway, by, as I like to think, the entire Sydney University English department. Or at least by those members of it who mattered. You hear divisiveness in that? You are meant to.

When you leave a boat you have been around the world on, you fear the ground will never again stay still beneath your feet. Barbara was unsteady on dry land for about a month. I was slower to recover. People who remember me from that period think I was drunk more often than I ought to have been; in fact I was simply giddy from the *Oriana* for most of the time I lived in Sydney. Imagine, then, one's condition at the very moment of disgorgement from the boat into the hydra hands of a splintered academic department. It was like coming off the high seas straight into a game of blind man's buff. Several games of blind man's buff, for every faction had its own supply of blindfolds and each turned you more violently than the other. All unknowingly, I had blundered into a theatre of war.

There are tales to tell, had I not already told some of them fictionally. Certainly it is tempting, with every day a new memoir of the Sydney English department in the Sixties appearing in Australia—as though the bottle of communal memory had suddenly popped its cork—to have my say. At the very least I would like to restore myself to history, some memoirists—Andrew Riemer in his sorry *Sandstone Gothic* will do as an example—having gone so far as to lobotomize their own minds in order to remove all trace of me, India-rubbering me out of the department, much in the way Milan Kundera describes the Czech Communists airbrushing Clementis out of all official photographs. Or I have been allowed to remain, as in Michael Wilding's indolently self-pitying account (in the magazine *Southerly*), but only on the most dubious tenure—where in truth an airbrush may have been a kindness—as a man possessed of 'a strangely eroticized' Leavisism, which turns out not to be so strange after all since Wilding also notes that it 'pervaded the department'.

Of all recollections of the Sixties, the least urgent, you might have thought, would be any that bore upon a brief English department contretemps in the University of Sydney, round about the time Australia was sending troops to fight in Vietnam. But war is war, however peripheral. And this may have been one of the last bloody ideological encounters in any literature department anywhere before theory took over and the universal darkness covered all.

To save time and spare everybody I will paint myself as a naive and wholly innocent participant. I came, found trouble, messed about in it for a while, and left. It was never really my fight. The real struggle was between Melbourne and Sydney. The long and the short of it was this: certain over-principled, live-wire personages from the University of Melbourne, 600 miles down the track, had been called in to invigorate a Laodicean department staffed, if that's not too active a verb, by an assortment of half-hearted scholars, old-fashioned bookworms, nest-featherers, tipplers and other variegated Sydney dossers—there's your scenario. The Melbournians overdid the principle and the live wire, the Sydney dossers fleetingly found the energy to defend their sinecures by fair means and foul, principally foul, the Melbournians were scuppered—there's your denouement.

But what, in the grand academic picture, was I doing there in the first place? Simple: I was a Leavisite. Forget the eroticized. That is merely a jealous reference to Frieda the Tit. I was a Leavisite full stop. And roughly speaking—because no other contemporary intellectual movement pertinent to the teaching of literature was more congenial to their native high-mindedness—the Melbournians thought of themselves as Leavisites. The reason I had been recruited was that I was fresh and still warm, like Adam, from the moulding hands of Leavis himself.

Hard to say what a Leavisite is, or rather was, when the whole point and art of being one was to refuse system and definition. To the degree that we couldn't describe what we were, we were Leavisites. Individually, we found our way into it experientially, untheoretically, learning as we went. As a group, one Leavisite simply recognized another Leavisite when he saw one.

I had gone to read English at Downing College, Cambridge, where F. R. Leavis presided, first and foremost because I had been taught by a pupil of Leavis's in the sixth form and he had told me that that was where I was going. Though well into his sixties when I in turn became his pupil, F. R. Leavis was still the enfant terrible of literary criticism. He seemed to be the only critic who didn't belong to one or other of the charmed circles of English cultural life. Neither a high table nor a Fleet Street man, he exuded principled exclusion, an outsiderism which might have been Bohemian had it been a trifle less puritanical. Thus he attracted students from working class grammar schools who felt themselves to be unromantically marginalized, and stiff-necked introverted Jews of the sort I was, inveterate choosers (to borrow a phrase of Dan Jacobson's) who approved of disapproving, who felt affronted by the contemporary, and in whom the practice of textual analysis stirred an ancient Talmudic disputatiousness, controversialism, a love of quibbling both for its own sake as an intellectual exercise, and as a sort of moral duty enjoined upon us by the Almighty.

The paradox of Leavisism, embraced wholeheartedly by the likes of me, was that from its position on the sidelines of English culture it offered to pronounce authoritatively on what it was—humanly, spiritually, as far as literature went at least—to be truly and centrally English.

An authoritativeness which, despite all its inbuilt ironies and inconsistencies, did not always go down well in a country as naturally rebellious as Australia. Much of what has fuelled the latest rush of English department memoirs is no more, I suspect, than an old aggrieved Jacobinism surfacing at the time of Australia's republican debate. While the politicians rouse the rabble with parodies of the English court of St James, academics and boulevardiers stoke the flames with cautionary recollections of a period of intellectual intransigence masterminded from Cambridge. That the Leavisites should figure as something so unlike themselves as marauding colonialists just shows how sloppy the republican debate has sometimes been.

I came, found trouble, messed about in it for a while, and left. Then the department died. I make no cause and effect connection. These things happen; there is such a thing as coincidence. Enough. In the end it's the wine-throwing and the arm-wrestling that make a difference to your life, not who says what about George Eliot. I loved being an academic, having a room with my own nameplate on the door to teach in, giving knockabout lectures to a thousand students at a time, but it was Sydney itself that bowled me over—Sydney the town, the benign Jewish accountant—not the university.

As an easily stimulated boy I had watched films in which people fall in love in Rome and Paris, and supposed as a consequence that only a crumbling Europe would do as backdrop to passion. Now here was Sydney with its burning bright harbour, its miles of romantic foreshore, a commingled smell of virgin sand and fresh Pacific surf which permeated the city's breathing as surely as the bridge dominated its skyline, making me feel I was always on holiday, no matter how black and bitter the departmental recriminations—always on holiday and always in love.

Read 'love' generously. What I loved, promiscuously, in my students—a thousand at a time—was the tone of the town. The touchy unusedness and the queer, almost overburdened knowledge; the harsh social combativeness and the sentimental mateship weepiness. 'You mad bastard, Jacobson,' someone I hardly knew said to me one night after a party. Though 'said' hardly renders the exceptional circumstances of the saying. He was standing over my bed, having shinned up a combination of drainpipes and balconies in the moonlight. Had he come to rob me of my wallet? Of my wife?

Was this something to do with my resembling a poofter? I lay very still under the covers, only my nose showing, waiting to see what he would do. He looked around the room for half a minute, laughed, then put his face very close to mine and bit the only part of me that was visible. After which he left the way he came. Later I learned he was an art critic.

Such a contradictory town. One half of it never out of a beach towel, the other half forever scuttling off to libraries and concert rooms, pale as the master of a Cambridge college. I don't know whether any educationalist has put his mind to why Australians have such a devotion to the arts of civilization. A strong self-improving working class culture, not undermined by class inferiority, may have something to do with it. And of course the pressure not to be thought provincial, not to be remote in mind merely because one is remote in body. Hence their encyclopedic knowledge of the contents of the great European galleries, before they've even visited them. Hence their passion for music. Once in a blue moon Claudio Arrau turned up to give a recital at the Sydney Town Hall (whereas in Manchester I could have gone to see him knocking up with the Halle any tick of the clock), yet you only had to play them ten seconds of a Schubert impromptu on your gramophone and they'd tell you who the pianist was, and who played it better. An argument for the cultural benefits of deprivation? The benefits incidentally accrued to me, whatever the explanation. If I am not a man of truly cultivated tastes today, that is only because I have never stayed in Australia long enough for cultivation to rub off.

For all the boisterous enticements of Sydney after Cambridge, I found it more conducive to work, to thinking and to writing, even if only to the writing of lectures. It helps you to concentrate if you can begin your day on the water. Whoever would have a clear head should go to work on a ferry. After an initial stay in a university flat in Drummoyne, Barbara and I had transferred to the North Shore, first to a harbourside studio and then to McMahon's Point and a pink-bricked shoebox with a balcony from which you felt you could reach out and pluck traffic off the bridge. Every morning I'd walk down an aromatic cliff, dense with blossom and foliage of such a polished green you could see your reflection in every leaf. Down,

down, with the sun on your neck, to a lurching wooden jetty where a little white boat waited to take you under the bridge—under the bridge at last!—to that house of mirth called Sydney University.

Seventeen minutes from McMahon's Point to Circular Quay, unless the ferry decided to call in to Neutral Bay first. Passengers less new to the experience read newspapers. I never did. I stared my eyeballs out and wondered how it could be I wasn't perfectly happy. I still wonder. You look and look at the harbour, trying to fathom the mystery of human dissatisfaction; then, in the evening, when the scarlet-streaked sky dies like a smile and the frowning gravity of royal blue takes over, you look and look at the lights and try to fathom the mystery again.

Leaving aside all my circumambient troubles—the restlessness of youth, an inexplicable homesickness for Manchester, the growing tension in the department—those evenings sitting on our tiny balcony with friends, looking across Lavender Bay to Luna Park, listening to the screams from the big dipper, or a Schubert impromptu coming from any one of a thousand music-loving flats, were among the happiest of my life. Forget the nightingale: whoever would cease upon the midnight with no pain should look out over Lavender Bay on a summer's evening. Or should have then, for it is a more agitated bay now, and less melodious.

It was from this balcony that we watched the Opera House go up, and with it the values of property, and with them the pulse rate of the city, and with that the word that Sydney was the place to be. Watched the style of domestic architecture change in harmony with the Opera House, as though it and it alone had suddenly woken the people to the idea that the harbour was now worth looking at. I often wondered about those previous generations of Sydneysiders who for years had lived bricked-up in dark, almost windowless apartment blocks, seemingly before the invention of glass. Were they so indifferent to the harbour that it didn't matter to them whether they had a view of it or not? Were they of another species? Or is harbour gazing like sunbathing: something you wouldn't think of bothering to do until someone else suggests it?

Sydney seemed to grow more turbulent as I watched. Very soon it would become a rest and recreation centre for American troops fighting in Vietnam. The city in my mind became restless with forebodings.

I made my plans to leave. How far university politics had anything to do with it I have never been sure; certainly there was no future for me at Melbourne, whither live wires were returning in ignominy to prepare for the coming of Marxism and deconstruction; nor was there anything for me under the restored regime at Sydney whose idea of a hot critical potato was to ask whether you could legitimately say one book was better than another. No, no future either way, but I still think the timing of my departure, at least, was more personal than professional. I had started to hate the bus ride between the ferry terminal and the university. The ugliness of George Street struck me as pestilential. I believed I was in a backwater, a place that had less going for it even than Manchester. I wrote letters to my mother saying I was rotting in Sydney, that I could hear my life's blood trickling away. How to explain that I do not know, because it was no less true that I was besotted with the place. This time it must have been existential; mid-twenties blues. And my wife too had grown unhappy. She had loved Sydney at first, our flat, the harbour, our friends, and was loved in return. But I ruined it for her. Too discontented; too unsettled by my own nature; too high on my own histrionics. A man of twenty-two who thinks he is a writer but isn't sure what he wants to write, who can't decide whether he's a Leavisite or a stand-up comedian, shouldn't bring a young wife to a place of so many glittering consolations. We separated a few years later, and though I returned to Australia, she never has. I am sorry for that. It counts against me in the final reckoning that I cast such a black cloud over Australia for her.

I say I returned, but it was Melbourne I went to first off, not Sydney, and to be a builder's labourer, not a teacher. Bit by bit, over time, I have tried to reclaim Sydney. But I find it hard. The city is indistinguishable from my youth. I can still smell myself in it, circa 1965. The unbearable bougainvillea smell of hope. And of distance, the first big distance I had ever put between home and the world. All I do when I go there now is take the little white wooden ferry under the bridge and try not to weep like the child I was. □

Long Tom Tjapanangka, 'ayers rock and irantji'. Acrylic on canvas, 153 x 137 cm, 1997

GRANTA

THE ROAD TO GINGER RILEY'S

Paul Toohey

The Road to Ginger Riley's

Mike Fordham lies under a makeshift canvas shelter at the turn-off, dying. It's only fifteen kilometres on to Maria Lagoon, where Ginger Riley, the Aboriginal painter, has his permanent outstation camp. Not far to go, considering we've already come more than a thousand. But now, after driving till three in the morning on a washed-out dirt track, exhaustion combined with the heavy midday heat and the morphine has rendered Fordham at best passingly conscious. He can go no further. As we contemplate his near corpse, it seems to us his only blessing is his oblivion to the flies that have started to settle on him.

'Leave me to sleep,' Fordham says, swigging morphine straight from the brown bottle. 'I need some time. I don't want to go to Ginger's camp looking and feeling like a maggot.'

We weren't even sure that Ginger Riley was at Maria Lagoon. Myself and my friend Dan Davis had driven Mike Fordham from Darwin to Borroloola in the south-west corner of the Gulf of Carpentaria. Ordinarily it was a morning-to-midnight journey, but with an overheating Toyota and a sick man groaning at every jolt, we had found ourselves driving long into a second day. Now we had to get to the tiny settlement where Riley lived. Cyclone rains had flooded the whole of the Gulf, prompting police warnings about the state of the roads. A week before a party had tried to get up the track to see if the painter needed a lift back down to dry land at Borroloola, but they had been forced to turn back, unable to cross the swollen Cox River. Army trucks had meanwhile come down from the north on exercise and churned the dirt highway into an impassable series of ruts, stranding the handful of people living at Maria Lagoon and the Limmen Bight Fishing Camp nearby.

At Borroloola we'd tried to find out more about the state of the road, which we knew was often impassable during the Wet, but no one had any news. We also wanted to find out whether it would be all right to take alcohol to Riley's, as some Aboriginal camps have a strict no-alcohol rule. Fordham went into the pub to ask and came out a few minutes later. 'I had a conversation with some fairly grotesque drinkers and learned that far from being a fretful painter who's abandoned alcohol for puritanical reasons, Riley's well on the

STEVE MCCURRY/MAGNUM PHOTOS

piss. And that's according to the sharper ones I spoke to.'

Some hours after leaving Borroloola, we'd been forced to stop, our progress halted by a ROAD CLOSED barrier. Dan and I got out of the truck and stood in the road, wondering whether Fordham would have the strength to survive if we got stranded. Chances were that if we tried to continue, we'd get bogged. We told Fordham that the decision to continue was his. He said he had a winch, his morphine. He told us to go on.

Ahead of us, Nathan River station was deserted, buried in seasonal speargrass. Beyond it the track was empty, unmarked by tyres. The country was trying to absorb the rain, its creatures gone to higher ground, its people for the most part gone to Katherine or Borroloola. There was no movement, no sign of life, just Dan and Fordham and myself inching slowly forward in the dark, and a pair of white owls which descended from the trees and took shifts to hang in the glow of the headlamps.

Today has brought wringing heat. Fordham looks to us as though he's slipping in and out of death. He says he is unable to distinguish whether he is at the edge of a terrifying abyss or about to take a shorter fall to somewhere soft. But given his sharp and shocking intakes of breath, which jolt him back to life with a look of horror on his face, it is a long way down for Fordham. Not hell, perhaps, but somewhere he doesn't want to go. Cancer has him by the throat. There's nothing we can do for him except make sure he can reach his morphine.

Dan and I build him a shelter among the speargrass and melaleucas, then leave him with the Cox River flies. We drive on to Ginger Riley's. There's a pretty freshwater crocodile tooling in a creek crossing, a welcoming little sentinel on the brink of Ginger's world. Then the track becomes uninterrupted mud, winding alongside a snaking grey-green creek overrun with pandanus. It's a sinister setting: an eerie, creeper-festooned stillness, the murky seclusion perfect for sheltering big saltwater crocodiles. More and more mud turns our fifteen-kilometre drive into an hour. At last we see the huts of Maria Lagoon, partly hidden from the road by the tall grass. There's just four cyclone-strength sheds on concrete slabs and a couple of shower blocks, fed by a generator which pumps water from the lagoon. There's no electricity.

As we pull up in front of the huts, Riley steps off his veranda to meet us, cowboy-legged, smacking his pants with his hat. Ten heeler-dingo hunting dogs precede him. Riley has an old, chewed-up face, but he still looks younger than we remember. Around his neck he wears a red bandanna and a stock whip, giving him the appearance of a bush bandit. Which he was once, briefly. The dogs back off us when Riley shows them the leather.

Dan and I settle on Riley's veranda and chase the cattle ticks away with our cigarette ends. There are two other men with him, one middle-aged, one teenaged; both are subdued. Riley doesn't introduce us. He says he got a message that we were coming, but what are we doing here?

I tell him that we've brought an old man from Darwin who is dying, with a couple of months to live at the outside. The quiet men look down, immediately accepting an alien's predicament as sad news; Riley shakes his head and says he's sorry to hear it. We tell him we've left the man asleep at the turn-off, that he's too weak to move after the long drive, but that we're hoping we can bring him to Maria Lagoon tonight. That the man saw Riley's exhibition two years ago in Melbourne, that it meant a lot to him. That he wants to talk to Riley before he dies. Riley shakes his head and lets a long silence hang, making us feel like Jehovahs who have just rung the Bishop's doorbell. 'Do I know him?' Riley asks, finally. No, he doesn't.

'Well, that's really good that he's come, that old fella, to see me,' Riley says, standing. 'I was going to Borroloola today, but I'll go later now. You go back and tell him I want to see him. Tell him I'll be waiting here for him, whenever.'

We tell Ginger we'll bring Fordham later, in the cool end of the day.

Before turning to leave, Davis asks Riley: 'Do you remember us?'

'Well,' he says, 'I was thinking, "I seen you fellas before..."'

We remind him of an afternoon we'd spent together a few years previously, just near here. We talked about a lot of things that day, but we didn't know Riley was an artist with works hanging in major galleries around the world. We didn't know because he never mentioned it.

'No,' says Riley, recalling the meeting. 'I didn't mention that.'

He signals us to stop as we drive away. 'Could you tell me, roughly, what month is it?'

It's the middle of March, we say.

Mike Fordham was a journalist. He had a reputation, but not as a journalist. He acquired the label of drunkard at eighteen, while working in an advertising agency in Melbourne, and it never left him. His drinking binges ran into one another and Fordham found himself on the way to becoming a mean husband and father. He may have wished for a long-suffering wife who would allow him drinker's latitude for the sake of his 'genius', but such wives only tend to turn up in the biographies of great writers.

Fordham's greatest work was writing Australia's famous Mortein insecticide theme song, 'Louie the Fly'. Or so people around Darwin say. 'That total bullshit,' says Fordham. 'Although I knew the bloke who claimed he wrote it.'

Fordham went from writing ads to journalism, reporting for the *Age* in Melbourne and the *Telegraph* in Sydney. In the mid-Seventies he moved to Darwin, leaving a collapsed marriage behind him. He continued to drink and began to write less and less.

Fordham couldn't get any proper work on ABC radio or with the *Northern Territory News*, Darwin's two main employers of journalists. He alarmed senior staff from both companies with his drunk and shambolic appearances, accusing them of cowardice in their political reporting of life under a crooked Northern Territory Government. It was easy for Fordham to be righteous. He had nothing to lose, least of all the job they wouldn't give him. Besides, most of his proposed stories reeked of legal suits; his investigations were frequently conducted in hotel bars with mysterious sources. Even if he was right about the corruption, he was travelling on instinct only. Editors could place neither him nor his stories. They were justified in not employing him. Fordham was more interested in the wider story than its detail and couldn't file a straight news report.

'That dog nearly bit me,' I'd said, after a blue heeler had gone for me when we'd stopped at the postmistress's house, earlier on our trip, to ask directions to Ginger's. 'No,' explained Fordham in a teacherly tone, 'it lunged at your throat.'

He started to write satirical columns for the smaller Darwin papers. He was good at it and the form excused him from conducting proper research. The suspicion that he was as good as or better than any journalist in town remained only that. As a junior journalist, I had to type up his weekly radio columns. He'd turn up in the newsroom, drunk, on Thursday afternoons, and start to recite his rants. Usually they were first-person accounts of Darwin politics from the viewpoint of a 'long-grasser', or a homeless drinker around town. The newsroom would empty. He became his characters, swinging air punches, bellowing in outrage at the answers to his own questions, grabbing me by the shirt collar when he wanted to make a point, and rolling his eyes horribly. Towards the end of the performance he would lower his voice in a deceptive moment of tender concern before exploding into a nasty, screeched finale. Then he would take the script I'd typed down to the studio and repeat the performance into a microphone. It suited his ego to have a 'boy' taking it all down. He claimed he had been a drinking buddy of Peter O' Toole's and Brendan Behan's years before, when he'd worked in London. Everything about him suggested this was true.

He had always hated communists and the rich; now he began to train his sights on everyone in between. His great capacity for hatred made Fordham's friends feel peculiarly privileged, a feeling which generally wore off when he needed to use the spare room for a few weeks. When Darwin's independent papers closed, Fordham had nowhere to go. That was fifteen, twenty years ago.

In his constant search for a semi-permanent bed, Fordham used up almost every yacht cabin and garden shed in town. My mate Dan had a mango farm down the track with a tin shack on it. I suggested he let Fordham rent it. The arrangement lasted a few months, until Dan got tired of Fordham ordering him to bring food and tobacco from town and never paying his rent. In the end he kicked him out. Not long after, Mike got word about his throat.

If things had gone as they might have, Fordham would have become an accomplished mid-to-elderly television journalist, toothily patronizing the outback in his white moleskin trousers, light-blue cotton drill shirt and elastic-sided R. M. Williams Yearling boots. He'd be off doing a well-earned 'easy' story about a marvellous, wise, far-flung and—most importantly—harmless blackfella with the great wisdom and patience so typical of elderly Aboriginal men who've had their goodwill tested since birth. But the elastic's gone in Fordham's boots, the zip is busted on his trousers and his shirt's been washed too many times for it still to be called blue. It's Riley who's doing fine—with money, fame and spangly clothes. 'Just sittin' on it,' is what Riley says. It's Fordham who's been broken.

Fordham denies his poverty or lack of success have made him bitter, but lying in the dirt at the turn-off he rants about how families no longer communicate because Rupert Murdoch and Kerry Packer have deliberately used their media networks to tear households apart. It seems to us, listening to this, that a dying man should have better things to worry about than Rupert and Kerry conspiracies.

'Besides, Fordham,' I say, 'your own family fell apart years ago, when television was still young and naive. Kerry Packer and Rupert Murdoch didn't ruin your family. You did.'

'Well,' he says, 'I was erratic. That's why my family broke up.' He went on to explain that 'information' would soon become the prevalent cancer-causing agent, on a par with the Log Cabin tobacco that had just about nailed him.

'My family probably think I haven't changed at all in forty years,' Fordham says. 'In their terms, I'm possibly something of a hopeless, raving failure.'

'Is that a wrong definition for you?' I ask him.

'Well, it's actually not a wrong definition for me.'

On the other hand, Fordham says that he's never wanted to live according to standard expectations. He may have gone about things the wrong way, he says, but he hasn't failed. Itinerants with no superannuation plan are widely viewed as failures; but it is possible, he says, that there's an element of choice in such a life. There was a time when drifters were respected for their cunning and envied for their weightlessness. Ginger Riley, after all, drifted for years.

Mid-afternoon, Riley drives out from Maria Lagoon to visit

Fordham, ahead of our arrangement. The little crocodile we saw in the creek earlier is sitting on the back seat of Ginger's LandCruiser, wearing a smile that momentarily distracts from the bullet hole through its head.

'I've just come,' says Riley, 'to say hello to that old fella, Mike, to make sure he's happy.' But Mike is in a deep morphine sleep and can't be roused from his swag. Riley drives back to his camp, tears in his eyes for someone he's never met.

Convinced Fordham is about to die, but hoping he'll be able to hang on until the sundown has a chance of reviving him, Dan and I start wondering about the protocol for dead bodies in these places. Perhaps the Borroloola police will take him off our hands. Or maybe we'll end up having to take him back to Darwin under a blue tarpaulin on the dinghy-trailer, covered in two-dollar bags of crushed ice.

'You needn't bother, you pricks,' says Fordham, leaning up on one elbow and staring at us with huge, faded blue eyes. 'If I die, you ask Ginger Riley if he's got a spare cave around here. You can put me in it with one of those precious bottles of vodka I know you're hoarding.'

We're not sure about Fordham's pharaonic notion of 'needing something for the journey'. It strikes us as a little selfish. 'We'll have to think about the vodka,' I say.

Fordham pulls a striped sheet over his head and asks us to go away.

At sundown, Fordham showers and shaves on the Cox River crossing, and steps into his cleanest dirty clothes.

'I just want,' he says, enjoying a moment of clarity before the next morphine cloud, 'to see one thing, one person, who may be able to help me leave this world believing that it is not a thoroughly detestable place.'

Three or four years previously Dan and I had driven along the same dirt highway. We'd decided to take a look at this part of the world that no one in Darwin ever seemed to talk about. As we passed a long, lily-covered waterhole, we caught sight of an old man seated on the ground next to a fire. Behind him was a blue Mazda Bongo van, its tyres completely shredded. As we were on a rarely used road we pulled in to see if the man needed a lift north to the service station at Roper Bar. He said no, that he was just sitting down for a few days.

A young man appeared over a sandy rise with a .22 magnum lever-action slung over his shoulder, feigning surprise to see visitors. As he got closer we could see that the rifle's barrel was noticeably bent, the stock strapped with string and electrical tape. The young man said that he was having trouble killing anything with the misshapen weapon; he was concerned that with the next round it might blow up in his face. We got the feeling he'd been watching us to make sure we weren't planning anything weird on the old man. The old man told us his name was Ginger Riley.

They were hanging out. Not camping, just stopping. Both seemed disconsolate but in no hurry to leave. They had nothing to eat but some kind of porridge, what looked like a mixture of flour and water, which was hardening in a pot on the fire. Dan had some small fish he'd throw-netted back at the Cox River crossing. He gave them to Ginger Riley, who tossed them into the pot.

'I don't like this fish,' Riley said shortly. 'You got a rifle?' Dan did. 'Maybe you can shoot me crocodile? There's one over there in the billabong. I'm hungry for some meat.'

Given the opportunity and permission to kill something big and protected, we went a little eagerly to the waterhole. On the face of it we were being propelled by sympathy for the old man's hunger, but really it was the same impulse that had made John Huston want to shoot an African bull elephant despite being warned: 'It's a crime to shoot an elephant.' 'It's not a crime, it's a sin,' Huston said. At least, he said it in Clint Eastwood's movie about him.

But we saw no crocodile. All we had for meat were some green supermarket sausages that had bloated repulsively in the Esky over the past few days. We'd been reluctant to mention them. 'They're still good!' Riley declared, shaking them straight on to the fire.

Only a few moments of that afternoon remain. Riley talked about the pygmies of the Limmen Bight region, vexatious human-spirits best avoided—if you meet one face to face and you don't beat it up with your fists, it'll come to your camp and steal fish or children, I don't remember which. If you do beat it up, it'll become an ingratiating friend for life. If you do happen to see one, he said, run away.

The young man added that he'd seen a family of hairy giants run out of a cave and flee along a ridge when the first machines started scraping around the huge McArthur River mine site not too far from where we were sitting. Feeling somewhat out-yarned, we apologized for having no such creatures where we came from.

Eventually Dan and I climbed back into our truck and continued our drive north to Darwin. In the years that followed we occasionally wondered about the superstitious old bushman drinking cold tea from a filthy tin cup, chain-packing a stemless pipe, minus a middle finger on his right hand from a bottle fight in Katherine town years before.

Witch doctor, we thought.

When the tests gave him only a few months to live, Fordham decided that he wanted to leave Australia and visit the art galleries of Lisbon and Seville. He'd been staring at a miserable dead end, unable to move about much, a prisoner of his disease and, he claimed, the monotonous national radio station. He couldn't turn it off, for fear of silence, but it was making him increasingly agitated. Every news bulletin seemed to carry items about a country being daily divided on racial grounds.

He'd never watched television and had grown too impatient to read books. He'd throw them down at the slightest objectionable word or idea. Dying men have no time for anything disagreeable. Besides, books are someone else's ideas and now, with his end in sight, he felt he needed his own.

Grappling with the religious art of Lisbon and the Moorish art of Seville would give death the right colour, he thought, and contemplation would distract him from its beckoning finger. Lisbon and Seville seemed a strange choice of destinations; it might be argued, after all, that these cities store some of Europe's least impressive art—Lorvao monastery's collection of abbot skulls dipped in silver aside. But they were the favourite cities of Fordham's estranged son. The trip would also serve as an eleventh-hour gesture to him.

Fordham's plan was to get drunk and fall down dead in a cafe, where no one would know him or claim him. It seemed a brave and selfish idea, but it also looked suspiciously like running away. Possibly he was afraid that, having burned so many bridges, he'd have no one to care for him while he was dying.

But he had no money and in the end the matter settled itself. He couldn't go.

Proud of the fact that he'd never lived for money, Fordham was facing his last months of life pension-poor on a sagging bed on a kind acquaintance's back veranda in Palmerston, a satellite suburb of Darwin that always makes room for the destitute. It was the only bed he could find. The palliative-care housing agency had told him seventeen other dying people were before him in the queue.

He was all right, in a forsaken way, just tired from a drug that would rather be accepted than argued with. He was pleased that his veranda had a ceiling fan to shake off the damp of the wet season; less enthusiastic that a view of a suburban back fence might be his last picture of the world. He wanted to go somewhere, anywhere. We suggested Limmen Bight—a brutal kind of place, a long way away. None of the art of Lisbon or Seville, but at least it was somewhere else.

'That's Ginger Riley's country!' Fordham said, and extolled his virtues as an artist and a revolutionary. We said we'd met a gnarly bloke at a waterhole a few years back who'd called himself Ginger Riley. He'd never mentioned anything to us about being a painter.

I wasn't that bent on finding Riley again, but I was interested in Fordham. I kept remembering an old Johnny Cash song in which a man happens upon a dying stranger lying on the ground. He gets down close to the man to hear his last words:

> I found him by the railroad track this morning
> I could see that he was nearly dead
> I knelt down beside him and I listened
> Just to hear the words a dyin' fella said...

Fordham has been given the verdict, but he's not so sure he feels as if he's dying. 'It's a curious thing,' he says, just before we drive on to Riley's. 'When I was first told, it didn't worry me much at all. It didn't seem to be me they were talking about. I'd wake up in the morning and say, "Now who's that fella that's dying?" And you know there's somebody in that bed who's dying, but you don't relate it to yourself. And then slowly the realization comes over that it is actually you, and you'd better start thinking about it.'

'Maybe you brought some beer?' asks Ginger Riley.

Maybe we did.

Riley has been beerless for weeks because of the floods. 'Anyway, later for that,' he says. Riley glances at Fordham and tells him: 'I know you know about Aboriginal people. I'm glad you've come to see me.'

Fordham first encountered Riley two years before at the National Gallery of Victoria. He had gone to see an Amish quilt exhibition, but had quickly tired of the tedious design precision. He wandered away and found a sign pointing to THE GINGER RILEY EXHIBITION. It cost sixteen dollars to see the quilts, nothing to see Ginger Riley.

Outside Melbourne was cold and grey, but inside the gallery there were great luminous canvases of magenta skies, rivers running out to seas, monsoonal rain clouds that appeared to be shower taps spitting little drops of rain. The paintings were rudimentary cartography, an unpretentious statement of country with no particular spiritual baggage. There were few questions unanswered, nothing to wrestle with.

Fordham remembered looking across the gallery floor and seeing Riley, a neat black cowboy crowded by fans. He wanted to go up to him, to tell him that he was also from the Northern Territory and liked the way he had painted it. But the crowd was assailing Riley with questions about the meaning in his art. They could not put his Aboriginality to one side—they wanted to know about spirit worlds and dreamings. Fordham wanted to tell them that Riley was just an artist—that they belittled both themselves and him by insisting on prefacing him and his art with the word 'Aboriginal'. Yet Riley didn't seem helpless or frustrated by the attention. In fact, he was drinking it up. His answers in no way matched the questions he was asked, but it didn't matter. It was Riley's moment and Fordham left him to it.

So it seems strange now when Riley claims a clear recollection of Fordham that day: 'You know, I did see you.'

'That could well be,' says Fordham, crashing gratefully on to some dog-worn furniture. He tells Riley his paintings are best appreciated at a distance, from the other side of a gallery. That they should be looked at simply as one might a take in a stretch of country.

'Not too many looked at those paintings like that,' says Riley. 'Not many understood that. What you say, about standing far away, that's what I always think in my mind,' says Riley. 'Some of that painting—doesn't matter Western [Australian] or Northern Territory painting, you don't see much. You gotta get over close and look. But my painting you can see it all from here to my Toyota over there'—fifteen metres—'or even further away. I mean those other paintings, doesn't matter who, but those paintings you can't hardly see.'

'Your paintings,' says Fordham, unwinding, 'they're just country. You've saved people the effort of climbing the hill to get a better look—everybody is put high above the land, at cloud level, watching the river running to the sea.'

'That's right,' says Riley. 'Just talking about it that way, my painting, everything that you can see, I make it bright, the tree and the hill and the river, bring it from outside and put it into one place—that's Limmen Bight station. Here. I collect things, in my mind...and put them here.'

Fordham says, 'So you're prepared to use anything from anywhere to create images, and it doesn't matter if in Limmen Bight country there's not this animal or a particular rock. If it appeals to you visually, you're prepared to put it there. Is that right?'

'That's right,' says Riley. 'What you think is not where you live. My paintings are what I think, not where I live. I collect the things I think and take them all here, cos I was born here. Maybe you can't see the things in my painting from here. Maybe they're not actually here. But I put them all in one place, that's here. Right here. And in my memory, I just sit there, in five minute, in five minute, I got that all in my mind and I start to work.'

Riley's been compared to European painters because well-known Aboriginal artists always are. He is polite about it, but doesn't need comparisons in order to evaluate himself—he's certain he's one of the greats. Asked who his favourite painter is, he names a woman from up the road. Whether he does this out of contempt for the art world, or whether he's simply telling the truth, I can't work out: 'I tell you one female. She used to paint like mine. This is Bessie Moore, an adoptive daughter of mine. She's in Urapunga. Just from Ngukkur across that [Roper] river. She could have been anybody. But she just work painting. She's good. I can't think no more—that's all I think on that. Bessie Moore.

'Some European painters, they have that same painting that I can see in my eye. And it's good. I don't, you know... I like paintings. I don't say no good about anybody. I don't say no good about me. Whatever I see. Whatever comes out I don't say no good. Not only myself, not only my painting. I love paintings from all people.'

With few exceptions, he paints this Limmen Bight country. One of his larger works can take twenty-four hours. He paints in short bursts, a few times each year. It seems almost conceited, the way he doesn't work at all on his technique, and he's certainly no detail-genius. His work is often described as 'rough' and 'childish', and not just by detractors. But as he explains, he is only about style. He is prepared to change his approach, but feels no need to rehearse. He prepares for change through contemplation.

'That's what I'm thinking now,' he says. 'Got to be change, going forward, not going back. Like when I'm doing my work, now I'm doing different painting, but still of the same country here. The colour is different. In Melbourne I did three or four really big ones. They're saying, "How come your painting's different?" I say, "It's the same country. You can see it—look." Only colour is different.'

Riley's got a horseman's bad lower back. When he was young, he was one of Lord Vestey's voluntary Aboriginal ringers on Nutwood Downs station. His wages were tea, sugar and bully beef. He rode through Central Australia, met the famous Albert Namatjira, liked his work and tried painting himself. He didn't like what he saw and put painting to one side, for decades. The law meanwhile changed and station owners had to pay Aborigines equal wages. Riley, like many others, found himself without work. He briefly resuscitated his riding career on the wrong side of the law and was busted rustling cattle west of Nutwood Downs. Questioned by a police sergeant, he immediately confessed. 'Aborigines have this hideous habit of telling the truth,' interjects Fordham. After three months' hard labour Riley went to Darwin, found himself drinking and wasting his time.

'I used to drink that flagon in Darwin,' he says. 'I used to drink that. Too much, too much. I think that beer's the best, but I used to like that big bottle instead of that little beer! Ha! Jingo! That used to drive me silly!' Riley does not look back on this period with regret, more amazement that he got out of it alive. His plan had always been to return to his mother's country, where he was born, where he is now.

Legal reckoning aside, Maria Lagoon and Limmen Bight—this whole part of the world—has fallen back to Aboriginal custody. Apart from fishermen, geologists and the Conservation Commission, only Aborigines use it. Nathan River and St Vidgeon, the cattle stations which officially override Aboriginal tenure, have long ceased to be viable. No cattle are run. The stations are officially 'working', but they have in fact been maintained as fronts to repel Aboriginal land claims.

Ginger Riley is the caretaker of the land on which he sits. The Mara people won a claim for coastal land just near here, at which he gave evidence (Riley is Mara). Riley is entitled to live on that land, but he prefers his private arrangement to occupy a small corner of St Vidgeon. It's where he was born—what he calls 'my mother's country'. Just off the coast lies Maria Island, although who this Maria is or was doesn't concern Riley. 'Some woman, innit? I call this place Wamangu, you can call it Maria Lagoon if you like.' Riley is independent of everyone, including Aborigines. He lights the fires to clear the long grass, hunts, slowly puzzles over his diesel Toyota's injector and electrical problems, visits places where he just sits down and thinks about himself and his country—which is what he was doing when we came past three years ago.

'I became a painter,' Riley says, 'just because my father and grandfather, they used to put mark on my coolamon when I was a baby. They said I was going to be a painter. I know straight away. And I run away from school, even from my father. Because my grandfather took me away somewhere to station. So I grow up at Nutwood Downs station. That was owned by Vesteys.'

'I'll wager Lord Vestey wouldn't have you sitting around painting—not when he's paying you nothing to break horses!'

screeches Fordham. England's Vestey family actually never clapped eyes on any of their Northern Territory land. Vesteys were knights and lords, High Anglican priest-like creatures who only visited their vast pastoral holdings through the reports of accountants.

'Oh no he wouldn't!' laughs Riley. 'But my father, he didn't say that, he didn't say, "You gotta be a painter". But maybe when I grow up I'd know what my painting was. And, after a while, I was rounding cattle, horsebreaking in, then maybe two three four five years then I pulled out. I went into Darwin, worked for government, clean up gardens, schools, everything. I used to clean that.

'After a while, maybe another five years gone, I'm just thinking, "I've got to get back to my people". So I go away from Darwin. So I come to Roper, to Ngukkur.

'And I'm working for council, I had a contract building a fence. It wasn't enough for me. Anyway a bloke—I don't where he is now, I never seen him—he put me in a course about painting. At Ngukkur. I just worked. It was different from them others, my painting, just because I was more from my father and my grandfather, in drawing. So, you see, I wasn't painting when I was young—I didn't know that. Just lately.'

When Riley began painting in 1986, he was discovered in a flash. Mimi Arts & Crafts, an Aboriginal gallery out of Katherine, received an invitation from the adult educator in Ngukkur to view an exhibition of new work by older people. Bob Gosford, now a Darwin lawyer but then a field officer for Mimi, attended. All the students were using fluorescent acrylics, which has come to define the so-called Ngukkur School.

'The exhibition was in a building that had been trashed—a community hall building,' Gosford said later. 'Ngukkur at the time looked like a war zone. We walked in and there was this burst of blazing colour. It was an entirely new spin on the material I was familiar with. It was the same subject matter, but the use of acrylic materials and the sheer number of new paintings...it was as if people had left bark and found something that opened all the doors that bark hadn't let them into. Although they were still traditional paintings.

'Ginger Riley's were the most fully developed and startling. As far as I know he hadn't painted before, and here were twenty-six landscapes—his first paintings. His love and respect for country was evident. In fact, it poured forth from these physical and psychic paintings. We bought the lot.'

Riley's very first painting from this exhibition shows him fidgeting with the more standard dot and cross-hatching styles, but Riley knew he was only doing what was expected of Aboriginal artists. He was faking it, and in doing so appalled himself. A few paintings later he'd left them alone. He hasn't touched a dot since.

'I don't catch up on this dot, really,' he says. 'I saw that dot dot dot. But I don't paint any tree dot dot dot. Doesn't mean anything to me. I can't understand. Can't even understand it! Some people can understand that, because they do things that way. People from Borroloola, around here, don't understand that, no they don't. They paint different way, trees and rivers, not that dot dot dot.'

Riley's paintings are big, clean and elementary. So much so they have alarmed critics and artists alike. His winning the 1992 Alice Prize reportedly provoked a 'stunned silence'. That such apparently simple imagery—a virtual stick figure of a bird on a one-colour background—should attract serious attention caused despair among painting's earnest toilers, white and black, but the buyers from the Robert Holmes à Court Collection had no doubt. Riley quickly became known, then famous, late in life.

But at Maria Lagoon there is no sign of artistic activity except for a pair of Riley's trousers covered in brush marks. Riley mostly paints in his manager's Spring Street gallery in Melbourne, seated on the ground with a big canvas stretched out before him.

'I never stand up and paint paintings,' he says. 'I just relax and sit down on the floor. That's how my work always done. Otherwise if I'm standing up the paint it will drip down into the canvas. That's why I don't like that way. On the floor I just move around slowly, better. I like that.'

Night has fallen on Maria Lagoon. 'What day is it?' asks Riley. Monday, we say.

'I think Tuesday, isn't it?' says Riley.

'They might have a different calendar in the Limmen Bight River,' says Fordham.

'No, we don't have different calendar. It's the same,' says Riley. 'Maybe when you were on the road you lost your minds somewhere? I'm just mentioning this because it's Tuesday. I'm only mentioning this because if I'm travelling, I just forget everything, what day it is. But I just sit here. You fellas been travelling. Very tired, drive, forget, tired. I'll bet fifty bucks it's Tuesday.'

I'm ready to take him up.

'No betting,' says Fordham. 'I despise betting.'

'OK, yes, sure, Mike,' says Riley.

'But I am about to lose my mind, Ginger,' says Fordham. 'These drugs are strong and I should like to talk to you before they start working. This is about...having an opportunity of living and dying with some understanding of why you—that is, I—have been here.'

'Are you there?' asks Riley.

'I was getting there, Ginger. I was almost there. And suddenly this unexpected thing has thrown me, mentally. I'm not in a screaming heap and I don't break down and cry in the middle of the night. I just feel slightly disappointed that I haven't got another two years. I've got doctors who've said maybe twelve months. Another has said maybe six. And some old gentleman with a bow tie running some palliative care unit in Darwin has said maybe two to three months, if I'm lucky. And that was well over a month and a half ago. So now perhaps I really shouldn't think about anything.'

Fordham has been contemplating the best means of approaching death without the assistance of institutions or religious organisations. Despite his avoidance of organized religion he's not an atheist; he feels there's a certain amount of credibility in what he calls the Aborigines' 'totemic system'. 'Aborigines look at the creation of the world and their own part in it. Their system, which is very close to the Hindu system, is fairly satisfactory,' he confides to Riley.

Riley broods on this for some time. Then he says, startled: 'Jingo!'

Riley is more stockman than sorcerer, trousers down to his arsecrack. He may participate in ceremonial business when the need arises, but mostly he follows his own schedule. Fordham can't draw him to talk about 'business'—to talk about it 'will kill you', he has said. Yet it's more than Riley being secretive. He seems to be saying that being Aboriginal is something that is in his mind, not on it.

Riley explains: 'I'm just...when I want to, I go city, stay, and come back to my place, the country here, and stay. It's just because I like it. I'm born here, I like the country, and I like myself. It doesn't matter. When I come back to my country, I'll always be happy. Understand what I mean?'

Then Riley says that he sees himself foremost as a Christian. Fordham doesn't seem to pick this up, perhaps because of the morphine overload. Or perhaps he doesn't want to hear. Fordham is explaining that indigenous artists from around the world, particularly carvers, have always presented gentle and mysterious images of their gods—unlike the 'blatant obscenity' of the image of a 'statue Jesus bleeding from his crown of thorns'. Riley puts his head down and mutters an apologetic prayer on Fordham's behalf.

Fordham is oblivious: 'I always find it extraordinary that whites have got this notion that there's actually some Jewish divinity,' he says. 'It's a bit like saying that the Rainbow Serpent [which features in many Aboriginal creation stories] was created by Captain Cook. "It's so mysterious that we must adopt it as a god!" Whereas in fact we're looking at something that is a great, fundamental creature. I don't find it difficult to believe in.'

I ask Riley if he has any idea what Mike's talking about. 'I'm catching up,' says Riley, annoyed, waving the question away.

'Last time I was in London,' says Fordham, 'I heard this conversation whereby someone was amazed to open the window of a council flat and shout, "LOOK, IT'S A BIRD!" And sure enough, there was a little sparrow scratching around on the lawn. And he, like some great explorer, had discovered...a SPARROW! And you just wonder what the ultimate relationship with the planet is. If someone had never seen a bird, what if they'd seen a thirty-foot python slithering around Piccadilly Circus? They might actually say, "It's a god!" And why not?'

'You got me there!' says Ginger.

'Well, I wouldn't fucking well kill it!' screams Fordham. 'It may very well be *the* God. Is that unreasonable? What we're looking at is a situation where human beings have for many years been trying to put something between themselves and a creator.'

Fordham falls back against his chair with a whimper.

The two other men with Riley at Maria Lagoon are Rowan Riley, Ginger's eighteen-year-old grandson, and Danny Riley, a middle-aged nephew with a face bent out of shape by drink—'grogface' is what they call it. Rowan is here to learn about this country from his grandfather; Danny is recovering, and looks to be in worse shape than Mike. Yet Danny is first to ask Fordham, 'Are you all right, old fella?'

'I'm all right, Danny,' Fordham complains, grinding Log Cabin tobacco into the heel of his palm. He smokes as much as it is possible to smoke.

'Anyway,' he says. 'I'd like to know how within the clan they face the prospect of people dying of cancer or tuberculosis. Does the Aboriginal man as he's getting older, does he think about life and death and do his cultural values allow him to approach it by himself, or does he need the assistance of his family? I'm going to die, but I certainly don't have a family or tribe around me.'

Ginger says, slowly, 'I wouldn't worry about it. Death is just death. You've lost your things, that's all. I don't catch up with death, really.'

Fordham asks Riley what his totem is.

'Barramundi,' Riley says. Every Aboriginal person is given a totem creature at birth, and afterwards they must not kill their totem—Riley can fish for shark or stingray but not for barramundi.

'When you die,' says Fordham, 'will you become a barramundi swimming around in Limmen Bight?'

'No. That's not right,' says Riley. 'I think it's the same place for all of us.'

I ask him whether he's talking about a Christian or Aboriginal religion, or a mix of both. 'I'm talking about a Christian entity,' says Riley. 'I believe in God, and I believe in Aboriginal culture. Do you see the difference?'

Finally it clicks with Fordham that he's followed a string only to find a Christian on the end of it.

Privately, I wonder if he's disappointed—it would have been easy enough for Fordham to round up a whole platoon of Christians back in town, all of whom would've been happy to gather around his deathbed and point out the exact direction he should be heading in next. Ginger Riley will not be painting himself in ochre and doing healing dance routines for Michael Fordham.

Riley packs a pipe. 'What's your church?' he says, turning to me.

Out here, everyone's got a church, even if the last time they saw it was at their own baptism. 'I have no church.'

'Why not?' he says, giving me a hard eye. I blame my teachers for being uninspiring catechists, which suddenly strikes me as lame. They deserved blame fifteen years ago, they can't be blamed forever.

'Just because you run away, is it?' says Riley, evidently satisfied by my fidgeting. 'My church is Church of England. When we die, we go the same place, in Heaven. I'll always be. I love God as myself. What else... I wouldn't mind say something to Paul. I'm just asking you, doesn't matter who you are, red or yellow, black or white or green, doesn't matter who you are, you are a human being. We made from the God—in Heaven Above. HEA-VEN A-BOVE. But, you know, I think he will live, long time, Mike.

'I think he'll live and maybe I will be gone,' says Riley. 'I just know Mike will live. Some person from Heaven Above told me. And God can just take my life any time. I'm sinner. I'm sinner. I chase the girls...and I drink too much. But I don't curse and I don't swear. I think He like me. I think it's true—He like me.'

The dogs explode into barking and Ginger shows them the whip.

'I dunno how,' says Riley, 'but all I just think, fast way maybe, I just know one place, this is in Heaven, nothing more or less. Look, I'm just satisfaction. I'm satisfied! Sometime I will be lonely in myself. But I still live in Maria Lagoon and that's it. Heaven, Heaven will come.'

'I said to my daughter the other day on the telephone,' says Fordham, 'that I thought I'd finally conquered loneliness. I've spent so much time by myself and I have thought too much about breaking this concept of loneliness. But I went about in it the wrong way and finally I think loneliness just conquered me.'

Fordham was fed up with society by the time he reached his late forties—about the same age Riley began impressing it as a painter. Fordham thought he could make the best of his exasperation by studying history, which would allow him to detach himself intellectually from frustration—be it his own poverty or what he saw as someone else's undeserved success. But he only enjoyed history when his head was in a book. When he looked up, the gloom was still with him—and he began to read his own circumstance as illustrative of the way all mankind was going.

Riley studied Aboriginal history as a young man, through his elders. Then he went wandering for decades, following the cattle or working subordinate jobs until he found his painting. He doesn't see the future as Fordham does—badness, where children will never have time to understand why they're human. He doesn't share Fordham's despair, even though he's felt harder than Fordham what it is to lose family to liquor and dumb fights. In Fordham's world, couples divorce and children never speak to their parents again. In Riley's, they die. Ginger Riley may not like death any more than we do, but he's more accustomed to it. He tells the not surprising news that the young man with the rifle we'd met three years before is dead, killed in a fight at Borroloola. Aborigines die young is how it is; why they get so drunk.

A few days before at the Top Camp in Borroloola, we'd had to turn the car around to allow two distraught Aboriginal women to drag a drunken, concussed man off the road. When Fordham mentions this, Riley shrugs—he sees it every time he goes to town. It's not that he doesn't care, he's just not prepared to be dragged in, and down.

'You got to be worried,' he says, with some emotion, possibly because one of his own children died in a campfire accident. 'Your children get hurt, you don't like to see that. I like my children. I don't want to lose my children or someone damage them. I love my children myself. They'll always be. Sometimes, especially when you have children—you gotta think. You don't want someone there to harm them.'

Fordham tells Riley none of it's an accident—there's a conscious plot afoot to destroy society: that's why no one cares about the open killings on the streets of Sydney and Melbourne; why no one bothers investigating who the arms manufacturers and drug dealers are; how synthesized alcoholic soda is being unleashed on the youth as a deliberately divisive plot. It's a rambling catalogue of unfocused complaints made by a fading man, but Riley is listening closely, nodding his head. He turns, imperiously, to me: 'Are you catching up with what Mike's saying, Paul?'

But neither Dan nor I are catching up. We're tired of Fordham's idea that everyone besides him is doomed to become the helpless victim of corporate evil, if they are not already. And it is becoming clear that Fordham has no desire to make peace with anyone, least of all himself. He will die a snarling ball of disgust that not even the buzzards will touch. At least, that's what we tell him.

Fordham is outraged. 'You little pricks—don't speak to me like that!' He staggers to his feet and shakes his fists at us. Riley intervenes. He orders that Mike's opinions be respected in his camp.

Give my love to Rose, please won't you mister?
Take her all my money, tell her buy some pretty clothes
Tell my boy that daddy's so proud of him...
And don't forget to give my love to Rose.

I think about this, the next verse of the song, where the guy gets to hear the dying man's last words. The truth is, while I liked the idea of the song—listening to a man's last words—I'd always been disappointed by what he heard. It was as if the songwriter had a good idea but stopped short when he found he couldn't put himself in a dying man's mind. But now I was beginning to think that the song was right all along: that a person on the brink of death is subject to the same petty concerns he always had. He is not entitled to any magnificent insights, because the imminence of death does not bestow them. He only cares about the people who loved him when he was fully alive. And most of all, he's scared of being alone.

All Fordham really wants is to see his daughter, who lives in Melbourne. But he's frightened of turning up on her doorstep, a virtual carcass.

Fordham's had enough. He tries to stand but forgets his legs and collapses. Danny is first to his side. Mike no longer has a big gut as tight as a drum, as he did when I first knew him. Carrying him under his arms to his bed, he feels light, as if he's been eaten out inside. His feet take cartoon running steps on the air. Ginger's prediction about Mike outlasting him doesn't seem at all right. He looks sick enough to prove the prophecy wrong this very night.

Danny Riley has dragged his own bowed wire bed across from his shed for Fordham. We help Fordham into it. All the while his breath is coming in great heaves, and he's constantly clearing his unclearable throat.

Suddenly he rouses himself, aware that we are looking down at him rather sadly.

'Look. I don't want the people who are close to me to ponder for the next ten years the fact that I am a drunken cunt, which I actually am not. Or that I was a total failure, which I am not. Because I've done a few things. I've shown total disregard for money. I've never felt any obligation to make money, which most people seem to. Despite what you all may think, being poor hasn't killed me—it's added another fifteen years to my life. Now leave me alone.'

Once Fordham is snoring, his breath coming in gasps, Riley is at my side. 'Bet you fifty bucks it's Tuesday,' he says. We shake.

Riley's first act of the next day is to sit up on his mattress and stare into his hands for a full half-hour. When he finally rises, the dogs stretch and stand with him. We don't ask him about it. He's the only monk in his own contemplative order.

Fordham wakes, stands upright for a moment, then falls and hits his head on a concrete slab with a thud that echoes around Maria Lagoon.

Sickness on this scale is something Dan and I know nothing about. Fordham must to be mothered to eat and does so in reluctant, measly amounts. A stent pries open the tumours on his oesophagus so that food can travel past it. He has no appetite, only an occasional disposition to live.

We go to the river. Fordham stays behind to read a volume of Derek Walcott's poems because, despite what he's said about seeing 'rivers stretching out to the sea' in Ginger's marvellous paintings, he's decided this morning that it's 'just another fucking river'. Ginger leaves Danny Riley to look after Fordham and the dogs.

We stop first at the Limmen Bight Fishing Camp to find out

what day it is. The woman there says it's Tuesday—she knows because she's counting the days till her husband returns with a truckload of supplies. Riley tries his best not to look put out.

The Limmen Bight enters the land via two wide mouths just above the south-west corner of the Gulf of Carpentaria. Upstream, the mud-clay banks hardly rise at all before leading on to featureless saltwater plains. There are a few deliberate hills on the near-horizon. 'Dangerous places' those hills, according to Riley. Last time Dan and I visited, we'd walked to one of them and found human bones in a cave. We were so accustomed to television death that it took a while to sink in that this wasn't murder, just a dead man's grave. The man of bones had a bag by his side—something for the journey.

'You shouldn't have gone there,' Riley says sternly. We tell him we weren't on Aboriginal land—that's on the north side of the river. 'It's not that,' he says, 'it's just dangerous. I think that man you saw got killed by snake. Or something.' The river is tidal, salt for a way then quickly fresh, shallow and dangerous.

The islands upriver are big enough to support animals. Many have fresh water. At a passing glance, nothing at all lives here, but time spent watching might reveal stingrays, king brown snakes, saltwater and freshwater crocodiles, sharks, dugongs, wallabies, flying foxes, eagles—and, living beneath the river's delta, a giant serpent-like creature. 'I don't have to see 'em, I know they're there. Sort of horny and whisker. But I don't call dragon, like you say—I just call Bulukbun,' Ginger tells us. Bulukbun appears in some of his paintings. I suspect this thing is actually one of his mates. It may exist as part of his culture but, by having it in his art, it also serves as a warning to others.

Before meeting Riley, Fordham had said: 'I think the Aborigines of this area must shake their heads and say, "Someone must have sung that Ginger fella". They probably consider him a defector. When I first looked at the paintings, I didn't know who Ginger Riley was, but I realized they were Aboriginal paintings of some sort. And they were quite revolutionary by anybody's standards—just because they work. Their revolutionary characteristics would inspire some fear from traditional Aboriginal painters. Therefore they'd probably dismiss them as "rubbish paintings".'

Fordham was right. Riley feels he needs protection. Nine dogs sleep on Riley's mattress, the tenth—head dog Whisky—under the mosquito net with him. They don't like anyone going near Riley in the day and at night the vigil is broadened to a circle of brindle and teeth. These are more than hunting dogs.

Around here are said to be clever men so adept at murder that if the victim feels anything at all it will be only a repercussive kick of a pointed bone; or creeping sickness from a bloodstream infiltrated with excrement; perhaps a tiny hole next to the neck where a long bone needle has painlessly punctured the lung of the sleeping man; or he awakes to find a nick on his lower back that wasn't there the night before. And then he's dead.

'I know those people,' Riley says, 'where they come from. They're always saying, "I take your kidney fat, you lose your fat". They're still using it. They'll always be. They got different Aborigine ways. Can be just take your fat out, kidney fat, and you be die. Just because—and I'm talking very easy way to you now—maybe you're not good people for them, maybe you get cranky for them, maybe you got girl from this country and they don't like you to get girl. And they will—take your kidney fat off and you're finished.'

But it's men with less subtle methods—those in Toyotas, with clubs—who require special heed. I'm not saying there's an Aboriginal fatwa on Ginger Riley, but there is bad blood. Riley says that Aborigines hate him, 'Because I got the painting, friend! I tell you, people, they are jealous of me. Because not traditional. In my mind, if I get mixed up with them, maybe sold together—I don't wanna be that way. I want to be separate from them mob. They got their painting, I got mine.

'I'm not different, I'm not something else. I'm just a human being. I'm just saying I'm different from other people. I'm the same human being. I'm not a tree. But they don't like them paintings. And I had trouble—a lot of trouble. Just because jealousy, people don't like me, just because I'm a high man.'

In 1993, after one of Riley's images was used on a postage stamp, he was accused by countrymen in Ngukkur and Borroloola of betraying sacred and secret images of the Mara people. This came after he'd won a string of major awards. The brethren seemed to be tiring of his remarkable success. Riley is contemptuous of the accusation. He believes his real problem is that he doesn't hang out in town, handing out his money to relatives for beer.

'That's why I'll always be at the white man's bar at Borroloola,' Riley says. 'They keep me away from nuisance people and the humbug. They look after me, always. They just keep me out from nuisance people robbing me for money, especially when they're drunk. If they ask, I'll give them drink. And if they don't ask, that's it, they can go their own way. Ah, jingo. It's money money money money.'

How, we wonder, do people around here even get to see Riley's work—most of it is done in the south, then sold and ferried out of the country to collectors.

'They always see because of newspaper, television,' says Riley. 'They see everything. Always see. You know, I don't hate them. I like them. They're still my friends. I don't run away from them—the paintings run away from them.'

'You'll want that fifty now,' says Riley, tugging one off a fat roll he keeps hidden down some snake hole.

If you bet you must be prepared to collect your winnings. And after being hit up a thousand times by Aborigines for cigarettes and small change, it seems a lost opportunity not to take money off Riley. But Fordham starts growling. I decline.

'I dunno why!' says Riley. 'I believe lots of people do that, but I don't know why you wouldn't take it.'

'It's wrong, that's why,' says Fordham.

'OK. Yes. Sure, Mike,' says Riley, rewadding the bill. 'OK, I appreciate that. I thought you'd take it now, Paul, but the old fella will kick your arse. Jingo!'

Maria Lagoon is uncommonly silent for a big pond. 'Toads,' says Riley. Poisonous toads have been marching slowly north from the Queensland sugar plantations for sixty years now, pushing aside small native animals and rudely settling in their place.

The others have gone to bed.

Riley's grant money comes from the government of the day, and he is studiously non-political. Asked if the government could treat

Aborigines better, he says, matter-of-fact, 'Oh yes. But the government always treat me well. I always get money from them [he was a 1997–98 grant recipient]. Maybe they could change that thing, can't think of that name, they always take money off me.'

Tax?

'Tax. I don't like that. They always take a lot of money. I think is not fair to me, but the government, I'll say nothing about that.'

Ginger Riley is one of the few Aborigines to discover that middle-income earners cop it something shocking in this country.

'This is yours,' Riley says, producing the fifty-dollar note once again. 'You got to understand,' he says, 'it's my law. I made a promise. You gotta take it.'

I take it.

'I like that old man, Mike,' says Riley, relieved to have jettisoned the freight of debt. 'I haven't met him before, but I met him. You know what I mean?'

'Do you mean you've met his type?'

'No, I don't mean that. I met him.'

'Then I don't really understand.'

Stopping outside Dan's mosquito net, I ask him what we are to make of someone who openly believes that a monster lives in his river. I'd like to know how Riley defines reality, but I suspect he doesn't draw a line. I define it as being awake—asleep is for monsters. What does he want a monster for? Can he see a parallel world that we can't see? Is he a fabricator? How come Aborigines claim rights to an invisible world?

'Fuck off,' says Dan.

We take photos of Ginger and Mike on the morning we leave. They pose helpfully, but the buddy scene feels strained. None of the shots worked out, anyway.

I hear Mike mentioning 'reconciliation' to Ginger. It too feels strained. It's a word that is used a lot in Australia and one I would have thought Fordham would despise. Besides, I don't see that he has anything to reconcile with Aborigines—he has always been straight with them. Ginger talks quietly to him. Fordham's head is bowed as if he's having a confession heard. Someone recently came up with a plan to absolve the nation's guilt: 'Sorry Books', in which every white Australian could sign their name and express their sorrow for what has happened to Aborigines in the past. If a Sorry Book was slapped in front of Fordham right now, he'd sign it. I don't know whether that indicates weakness or strength.

'I had my teeth bashed out last year outside a railway station in Sydney by a group of urban Redfern young fellas,' Fordham tells Riley. Redfern is Sydney's wrecked Aboriginal quarter. 'I didn't really react against that. I just had to face the fact I was in a city I hadn't been to for many, many years, and I was in the wrong place at the wrong time. They rounded me up and smashed my face into the ground and I ended up in Sydney Hospital. It had more to do with my stupidity than their thieving and their aggression.

'And if there was some residual animosity, then by finding you I've actually absolved myself of any feelings of resentment against a race of people who have got absolutely nothing to do with this unnatural brutality.'

Fordham goes on: 'I really wanted to run away from this country, Ginger. I felt the lack of soul in Australia to be dispiriting—I felt that I was going through a whole state of unnecessary depression that had nothing to do with this disease I've got. I thought, "What is it that's lacking in this place? What makes people's lives so dependent on frivolous amusement? Why is there a middle-class paralysis where people need to be entertained and at the same time learn nothing?"

'I never used to think about "blacks and whites". And now I'm constantly trying to avoid the question. In Australia, every minor issue becomes a major one.

'But what am I doing running around villages in Portugal or Spain, heading off to the Basque country? The proposition of seeing you was a similar solution to the one I had—that I might go through a process of rediscovery in the Northern Territory, feel the way I felt when I first came here, look for some sort of inner non-religious strength that will help me face whatever I have to face in the next couple of months. And perhaps a staff to use as I'm stumbling towards what perhaps is inevitable darkness. And I think I have found that.'

Riley again has tears for Fordham. He talks to Mike about making some plans to see him, somewhere, later. Mike tells him plans probably aren't a good idea.

Later, I ask Fordham what right we had to take his burden to that man. 'I don't think we had any right in some ways, but I think he knew this was going to happen. I think he knew we were coming.' Fordham enters the unloggable terrain of telepathy, so leave it at that. Such talk is for the insane, the Aborigines, and the dead.

Fordham says there was a time when the bunghole highway towns of the Northern Territory weren't populated by sneering men and women leaning on the bar never having to ask for a drink because the barman knows what they drink, by crikey.

It's the same everywhere. Every pub has its sullen barman who won't even return a simple good morning. Until, unwittingly, you utter some mystery keyword, and then you can't shut the bastard up. The many foreigners, travelling Australia, who have been assured that goodwill and bush ballads are free to all who pass, sit stranded in the corners. They are confused, as well, by the ever-present pissed Aborigines.

The traveller's crime is that he or she has not lived in the outback; they know nothing of heat and hardship and mongrel blacks. Therefore, they know nothing.

On the way back to Darwin we stop for another drink. A middle-aged barman tells us how he nearly got to have sex with a twenty-one-year-old Danish traveller who was working here, behind his bar. Dan and I thump the bar: 'Nearly?'

'Yeah, but on the night we were lined up she jumped in a truck and went to Darwin.' He actually believes the barmaid is the loser in this story.

'Oh, fuck,' Fordham eventually yells, slamming his glass on the counter in despair: at us, his two pesky companions for five days; at his throat; at it all, in fact, but particularly at the new settlers of this old country who believe that wearing an oil-stained hat at a certain tilt endows them with the gift of character.

Dan, consoling, suggests this must be the origin of the expression 'galahs'—senseless men and women with grey work clothes and sunburned pink faces, who are rude to this polite man who has to bunch up his pants because his once-huge stomach is receding faster than he can punch holes in his belt.

Riley would get worse treatment. Partly because his pants fall down too, mostly on account of his black skin. He may even—still—be told that there are nice chairs for his type outside. He rode horses and cattle through here when these people were kittens.

Mike Fordham died in hospital a few months later. His daughter was with him.

As for Ginger Riley, the road past his place has been improved and his world has become a little more accessible. In December 1999 stories appeared in the newspapers claiming that fake Riley artworks were flooding the Australian market. The works carried Riley's distinctive missing-finger hand signature, but he insisted they weren't his. He told police that a group of people had turned up at his outstation with canvases and begun painting in his style. He said he was persuaded to sign the paintings after the interlopers had got him horribly drunk.

The truth may be more complicated. Some people believe that Riley has dug himself into a hole. That he did in fact paint the works, but panicked when his Melbourne-based manager pointed out that he had signed an exclusive contract with her. Lawyers are now involved. □

GRANTA

GROG

Photographs and interviews by Polly Borland

Galiamble is a twenty-four-hour residential centre for Aboriginal men with alcohol or drug problems. Winja Ulupna is its sister home for Aboriginal women. They are both in St Kilda, Melbourne, Victoria.

10 MITCHELL
Galiamble
HOUSE RULES
Any person under the influence of alcohol will not be permitted entry
WELCOME
TO
GALIAMBLE
MILO

STREET

AUNTIE ALMA

Yes, I do remember, love. We lived on a little place out in Framlingham, that's where my mother comes from, and one day she was in town and all of a sudden they came and took us, like that. There were six of us, two brothers and four sisters. And that was the last time we sort of seen Mum and Dad for a long time.

They put us in different homes, I went to an older girls' home. I stayed there till I was sixteen, then I went to a live-in job for twelve months. But I sort of ran away, so they sent me back to the girls' home and let me out when I turned eighteen. Then I lived in a hostel in Northcote. And then we all sort of found each other. We didn't find one, that was Archie, he was the baby. But as he got older, he come looking for us and he found us.

See I didn't know much then, love. The places I did go to, I was treated like one of the family. In the home we all got treated equal. I never ever had any trouble there. But I still think it was wrong. It was sad when they were taking us, my poor old mum and dad running after the police car. They couldn't do anything.

Afterwards Mum and Dad separated. They'd hit the grog heavy, you know. Then I got settled down. Me and my husband Arnold. He was German. Well we got on fantastic before we had children. He was a cook, and we used to travel with the shows. He used to cook toffee apples and hot dogs, and that. Then we come down to Melbourne and we settled in Collingwood and had the children.

When I got separated from my husband, that's when I hit the grog heavy. I thought there was nothing else. I don't know, it's such a horrible stuff, I suppose, alcohol. I worked and worked and all of a sudden we just drifted apart. There was no social service hardly and I only had a casual permit job in a fish factory. So my nerves were going and they had some foster people that took the three children, and that's where they grew up.

It must be nearly ten months since I had a drink. My memory's gone a bit with the booze. I said to my daughter—I call her 'daught'—I said, 'Daught, I can't remember your birthday.' And she said, 'Oh, don't worry, Mum, I know. Too much *[mimes a drink]*.' And I said, 'Yeah.' I'm fifty-eight, love. I'm happy I'm not drinking. I'm looking forward to leaving this place. I'm not touching that dirty stuff no more.

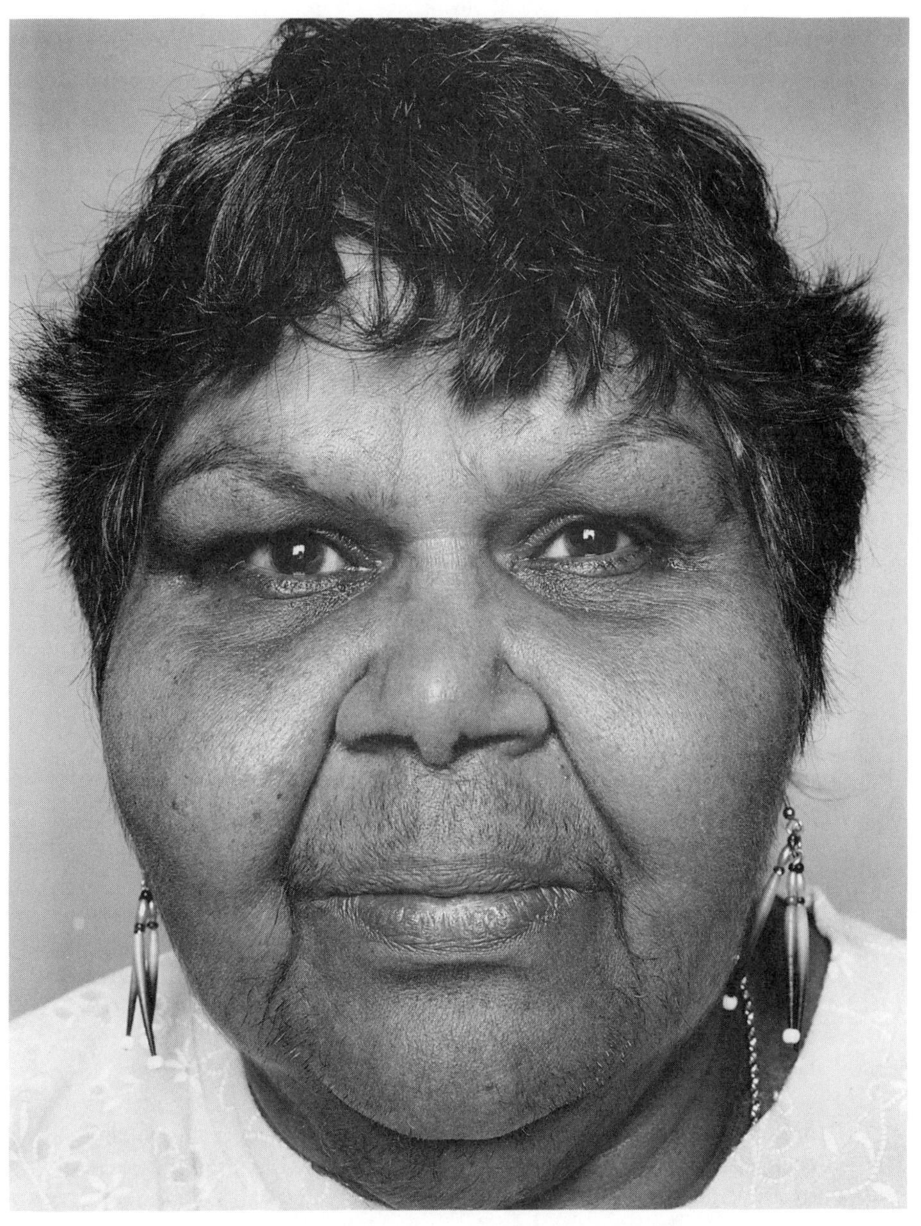

MELISSA STANLEY (MISSY)

My mother's full Aboriginal. My father's white. My sister's full Aboriginal, she's the darkest of the family. I'm the lightest out of the lot of us kids. My mum was anaemic when she had me and she was donated three bags of blood, so I inherited a white skin—well, not quite white. I would love to be full-blooded but there's nothing I can do about that.

My mum was part of the stolen generation. She was shifted around different homes until she met my brother's dad. He left her when he found out she was pregnant, and then she met my father.

I was fostered out for a little while when I was a baby just so Mum could have a break. They used to have programmes going through the Aboriginal co-op and family charities and my brother and I used to go for two or three weeks for a holiday. My brother's doing really well for himself now. He works at Mirana Creations, Aboriginal Arts and Crafts on Torquay Road. He's engaged to be married, he's got two daughters, Rebecca and Megan.

My children have been in care about a year and a half now. I just had a really bad problem with marijuana that I couldn't break free from. My son was taken off me three days after I gave birth to him. I'd just finished seeing some visitors off and I turned my back and there's a lady asking me if I was Melissa Stanley and I said yes and she said would I go into this room and I walked in and there was five or six people sitting there and I knew straight away what was going on, and I just flipped. They just didn't give me a chance to show what I could do. They thought if I took him home he wasn't going to be cared for properly, because of the people that I used to have staying with me, that was the main problem, and the dope, and my ex. Once my son was gone as well, then things got a lot worse.

On Wednesday it'll be twenty months that I've been here. I've had so much support from the workers; they're trying hard to get my children back. Lots of things are looking up for me now. I only get the kids two hours once a week, but soon we're going to push for weekend access, and hopefully then I'll have a house of my own. Definitely in Melbourne. I can't go back to Geelong, too many memories, too many enemies, too many fights, too many drugs. All my friends are smokers or drinkers, and I can't be around that and neither can my kids.

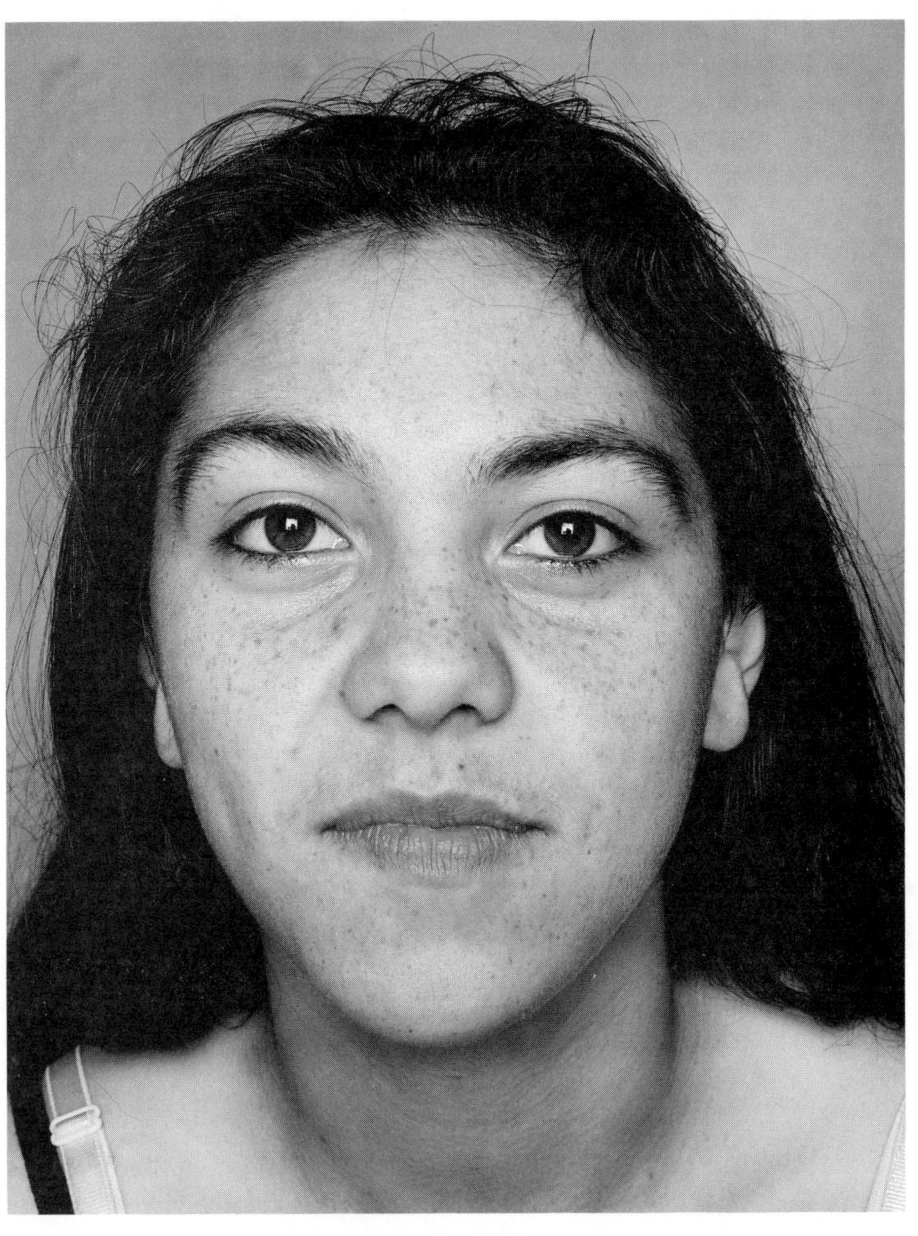

TRACY (left)

I was fifteen or sixteen when I started. I haven't got an alcohol problem. My problem is the pills. After my mum died I just got into the drugs more and more. She overdosed accidentally on drugs, when I was nineteen. After that my dad looked after me. He was a good father. He wasn't a drinker. He's in an elderly home now.

My sister's an alcoholic at the moment. My brother's been clean for the last two years. He did all of it, speed and alcohol, pills. Now he's a Christian, he's just married last year. My other brother—his girlfriend straightened him out. She's having a baby. They're both fine now. But my sister, she just can't get off it.

This is about my fifth time in here. Before I've just come in short term and taken off again. But this time I've been clean for four months. That's a miracle for me.

When I was younger, I used to wish I was a gubba, a white person. I used to be called 'Abo' and hideous names all the time. It made me feel terrible, but there wasn't much I could do about it. At school I had some friends who were white and they were nice.

I wouldn't have a clue about my culture. I would be sort of interested in learning more about it maybe, but just at the moment I've got to get myself better first.

I hate having my photo taken. I just hate myself at the moment. I hated you. You used to really piss me off, I just didn't like being around you. I'm fine now. It was nothing to do with you being white. I think it's that I didn't trust you. But it's all right now.

CRYSTAL HARRISON (right)

I'm from the Yorta-Yorta tribe. I'm not sure if I'm full-blooded but both my parents were dark like me. I've got two sisters and two brothers. We all lived with my grandma, because my mum died when I was five and my nan came and picked us up and our toys from the mission and took us back to Shepparton, where we grew up.

My dad wasn't a drinker but he started drinking when my mum died, because he couldn't look after us. He used to flog me. I had a lot of floggings from my dad, actually. Maybe it was because I looked like my mum. He drank an awful lot. That's why my nan picked us up, because there was white people going to take us away, they were

going to split us up, my sister was only six months old.

Just me and my big brother are drinkers. First I was smoking marijuana, then I got off that and ended up on heroin. I started drinking at sixteen, as soon as my nan died. I didn't know what to do, my dad wasn't there, so I just started drinking, I drank and drank, I was drunk right up until now. I drank with heroin once, and I OD'd. The ambulance man said another five minutes and I'd have been dead.

My cousin came down to my nan's funeral and said would you like to come to Melbourne for a couple of weeks and since then I just moved back and forth. Sometimes I didn't live anywhere, I lived on the streets. I've done a lot of things, terrible things. To get by.

I'll have been here two weeks on Wednesday. I was sick, my body was sick, I was just sick of using, I'm sick of doing the things I had to do to get it. I've just had enough.

LUBBY MOORE (right, with Crystal Harrison)

My father called me Lubby when I was little. I must have been a lovable baby, I suppose. I'm twenty-nine now. I grew up in Swan Hill, on the river bank. We lived in tin sheds or tents or caravans. That was our tribal grounds. I'm full-blooded. There aren't many full-blooded in Victoria now, but up in the Northern Territories there are.

There was a lot of racism at school. They called us 'Abos', 'niggers', 'hot chocolate'. But our parents taught us to stand up for our rights. If someone said, 'You black so-and-so,' they said I had to stand up to them and say they weren't any different from us just because they had a different colour skin.

Where I come from we started from scratch, building our own huts and then, as we grew older, my uncles and aunties moved into caravans and then into real houses. We got a water system, grew our own vegetables, made our own clothes. Now we work in offices and all that. White people thought we didn't have the brains they had and couldn't do the things they did, but we proved them wrong.

I resent that the white people took our heritage away, everything we loved, our language, our homes, our children. When they took our children they took our identity as well. But if somebody was to say, 'You can be white,' I'd say no. I was born black and I want to die black. The inside of me is exactly the same as a white person.

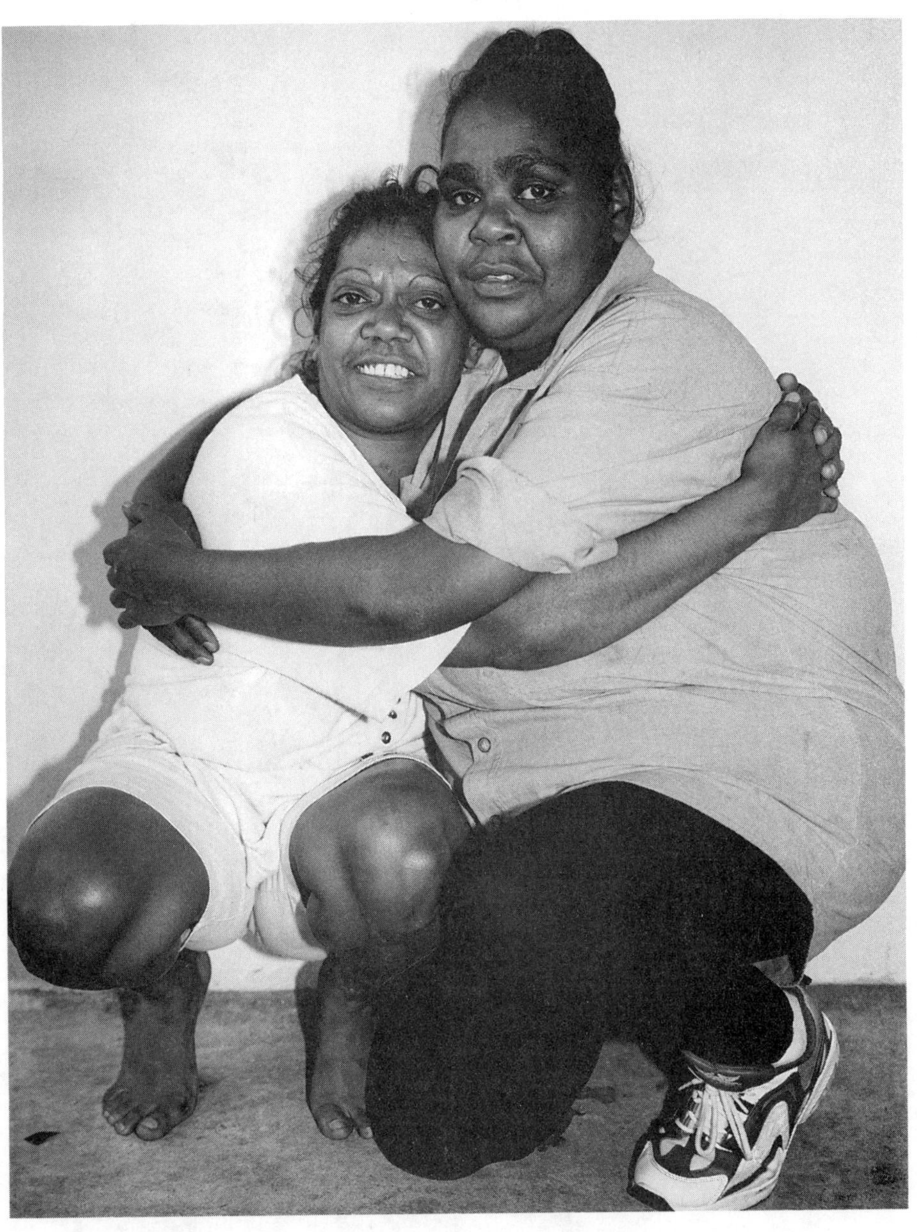

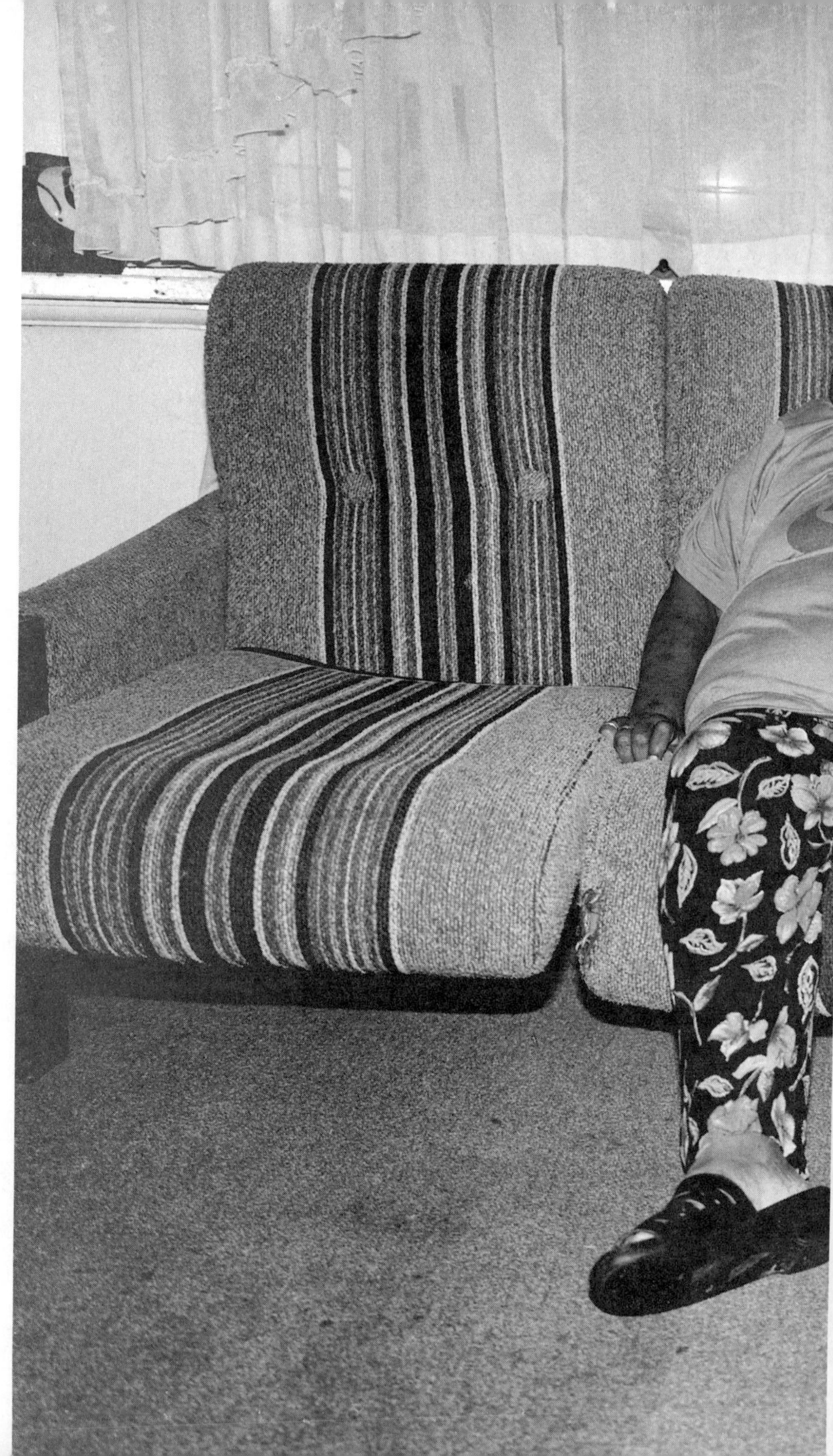

adidas
RESPONSE
adidas

TEAC

FRED ANDREWS

I'm confused with my Aboriginal identity. First of all, my mother was Aboriginal, and she was taken off her parents and put in homes. This was before the policy law, in the time leading up to it. Anyway, she got out, married an Aboriginal fella, had two kids and two miscarriages, and they're my older brothers, they're really dark. They got taken off my mother, I don't know all the circumstances because my mum wouldn't say too much. Then she married my dad, who was a whitefella, and got her children back. She lived with him and twenty years later she married him. I've also got a sister that's a throwback, fairly dark, from my grandfather. I was a lot like my mother.

It was in my teens that I started to hang around with other Aboriginal people. At first, when I'd waved at them down the street they thought I was giving cheek, a whitefella waving to the blacks. After a while, though, I didn't want to know them. I thought all they did was get drunk and fight all the time. But as I got older and spent time in jail and stuff like that, I got to know more about it.

It's a hard issue; you add grog and it makes the issue even harder. It's always been about land rights and recognition—that we're not dumb, we aren't useless, we aren't all alcoholics, you know. But you end up sending us to the pub and drinking. I probably lost my own self-esteem because even places where I worked I'd hear 'dirty black bastards', 'Abo bastards', stuff like that. And I'm an Abo, yet my skin's white.

I can hide in society because of my white skin, if I don't bring up my Aboriginality. That's like being split in half. Trying to be someone I'm not. I can definitely see how for other Aboriginals with dark skins, trying to fight against that, it's like a slippery pole. Every time you try to build your way up in society, you slip right back down, because you just don't fit in with white society. There's no way that a black Aboriginal is going to be a boss over white people. They just don't like it. It's just the way it is.

I know a lot about my culture now, but only because I searched for answers. I haven't gone back to my tribe, but I've studied other Aboriginal cultures from different tribes, I definitely understand other people's culture a little bit, and that's how I know about mine. I've studied it, and I know I'm a rare example of the white Aboriginal.

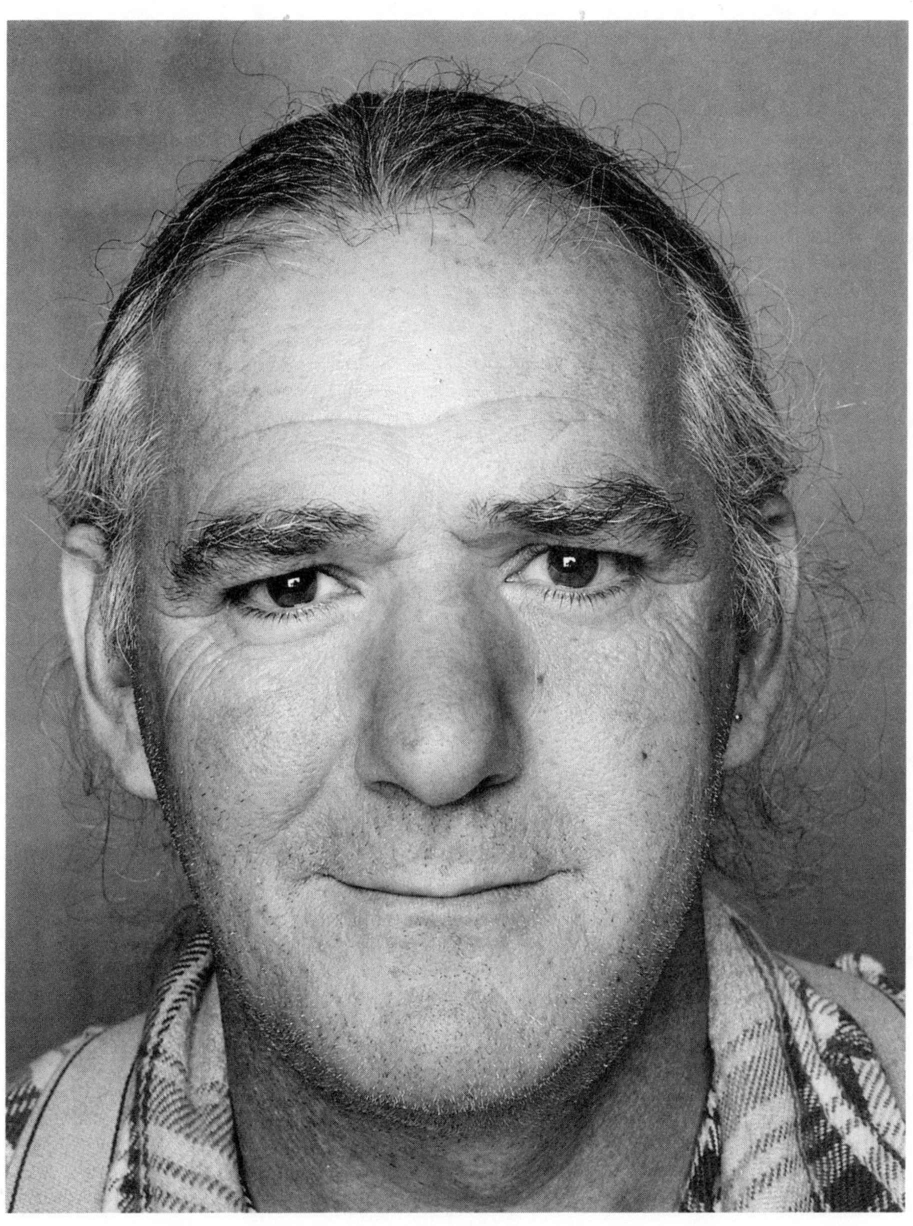

CLIFFORD DALLAS LYMBURNER

We were originally from up in Cape York, via my grandmother, who was a half-caste. Her father was Irish, married a full-blood and she was the product. Her name was Bessie Lymburner. There's a poem about her, it goes like this:

Our Kanju Queen,
You are blessing from above,
Purely formed out of love.
Your life had started a long time ago,
Born far north Cape York we know.
The tribe name is Kanju.
Out of them we were blessed with you.
You paid the price for being a half-caste,
The government treated you as a outcast.
They sent you far far away,
To a small island bay,
Known as Palm Island to this day.
There you grew up in a dormitory,
Among one another sharing stories.
Your heart still ached, and tears still rolled,
To be with your Kanju family, as a whole.
God had other plans installed,
For you to walk strong and tall.
As you grew you came of age,
You were set free like a bird from its cage.
There you met the man of your dreams,
Your life started flowing like a stream.
Times were tough living under the Act,
You carried on forward, and that's a fact.
When you was in your twenties,
You gave your heart to God Almighty.
There it was you became a mother,
You had four daughters and a son.
Out of them you started to plan,
Your very own little Kanju clan...

She only died last year. She could chuck a broom just like chucking a boomerang.

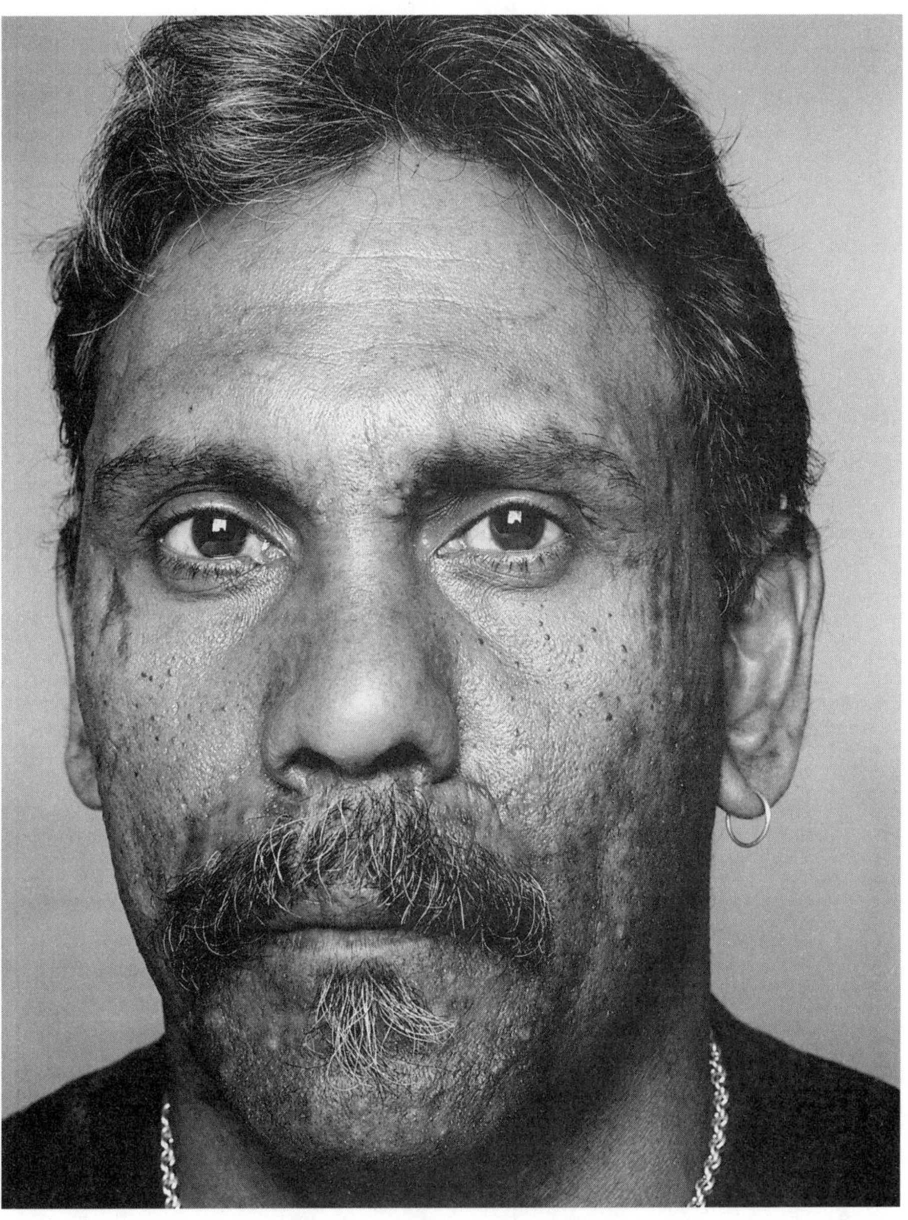

GARY RYAN

I was born in Melbourne in the suburbs area, I'm originally from the Lake Tyers Mission, but I never seen my black parents very much, they were alcoholics. I was adopted by my white parents. I started drinking when I was playing football at weekends. I started in the junior league, just watching my mates drink, and by the time I was in the senior league I was drinking seven days a week twenty-four hours a day. My white parents never drank in their lives, and I was asked to leave home because of my drinking. I lived with a cousin of mine, an Aboriginal, he was seventeenth in the family, he was drinking all the time.

Anyway, I got a job, I'm a builder by trade. I was a good worker, been working seven or eight years, I had a car, motorbike. But I just wanted money to buy more grog. I was drunk every morning, drunk every night. I had the police on to me a lot of the time. They tried to put me back on my parents' farm where there was no drink. I wasn't allowed to go off their farm, wasn't allowed into town on my own.

Last year in March my parents went on holiday and they didn't trust me to be at home on my own. So I had to go to court and they said I had to go to Galiamble. I been here nearly fifteen months off the grog, been in court about five times or six times last year, and they know I'm a good bloke, that I'm not drunk any more.

I try to stay away from my Aboriginal family because I think they'll get me back on the drink. My older sister doesn't drink, so I spend a lot of time with her and my little niece.

Last Sunday, I got up and told [the supervisor] I wanted to go home. I told him I'm very close to getting drunk. So I went home for a couple of days. Then my dad, my mum and my auntie came back here and they went to meetings to support me. They'd never been here in their lives. And there was a lot of people at the meeting and Mum and Dad had to talk. And I saw them after and I said, 'What did you reckon?' And they said they'd loved it.

Sometimes things go funny in my head. I've been thinking too much about my court case, it's on a serious charge. I tell them in meetings about how I got in trouble but I don't tell them the charge. I can't remember what happened. They say there's a fifty-fifty chance of getting me back in here, and I hope it works.

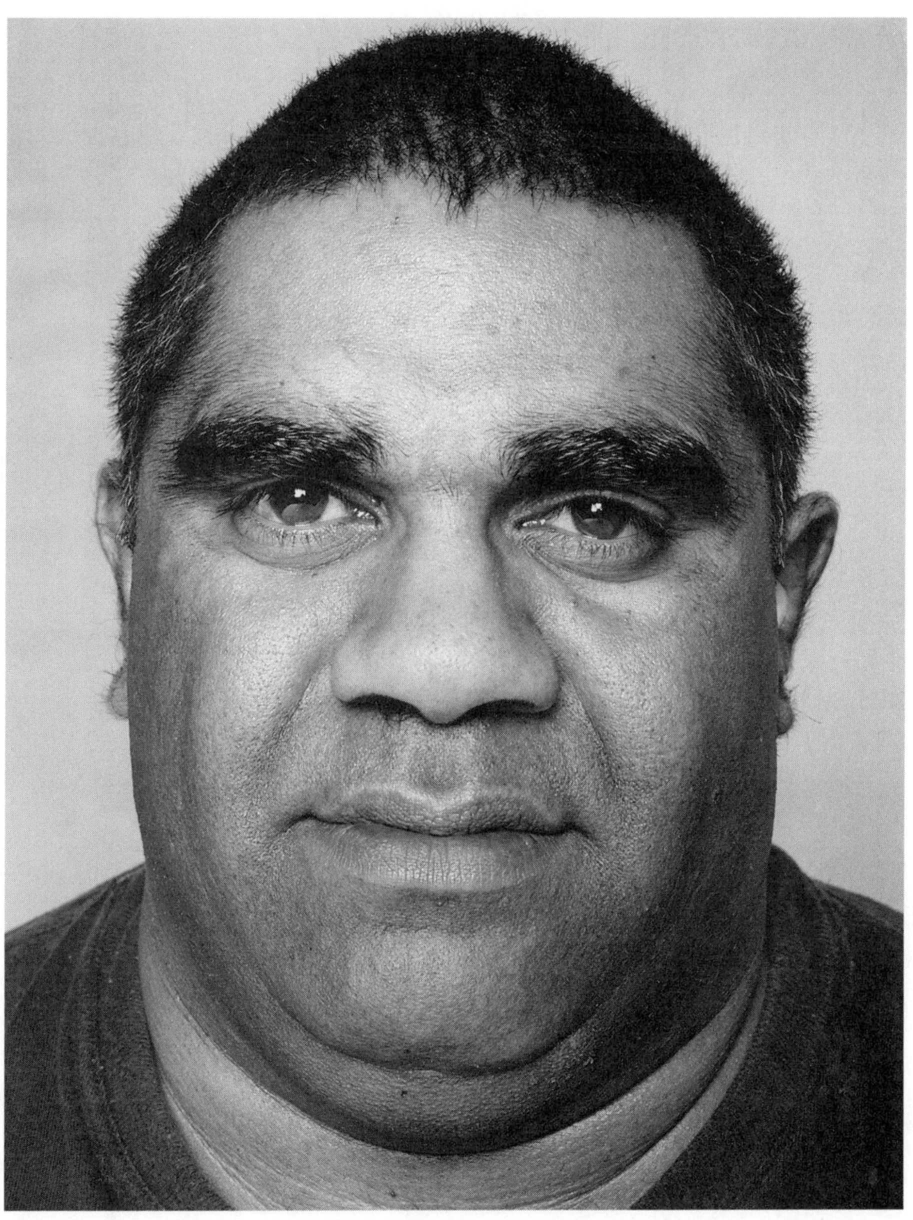

GEOFFREY W. BLACK (BLACKY)

I was told if I'd had the right education and done the right things, then I'd be normal. Most of my friends never got to high school. When I left school I went for heaps of jobs, and I had those jobs over the phone, yet the minute I walked through the door, I would see the person's eyes change and there were always excuses. The job wasn't there any more, sorry, they'd given it to somebody else. Then I'd see other people going in, and I'd ask what they were going for, and they'd say, 'Oh, for a job, mate,' and it would still be open. Also you run into a lot of that coconut stuff when you're younger. You try working in the white community you're a 'coconut'. Then your black cousins won't have anything to do with you, and white people won't, either. Coconut? It means brown on the outside, white on the inside.

I started drinking when I was about eighteen, I suppose. I never wanted to drink, but after a football game it'd be: 'Oh, have a drink, man, have a drink.' And in the end, I'd have a drink. Then with girls it was a confidence booster. As soon as I got my licence, I'd go partying, have a beer. I hung out with Aboriginals, but I knew lots of white mates. Sometimes they want you around, other times they don't. There's a lot of passive racism. Someone will shake your hand, tell you you're a good person, then walk away and wipe their hands. They'll pay you lip service, but then want nothing to do with you privately.

In my book we have to accept the past, find an equilibrium and move forward. It's not going to happen in my lifetime, because there's black people want everything back and that's just impractical. You can't expect white people to give up land they've worked on for generations. Some land should be given back, or if not money. But why can't they do something for the young Aboriginal people? Look what alcohol's doing to the missions now, to the full-blooded Aboriginals out there. They're destroyed by alcohol, glue and petrol. And it could be fixed up, you know. But there's always something to stop that happening. All I see is the government has given up the assimilation policy but taken up one that's unwritten. That's why they're moving black people into town off the missions. So a white man can get with a black woman and their kids will be a little less black, and their kids will be less black still, and within ten generations there won't be a full-blooded Aboriginal person in Australia anyway.

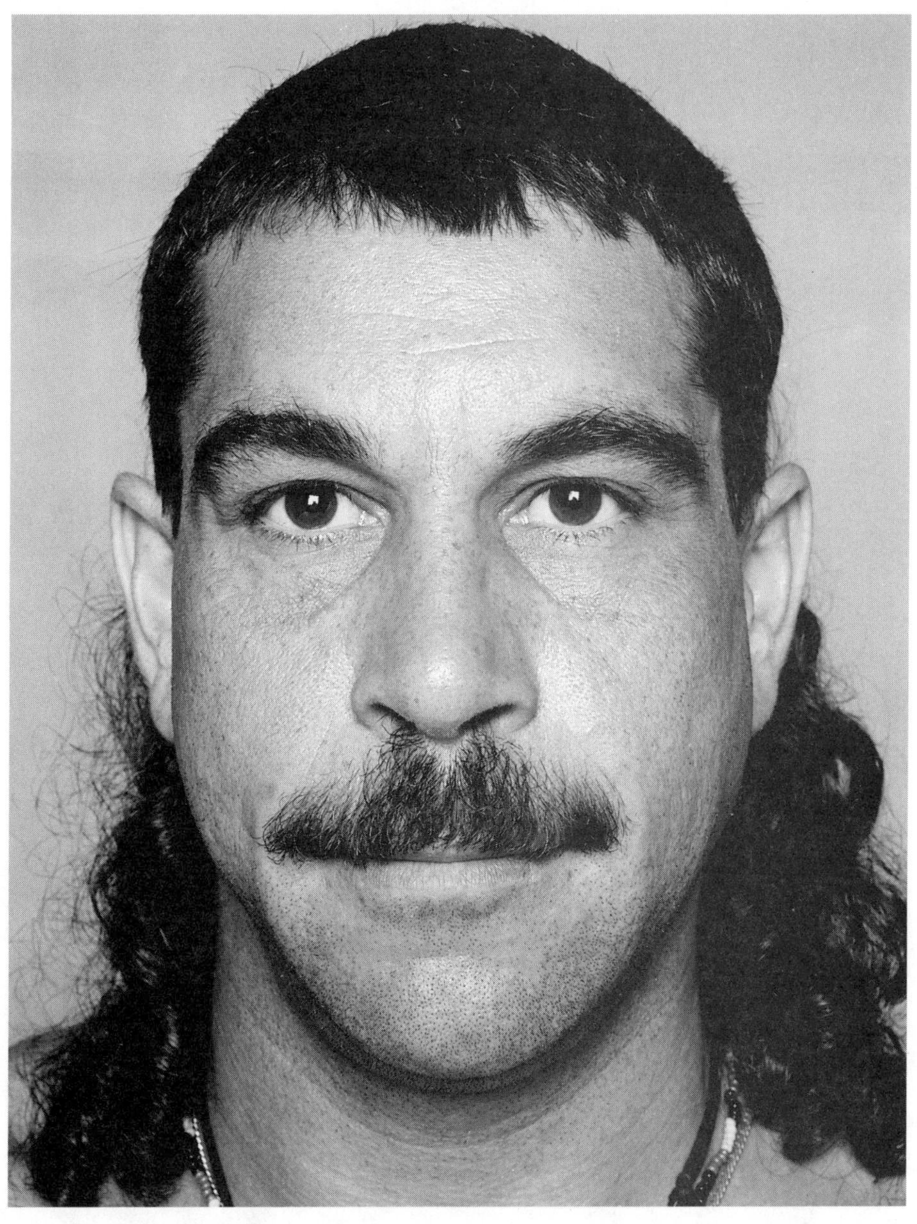

WILLIAM TALGART

I'm forty-one, from Mount Barker in Western Australia. My grandmother was my first mother, because my natural mother had another baby to a fair Aboriginal and he used to bash me the whole time and tried to run me over with a tractor, and my grandmother saw that. So she took me under her wing. Then when she died I went back to my natural mother, because she'd got rid of that relationship.

In 1969 I was moved to a mission and everything changed for me. They taught me a lot of things, how to get rid of racism and treat people for what they are. You had to do what they said. It was white-run. In those days if you got a pair of shoes it was a bonus. Some days we used to piss on our feet because the ground was so cold.

I've got cousins at Warburton Mission in Western Australia, which is run by Aboriginals. Our totem is the serpent. If you go to Darwin or Kununurra, they respect the crocodiles. Some Aboriginals are emu, some are birds, some even snakes. We go on 'walkabout'—which means hunting with spears, sticks, boomerangs. Most of them these days, they just get cars, but some still go by walking.

Up in the Kimberleys, before they walk about their burial grounds, they have to shout out to let the ancestors know it's a tribal person coming through. They talk in their lingo, so the spirits understand who it is. It's the same with the instrument we play, the didge. If you give your didge to somebody else, that person is taking your spirit.

My mother was a tribal woman. There's men's secrets and there's women's secrets. The different tribes have a queen, princesses, all the way down. The king makes the decisions and the queen sits on his left-hand side. If you have a problem, they sort it out.

I spent about twenty-five years drinking, and I spent most of my life in a prison. Now I'm going to school and doing indigenous perfoming arts. We're all Aboriginal, we're a strong group. I've got a bit of a play I want to get on, and I'm doing some counselling work.

Before my brother died, he told me my stepfather was being paid back. I had everything planned against him. I was going to cut his feet, do things to him that weren't nice. And my brother pointed at him and said, 'Don't worry. See that light? He'll walk under it into the dark and then run back.' And I said, 'Why?' And he said, 'Because Mum's in there and she's going to torment him until he's died.'

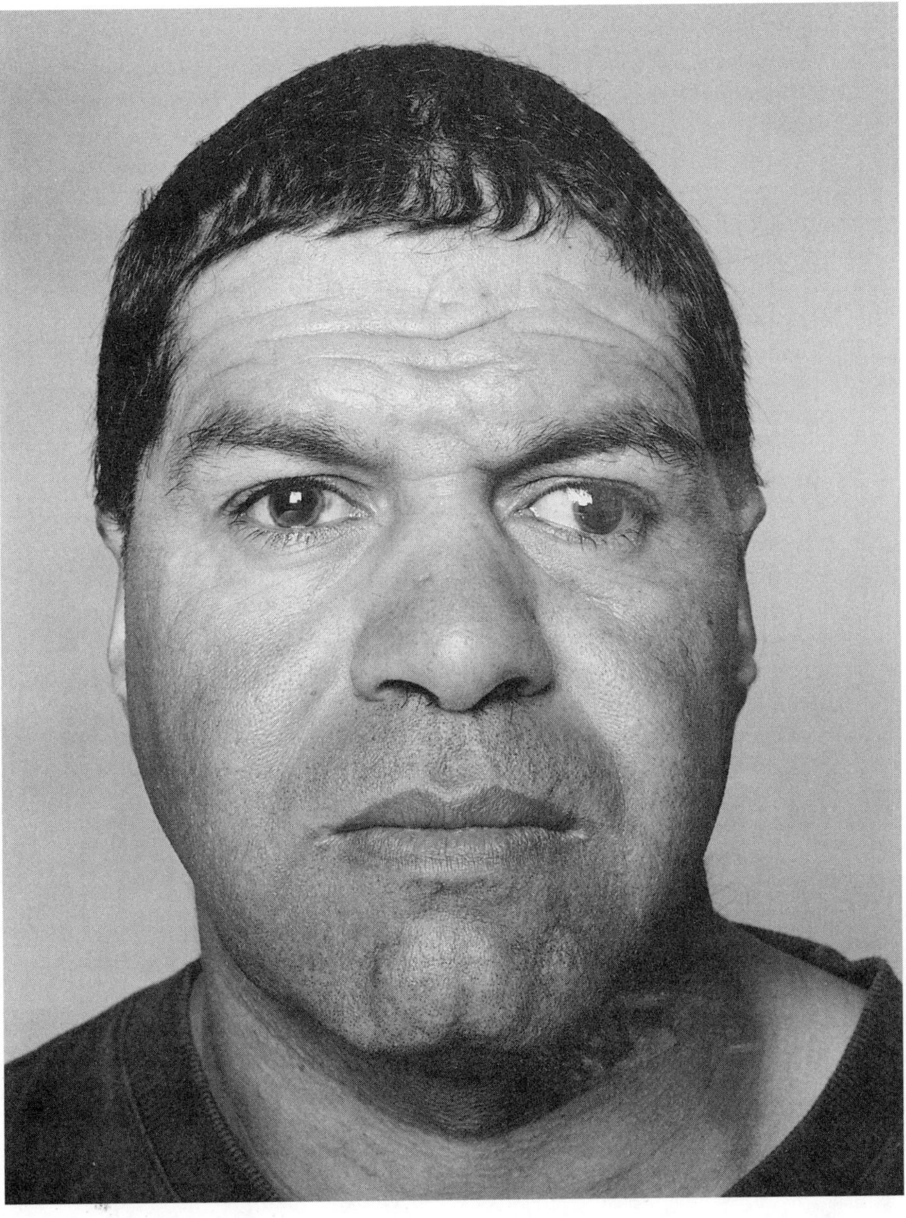

FES PIKE

I was born in Swan Hill in Victoria. The tribe is known as Wombaya. When I was growing up it was mostly in foster homes, because I was part of the stolen generation thing that was going on. It was late Sixties, early Seventies. I suppose it was because the government thought they knew best and just because my mum and dad was drinking, the government thought they couldn't take care of me, so I was fostered out at the age of five.

I was in about ten or eleven homes. They tried bringing me up as a white child—I've got nothing against white people—but, school uniforms, they put me in cubs and scouts, I really didn't like that. We only saw our parents on supervised visits. My foster parents would ring my mum and ask her if she wanted to see us, and she would come, but not like every week or anything. I would have been quite happy to stay on the mission with my mother.

They say that the biggest killer that the white man brought in was sugar. Aboriginal people died of sugar diabetes, and now there's alcohol and drugs. Aboriginal people are getting drawn to the city. They like the nightlife, drink, drugs, it's more exciting. I don't know many Aboriginals that work, the ones I know are mostly on the dole. For a long time there's been a myth that Aboriginal people are dirty and lazy. But when they see us out in the parks or on the river banks or drinking under a tree, it's not that we're dirty or lazy, we just don't like to drink indoors, we like to go out and enjoy the outdoors.

I think you'll always get racism, doesn't matter what race you are, you'll get it in any culture. I mean I see my dislike of some of those white people as being racist myself. I think, 'Oh, you white so-and-so,' and without me knowing it I'm being racist too.

I have three daughters, Kayla, Keera and Ivy. Two are five and the youngest is four. Their mother is Aboriginal. I think, for me—I've got to be careful here, so I don't make a racist statement!—but I think you understand one another better, not only as husband and wife, but as Aboriginal people, and you can install the child's identity.

We need to live in harmony. We don't need white people any longer to come and rip us apart, we're ripping each other apart by drugs and alcohol, we're fighting each other, we don't need another nationality to come in and destroy us, we're doing it ourselves.

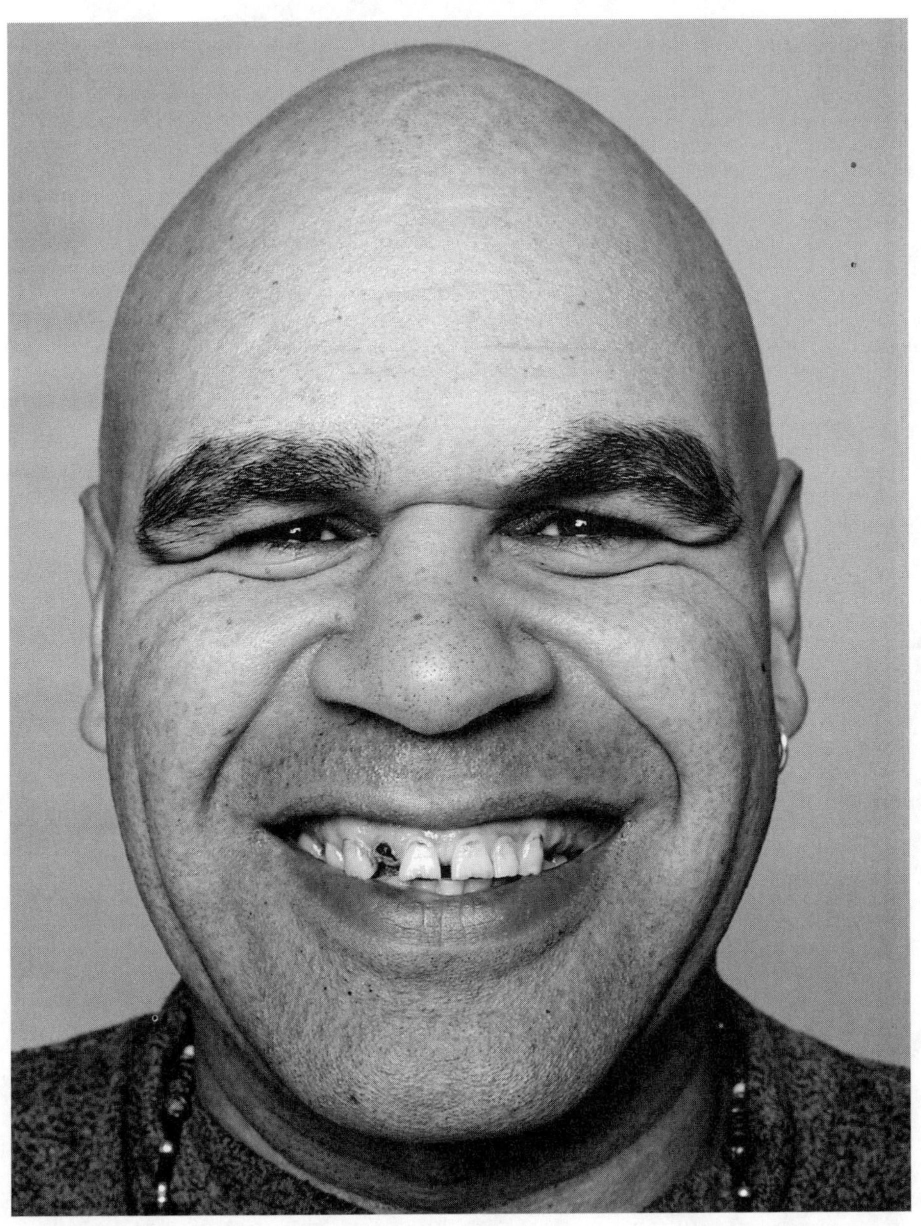

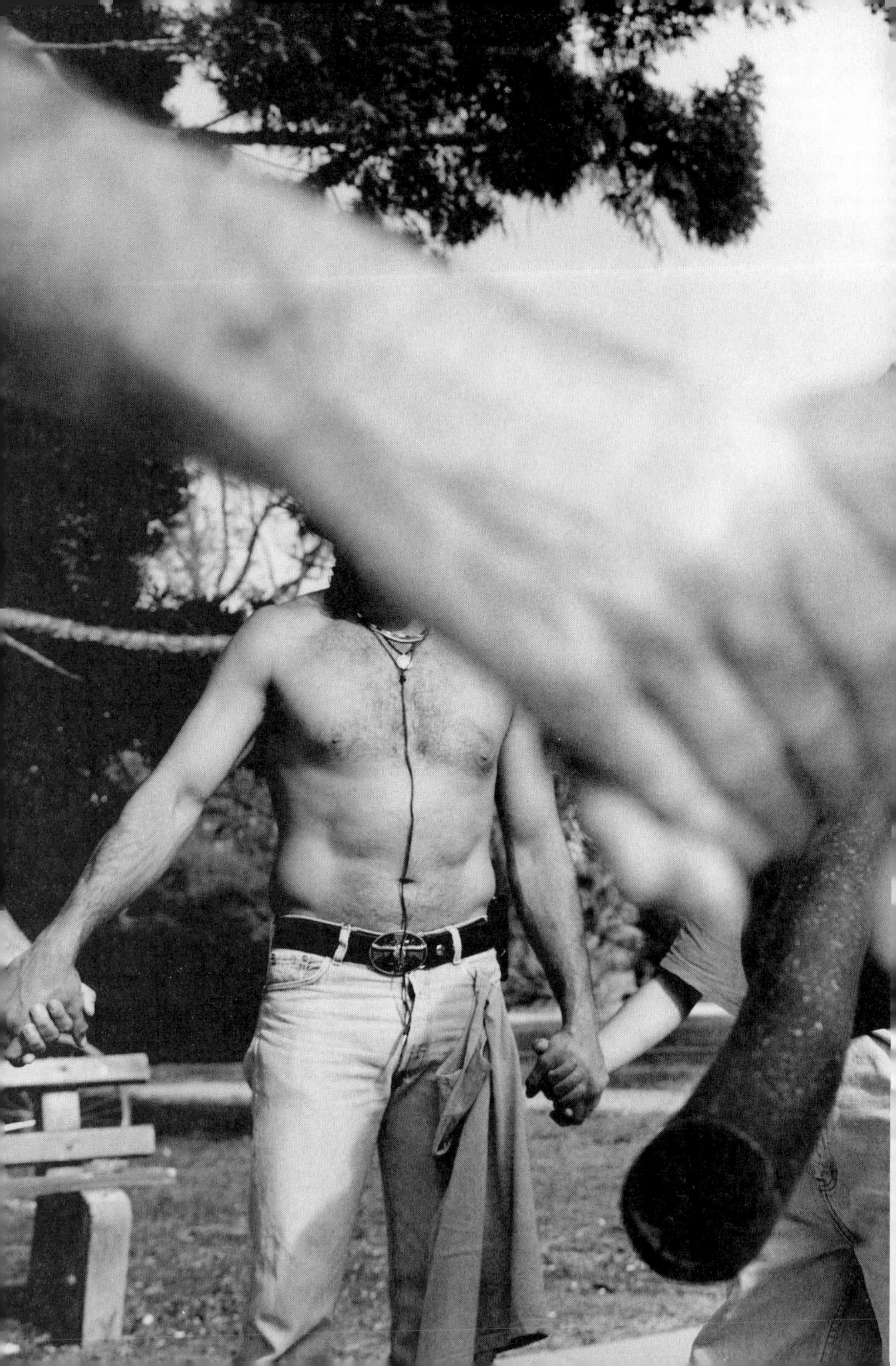

AFTERWORD

As a child my father used to take me and my sisters and brother on some of his work trips. A couple of times he took to Echuca to visit the Aboriginal community there. My father was an architect, who in his university days had been a member of the Communist Party. He had a keen sense of social justice and often designed buildings free of charge for people he felt he could help. In Echuca he had agreed to help them plan a schoolhouse. The building was designed as much by the people there as by my father and is still in use today.

When I went back to Melbourne at the end of 1999 I wanted to contact some of Victoria's indigenous people to photograph them. I had always known that the introduction of alcohol had helped to destroy the Aboriginal communities. What I hadn't realized was how the use of heroin, which had accelerated in the white community, had now infiltrated the indigenous population too. I found the story I wanted to cover at Galiamble and Winja. Here was a group of people who were trying to fight their way back.

When I'd told my friends what I intended to do, I got a variety of reactions. Some of them thought I had no right as a white Australian to document indigenous people. Others asked me where all the Aboriginals in Melbourne were. Some of them had never met an Aboriginal. It made me realize how invisible the native people were, particularly in the city, and how convenient this was for the white community: they could literally forget they were there.

I knew I would be regarded as a foreigner. I didn't even live in Australia. My only connection with the people I met was that I, too, had been dependent on alcohol, and my mother died, aged forty-nine, from alcohol- and tobacco-related illnesses. After a lot of arguments I decided that political correctness only boxed me in and reinforced the status quo. I wasn't under the illusion I could make a difference to their lives, but I hope the exchange between us was a fleeting positive experience, one in which I tried not to presume anything.

I would like to thank everyone at Galiamble and Winja for letting me inside their lives for a short time, and Brendan, whose troupe performed some of their dances for me. As this issue went to press, I learned that Crystal Harrison, who had left Winja, had been found dead of a heroin overdose. She was twenty-seven. POLLY BORLAND

GRANTA

THE GERMAINE TAPE

Georgia Blain

Germaine Greer, 1975

HULTON GETTY

The Germaine Tape

It was 1972 when my father interviewed Germaine Greer for the Australian Broadcasting Corporation in Sydney. I was eight at the time, and although I had heard of his guest, I certainly didn't have enough interest in what she had to say to actually sit and listen to his programme. But then, I never listened to any of his broadcasts, not even when he interviewed Elton John. His show was all talk and no music; it was quality adult listening, or so I believed, and as such it held no attraction for a child, not even his daughter.

My father's programme, *Let's Find Out*, was particularly popular with women. Years later, I still come across his listeners who tell me what a wonderful voice my father had and what a perceptive and intelligent interviewer he was.

My first reaction is usually one of surprise. I am more used to people wanting to talk about my mother and how her work in mental illness or feminism has changed their lives. When they approach me, this is the conversation I am expecting and most of the time this is what I get. But sometimes I am taken off guard. I stand awkwardly, forced to listen politely to anecdotes about my father, to share in someone else's memories of him, all the time waiting for a chance to extract myself.

It was my father's third wife who taped the interview when they replayed it on the ABC, and my mother (his second wife) who rang to tell me she had a copy.

She offered to drop it round, she told me I would find it 'interesting', and although I was curious, I also had some trepidation about hearing that voice again, the crispness of those consonants, the roundness of those vowels, the boom that could carry from one end of the house to the other.

It would not be the first time I had heard him since he had died, and I was surprised at the apprehension I still felt at the prospect of listening to a recording of him. I have photographs of him and me together, and letters he wrote to me when he separated from my mother (usually asking me to tell her something he refused to communicate directly). It is rare that I look at them with any more than a detached curiosity about him, similar to the kind of interest I might feel on seeing a photograph of a stranger whose eyes or smile have momentarily caught my attention.

His voice, however, was a different prospect. I was not prepared for how it would affect me the first time I heard it, about two years after he became ill with a cancer that killed him in a matter of months. I was sixteen at the time, and I listened, lights out, alone, to one of his programmes replayed on late night radio. It was not his words I heard, I do not even remember who it was he was interviewing, it was just that voice, filling my room, bringing him back, and after five minutes, I turned it off. I could not bear the confused feelings it caused in me.

My father was proud of his ABC voice, a voice that was cultivated to sound as close to the required BBC standard, with as little trace of an Australian accent, as possible.

When I was about five years old, and my brother eight, he would call us into his study, one by one, to interview us. I would wait outside his door for my turn, looking forward to the microphone, the immaculate Nagra which he always handled with a cloth, the click of the smooth metal switch, followed by the turn of the tape reels, and then that extraordinary capturing of our voices.

'Tell me,' he would say, 'about your day.'

And although I was always the most compliant in nearly every aspect of our lives, although I put all my toys away, made sure that I never stepped on the white border of his Chinese rug, never touched the windows of his car (an act that would cause him to pull over immediately and angrily wipe off any fingerprints with a chamois); in the interview room, I rebelled.

'No,' I would say.

I did not want to be interviewed, I did not want to do as he had told me. I wanted to sing, and it was always the same song, 'Go Tell it on the Mountain', that I insisted upon warbling into the microphone.

He would try again, promising me I could have my way once I had answered his questions.

'No,' I would insist, and he would take out a clean, neatly ironed white handkerchief and wipe away the slight sheen of sweat on his forehead.

It was a warning sign my brother would have heeded immediately, but one that I knew I could ignore. I was the favourite, and from an early age I was aware I could push him further than anyone else would have dared. I would look him straight in the eye and sing, that same chorus, over and over again, while he waited impatiently for a chance to break in with a question I would once again refuse to answer.

By 1972, when Germaine was a guest on his programme, we were too old for the home interviews. I had started at a new primary school, set up by the government for a handful of state-wide selected children. Our teacher, Mrs Brown, was also specially selected, and having just visited China, she was all enthusiasm for injecting Maoist principles into the classroom. We had re-education groups, cadres, compulsory early morning exercises and no maths, and on our first day, she did the unspeakable and asked us what our parents voted.

'Raise your hands if they vote for the Liberal Party,' she commanded, and when I saw everyone in the class, bar one girl, put up their hand, I quickly lied and followed suit.

Gough Whitlam and the Labor Party had just come to power, and my mother had been one of the many who voted for him. Shortly after he was elected she was asked to sit on his newly established Royal Commission into Human Relationships as a Commissioner. They were looking at everything: homosexuality, abortion, the age of consent, domestic violence; in fact they were examining issues that were still considered unsuitable for private discussion let alone public investigation.

I do not know how my father voted. But I do know he had taken to calling himself by my mother's surname in a loud voice when he got drunk at parties. As his fame was slipping, hers was on the rise.

When my mother dropped the tape off at my house, I didn't listen to it straight away. In fact, it was several days before I heard it. She left it in the letter box and I picked it up as I was heading out on an errand. On my way home, I left the tape in the car.

I rarely talk about my father, even with my closest friends. When I was younger I would sometimes tell stories of his physical violence. I would recount the facts of particular episodes, some I had seen, some my mother had told me about later. After a while I realized I was testing myself, recounting the details to show that my father had not affected me and that I had come to terms with who he was, a lie that I gradually learned not to inflict upon myself any longer. It was not just those extreme physical outbursts that made up who he was, nor did they alone account for the ambivalent feelings I have towards him. There was so much I could not describe in neat episodes; the constant threat in his presence and the tension we all lived under; eating dinner in silence and knowing that the wrong word, a dropped piece of cutlery, even the scrape of a chair could set him off; the moments when he would slam his fist down and we would wait uncertain as to whether worse would follow; the occasional shove against a wall; the relief we felt each time he left the house and the fear each time he returned. I changed tack; if I spoke of him at all it would be to tell one of a selected range of stories concerning his obsessive behaviour, an anecdote we could all laugh at. Eventually I gave up telling even the 'funny' stories. I would be halfway through recounting a particular episode when it would slowly become obvious that what I'd intended to be a light amusing tale had become painfully awkward.

I did not know how the tape would affect me. I wanted to listen to it, I was curious about the kind of questions he would ask, but it was not until several days later when I was driving to visit a friend, that I slipped it into the player. It was raining and the traffic was heavy. As I waited at the lights, trying to clear a patch of vision in the fogged-up windscreen, my father's voice, with all its theatricality, filled the car; 'I confess I feel myself somewhat challenged,' as clear as if he were sitting next to me; 'my guest is the redoubtable Germaine Greer.'

Redoubtable. Formidable. This was how my father described my mother when he was in a good mood and performing, usually at a dinner party, glass of red in one hand, guests gathered around him. They were words he used with mock fear, and mock humbleness in the face of her achievements.

As far as I know he never questioned my mother's desire to work and have a career, although I think he found her popularity and success difficult to deal with. In order to counter this, we were always led to believe, probably more so by her than by him, that although she may have had the greater fame (she had a radio show, a daily newspaper column, and made regular television appearances prior to her work on the Commission), he was the 'proper' journalist and the better interviewer. As for issues such as child care and housekeeping (which were the extent of his understanding of feminism), they were taken care of by cleaners and live-in nannies. Women's libbers, bra burning and the redoubtable Ms Greer were happening on the outside; they had little to do with our lives, or so he would have liked to believe.

Shortly after starting her work on the Commission, my mother began to realize she was going to leave him. It was a process that took a few years. As her resolve grew, and became more obvious, my father retreated to his study increasingly often. Sometimes we wouldn't see him for an entire day. He would close the door, turn out the lights, draw the curtains, and sit in his armchair in the near darkness, legs stretched in front of him so that his feet did not rest on the white border of the rug, hands covering his face.

His absence should have been a relief, but in fact his despair created as palpable an atmosphere as his anger. I would try to ignore it, but I often found myself outside his study door. Knowing that I was the only one likely to be allowed in, I would knock tentatively, and then wish I hadn't as soon as I stepped into the gloom.

'Since your mother discovered feminism,' he would say, referring to her work on the Commission, 'she wants to get rid of me. None of you love me. None of you care.' He would take his hands away from his face for a moment and look at me. 'Except you,' he would say. 'You are the only one who would mind if I died.'

It was a weight I did not want to carry. I would stand in front of him, fists clenched, digging the heels of my shoes into the carpet, hoping I was making the border filthy, and hating everything; my father, my mother and even women's liberationists.

Of course, my mother didn't simply embrace feminism and decide to change her life. But as her confidence grew, as she became more involved with her work and the people she met through it, she realized she didn't have to live with the fear he inflicted. I have often wondered why it took her so long. I have often wished it had happened sooner.

As I listened to his interview, the rat-a-tat firing of questions that constituted his idea of a 'lively' programme, I cringed. He sounded like a man who didn't listen, who wouldn't stretch himself to take in a different viewpoint. I suspected he hadn't really thought about any of the issues they were discussing, let alone read any of Germaine Greer's work. He was clearly out of his depth, and the embarrassment I felt escalated as the interview progressed, reaching a peak when the conversation turned to lesbians. As Germaine laughingly stated that nearly every man believed that all a lesbian needed was him, my father, sounding uncomfortable, said that her comment was 'something of a whack under the belt'.

'Why?' she asked him.

'I don't know,' he replied.

'If you think I have any interest in what's pattering about under your belt, you are mistaken,' she retorted, as he urged her to change the subject. I blushed for him. It was clear that she was the consummate performer, far more adept than my father at handling an interview.

Recently my mother told me a little of the background to the programme. It was part of a day-long press call. Germaine was ensconced in a hotel suite, dressed in white, a half bottle of champagne on the table in front of her. My mother was one of the people interviewing her in the morning, my father was on the afternoon roll-call.

My mother's interview was for another radio station. She had a young photographer with her who was taking publicity stills. He was so entranced by his subject that he took his pictures hanging from the lights, the table, the bed, all in an attempt to impress her ('like something out of *Blow-Up*,' my mother said), only to discover at the end of the shoot that he had forgotten to put any film in his camera.

Halfway through the session with my mother, Germaine jumped up and started making a fuss. She had menstrual blood on her skirt. 'Look,' she said, with delight, pointing it out to everyone in the room, and sure enough, there it was.

It was a performance that was apparently repeated for my father, with the same surprise and the same fuss.

I don't think my father would have been horrified by menstrual blood as such, other than by the possibility of its causing a stain. In any event, the episode never made it on to tape, luckily. I found listening to his attempts at dealing with Germaine's comments about lesbians difficult enough, and I turned the volume down a couple of notches.

He had lost control, something I knew he could not bear to do. This was a man who regularly measured the distance between the candlesticks on the sideboard, adjusting them if they were even slightly out, who made us watch him while he remade the beds (no housekeeper was ever capable of doing the job to his satisfaction) so that we could learn how to get each hospital corner perfect, who always had a Wettex in his hand and who would darken with rage at a mark on a wall, crease in a sheet or crumb on the floor.

Although I was never on the receiving end of his violence, I was often a witness to it. Pressed against the wall or crouched on the stairs, my pleading never managed to stop him, even though he'd told me I was the only one who loved him, the only one who cared.

My mother remembers the day I challenged my father and broke away from the oppressive hold he had over all of us. Strangely, I don't.

She says it was during the time she was trying to leave, when he had retreated into his study. He would emerge only at dinner, then sit at the table, head in his hands, hardly speaking. We'd ask him if he wanted vegetables and if he did respond, it would only be to ask us what we cared, what any of us cared; in fact he could die and none of us would care, he would say, without looking up.

My mother says that one day I finally told him he was the one who didn't care, how could he behave like this if he loved us. I pushed my chair back, scraping it loudly on the kitchen floor, and left the table without being excused.

I don't remember. I wish I could, but I don't.

As the interview progressed, my father abandoned the sticky subject of lesbians and feminists and asked Germaine about her childhood. From the boredom in her voice, I guessed she found this line of questioning dull. As I listened, I found myself remembering the little I knew about my father's own childhood, the few stories he had told us, so few I could count the bare, stark summaries on the fingers of one hand.

He was the only child of a solicitor called Norman and a frustrated would-be opera singer, called Maisie. Maisie used to whip herself rather than him whenever he misbehaved. Every Sunday he went to his very strict and very religious paternal grandmother's for the day, where he had to stay in a darkened room with only bread and water and a copy of the *Pilgrim's Progress*. He was sent to Bedales in England for a short period, which he hated.

I didn't know anything else.

I was always particularly fascinated by the story of the paternal grandmother, the sheer gothic horror of it.

'But didn't you starve?' I would ask him, wide-eyed and wanting to know more.

'I was very, very hungry,' he would tell me.

Although the tale of Maisie whipping herself was even more horrific, I stayed away from it, sensing that it might be too much even for my melodramatic tastes. He never volunteered anything further about it.

I never met either of his parents, both of whom died before he married my mother. I also never knew, until shortly before my father's own death, that Norman had killed himself.

My father called me into his study at his third wife's house (a replica of the study he had had in our own house), and told me that he had been writing his autobiography and he wanted me to read it. He gave me the first chapter, the only one he had written.

Norman, he wrote, had been a solicitor who had gone broke in the depression and had not been able to bear the shame of telling anyone. The night my father finished his final law exams, they sat down together and went through the answers he had given. Convinced my father had passed and would be able to support Maisie, Norman stuck his head in the gas oven and killed himself. Shortly afterwards, my father found out he had failed.

I relayed the story to my mother and asked her why no one had ever told me this before. I was thirteen at the time, and it seemed a very significant tragedy that helped to make sense of so much that was difficult in my father.

My mother was surprised. Norman, she said, had killed himself, but he had not gone broke. He had swindled the firm's trust fund and was about to be tried. Furthermore, my father had never gone past his first year of law.

After this conversation I began to doubt every other story my father had told me.

As I turned the car into my friend's street, the interview began to veer away from the relatively straightforward topic of Germaine's childhood, slipping back into more difficult territory. I wished the tape would end. It was difficult to listen to, and not for the reasons I had anticipated.

Germaine was telling a story about a man losing his virginity that had very little to do with sexual politics, and could hardly be called threatening. My father interrupted her. He sounded patronizing.

'So many of these little anecdotes of yours,' he said, 'which are delightful and illustrative or tragic and poignant or whatever they may be, they all appear to relate to men. I wonder if you have a similar fund about women.'

I was holding my breath as I waited for her response.

'I am really baffled by that statement,' she said, and the surprise in her voice was genuine, her entire performance momentarily floundering as she searched for a way to respond.

The few minutes of the interview that remained descended into a shambles. My father's responses seemed to come increasingly from the hip, and made less and less sense. I pulled up at my friend's house, feeling excruciatingly embarrassed for him. I was amazed at how quickly that voice had lost all of its power.

It was the first time in my adult life that I had listened to one of my father's interviews, and I found myself hating this rapid dissolution of the last shred of respect I had held for him. I was surprised at how much I still wanted to believe he was a good interviewer.

The programme was tail-ended by a panel discussion among contemporary feminists. They discussed my father's attitudes; one woman mentioned that he had been married to one of Australia's better-known feminists.

I did not want to listen to them, and I found myself wanting to defend him. It was the times, I wanted to say. That was how it was.

What about men? he'd kept asking on the programme. Surely women's liberation wouldn't bring the sexes any closer? Surely it would only cause resentment and anger in men? Surely some women liked the way things were?

I wasn't even sure if this was really what he thought, despite the fact that he'd always told us that feminism caused the breakdown of his marriage to my mother. I had no idea what his attitudes were. I was a child when he died. If I'd had a chance as an adult to say what I couldn't say when I was young, and if he had listened and explained, we might have moved into the world of his likes and dislikes, his beliefs and his fears. But I never got the opportunity. All I could say in his defence was that he was an ABC interviewer who wanted to have a bit of a joust on his programme with the infamous Ms Greer because it would make for entertaining listening, and that was his job, a job we were always told he was very good at. He may have been, this one interview may have been an aberration. Although I don't remember him as a man who had a great passion or love for his work.

It was during the last part of his life, after he'd retired and before he became ill, that my father seemed to be happiest. He could do what he liked; listen to music, walk and take photographs; and that was what he did, usually by himself, sometimes with me when I stayed with him on the weekends.

But even though life at home became more peaceful once he'd left and remarried, I felt hardened towards him, to such an extent that when he came to tell me had cancer, I sat opposite him and thought 'what now?'

I only saw him a couple of times after he told me, and I did not see him at all in the last few months of his life. When we heard he had died, I did not cry. It was Christmas and we were staying in a tiny town by the beach. Each morning we would walk up to the phone box in the heat and wait while my mother rang Sydney for the news. I remember sometimes kicking at the dust and wishing he would hurry up so that we could enjoy our holiday. I remember a small part of me believing that he was hanging on for the drama of it.

When he finally died on Christmas Eve, we flew back for the funeral. Once again, I stayed dry-eyed, unable to mourn for a man I had shut out of my heart and refused to let back in. In fact, I felt more bemused than sad as I listened to the priest get his name wrong and describe him as a 'gentle man', a 'peaceful man', in a eulogy that had clearly been written for someone the priest had never met.

The only time I come close to crying for him is when I look at a photo of him as a young boy. My mother gave it to me when I was about seventeen and I keep it tucked away in a bottom drawer, not out of anger, but because there is something painful in the shyness of that gaze, the stiffness of the formal pose, the plumpness of his legs, something that's hard to confront.

I waited for the rain to ease before I got out of the car. As I sat in the silence I could picture him clearly. I could see his face, his silver-white hair, his immaculately pressed open-necked shirts and slacks, the small leather handbag he'd always carried, to my embarrassment.

The rain stopped momentarily. 'If there is enough blue sky to make a pair of sailor's pants,' my father used to say, 'it's on its way to clearing.' □

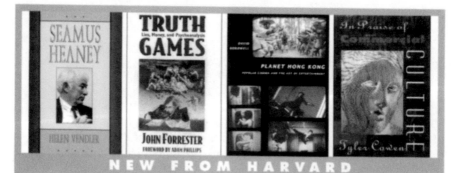

GRANTA

WAR WORK

Frank Moorhouse

Sydney 1936: there in the Cahill's cafe, a strange male voice intruded, 'Edith—Alva—haven't seen you both for years.' It was like the voice from a gramophone with a worn needle.

They looked up at a man dressed in a faded brown corduroy suit and wearing a beret, with a returned soldier badge on his jacket and with a face that looked like that of a mummy. It had obviously been surgically rehabilitated. The skin was tightly stretched emphasizing the cheekbones which seemed about to poke through the skin which was an unnatural deep brown. The eyes looked as though they were made of glass but he was obviously not blind. He had no eyebrows or eyelashes.

They both stared at him and then Edith glanced at Alva for help in recognizing the man.

'You're a fine couple of friends—not remembering an old mate.'

The voice was sardonic.

Edith remembered the voice, even if a damaged version. But couldn't find a name for it.

'Scraper Somerville,' he said.

'Scraper!' Edith said, furiously trying to recall him, rising to her feet and shaking his crumpled hand. 'It's been so long I didn't recognize you at first.'

Alva also rose and shook his hand. 'Scraper—good to see you.'

'You don't both have to be so polite, I know I look like an Egyptian mummy. It shouldn't be "good" to see me.'

Edith and Alva stood, rendered mute.

'Oh, sit down, sit down—no need for all these Red Cross faces—stop being solicitous.'

They sat down in a shot, like school girls. He dragged over a chair.

He seemed to have to blink more often than most people. His hands had also been reconstructed. They were bent and buckled and looked like hen's feet.

She couldn't remember his first name. He'd been nicknamed Scraper because of his height—skyscraper.

'Skyscraper,' she said to Alva. She caught herself talking about the student boy, Scraper, as if he was unrelated to this disfigured man seated with them.

'Half the students thought it was skyscraper and half thought it was boot scraper,' he said. 'Useful. Let me know who were my friends and who were not. Scraping the bottom of the barrel is another way I think of it. Scraping the bottom of life's barrel.'

'Sit down with us,' Edith said, unnecessarily, bringing herself back to self-control, and taking him at his word about excessive politeness, added, 'though you seem to have done so, already.'

Laughing from unease.

Scraper ordered tea. The waitress seemed to know him well.

He looked Edith over, a disconcerting experience because the appearance of his face made him seem to find looking an act of some effort. His neck did not move freely. 'You're a big wheel in the League of Nations, Edith, that's what I hear.'

'Edith gave a fine lecture this afternoon in the history lecture theatre,' Alva said.

Was it so 'fine'? Was Alva being polite?

'Would've come if I'd known. Interested in the future of war.'

The three of them lapsed into another silence. The tea arrived and when the waitress had left them, Edith offered brandy and he accepted with alacrity. She gave Alva and herself another boost.

'Tell me what you've been doing, Scraper? You did law?' Edith said, taking a stab at it, still only vaguely recalling the student named 'Scraper'.

'I practise law in a small way. A very small way. I practise away from the public gaze. Whatever scraps of work are thrown on my plate. And I write, you know.'

'Novels?'

'Verse.'

'I'm sure my father warned me about lawyers who practised "a little law" and who write poetry,' Edith said, laughing, trying to be light-hearted in the presence of such physical tribulation. 'Married?' she asked, regretting the almost certain insensitivity of the question, knowing that his appearance was such that it could not be lived with. No one could look at his face for long.

He laughed darkly. 'Stop being conventional, Edith. You never were before. Or was it a cruel question? And, no. The answer is no.'

'Alva hasn't married either,' she said, disobeying his rule on convention, and realizing that, in a more conventional situation, it would be a horrible joke towards matchmaking.

Oh dear, what a day. She'd spoken at her old university, had argued that the League was not a sinking ship, and still didn't know how well or badly the talk had gone and whether she believed it at all, and Alva, her oldest friend, had come out as an admirer of Mussolini. And she was now uncertain whether Alva was a friend or not.

And Scraper had appeared like an apparition.

He seemed to examine the question and the additional statement for possible motive. And then he became black as a storm, 'Don't pretend I'm normal. And don't pretend to flirt. I have no stomach for that style of patronizing.'

Edith could not imagine anything more remote from her capacities or intentions than flirting with this wreck of a man.

He then changed immediately, the black cloud passing, looked at them and laughed, '"The Newtown Tarts".'

'You remember!' Edith exclaimed. She turned to Alva: 'See, he remembers.' She turned to Scraper: 'We were talking about that just now. Alva claims not to remember. I think it's because she's a reformed woman. Putting her wicked past behind her.'

'I may indeed be a reformed woman,' Alva said, laughing, but her voice indicated that she was heartily dissatisfied by the way the conversations had gone and the inclusion of herself in the references to 'tarts'.

'You boys at the Union used to call us Women's College girls "the Newtown tarts"?' Edith said, feeling an urgent need to keep talking.

'Weren't you?' Scraper said.

'After you began calling us the Newtown tarts—undergraduate joke in bad taste—or what you thought was bad taste—our group adopted it and we called ourselves "the Newtown Tarts". Although Alva claims not to remember.'

'I don't. And I wasn't.'

'And we all hoped that you were really tarts,' said Scraper. 'And worse.'

'I rather liked being *called* a tart back then,' Edith said, looking at Scraper, wondering if he was hearing this correctly, feeling rather risqué and wanting also to say it as a way of pinching Alva's arm. 'And I liked being identified with slummy Newtown which I privately thought of as demi-monde, a world of devilish mysteries.'

'Edith! We never went there,' Alva complained.

'It was an unexplored place. It was a metaphorical place.'

'I seem to remember that we weren't allowed to go there,' Alva persisted.

'I didn't think of it as working class. I thought of it as The Underworld,' Edith said, wondering what Newtown had really been like.

'I was there a lot—identifying with the working class,' Scraper said. 'But they never identified with me.'

Scraper slurped down his tea, holding the cup in both hands, wanting the brandy, impervious to the heat of the tea.

Alva chose at this time to excuse herself, looking deliberately at her watch and saying, 'Time flies.'

The coward. How could she!

Edith had had enough of 'social life' for the day. Regardless of how callous it seemed, she also grabbed at the opportunity to leave, 'I suppose I, too, must go.'

He looked at them with a cynical smile. 'Don't like the look of the face of war?'

Edith was conscious of how the word *face* intruded into his retort.

Alva and she both coloured.

Edith made no effort to leave, knowing that it was now impossible. 'The war is a long time over,' Edith said, rather harshly.

'For me it's never over.'

'Touché.'

Edith gave in to the idea that she was stuck.

'Please stay,' he said in a more courtly tone. 'Conversation is hard to snare, these days. And you are just as I remember you, Edith. If you take away the conventional gambits.' Edith now began to picture Scraper before his injuries, the boy Scraper was coming back to her memory. He'd been so cocky, and so much the child of the sheep station.

Alva held to her resolve to leave, gathered her things, held out her hand to Scraper, shook it and then shook Edith's hand. 'I hope we can all get together again before Edith goes back to her fine life in Geneva. And, Scraper, you must look me up—I'm working at the Commonwealth Laboratories. Call me some time.'

'I do hope we have another chance to talk, too,' Edith said, feeling trapped and abandoned.

Alva left, saying to Edith, 'I'll contact you at the Victoria Club, tomorrow.'

'Do that, Al, please.'

'I will.'

The wretch. Leaving her like that. Unforgivable. She didn't care if she saw her again or not.

Scraper turned to Edith. 'Don't stay from compassion.'

'Why not from compassion? Won't that do?'

He moved his mouth in what was probably the shadow of a grin. 'That's better. Edith, the implacable foe of cant and humbug. Compassion will do. Anything that wins me a conversation will do. Some days I feel I would be happy to pay for conversation.

'You aren't married?' he asked.

Edith to her consternation again found herself considering her answer. Had she become totally duplicitous?

'I am,' she answered as firmly as she could.

'Australian?'

'British.'

'In the war?'

Must the war remain the pivot of all their lives? Yes.

'Dardanelles. Lancashire Fusiliers.'

'Rank?'

'Captain. He was wounded at the Dardanelles. Shrapnel.'

'Are you happily married?'

She again considered her answer. Some people did not deserve to be trusted with the truth. Could this freakish man be trusted with her truths? She decided that she had to lie to him. 'Yes, perfectly.'

Hesitating and then adding the word perfectly was a mistake, a revealing exaggeration if he were clever enough to pick it.

He looked down at his tea. '"Perfectly".'

He made a smile with his tight, unnatural mouth. 'Why no ring?'

She gave her explanation about having forgotten to put it on after hand-washing.

He smiled his twisted smile. 'Have you read much Freud?'

She nodded. 'I've been analysed,' she boasted.

'You must know about "forgetting things" and "losing things"—they're signals to ourselves.'

'Sometimes we just forget.'

'There are no accidents.'

She nearly said, oh and what about you being so shockingly wounded?

The waitress cleared away the things. 'Leave them,' he said. The waitress shrugged as if accustomed to his ways, and went off. 'Have you any more of that cognac?'

Edith took out the flask and poured them two more drinks in the cups. She left the flask on the table.

'I like a little harsh honesty. It is how I remember you. Given the way I am, I'm denied anything to do with honesty. Except by the mirror. Are you back here because the League is finished?'

How astute he was. He was not so far submerged in his self-pity that he was unable to see what others were doing around him. And by praising her honesty he was demanding it from her.

He pointed his question more sharply. 'Jumping ship?' he said.

She had to work out then in reasonably honest conversational terms—as demanded—just what it was she was doing. Was she a married woman? Or only 'sometimes'?! Was she deserting the League?

'Very interesting. Your answer is a long time coming and I can't read your mind on this,' he said. 'Ah, we have an interesting case here, in our dashing Edith. You can have time to answer and you may revise your answer to the marriage question.'

'I can't read my own mind. I'm here on home leave. I'll go to Canberra to look at the possibilities of working there. Yes.'

'From Geneva to Canberra?' He seemed to find this incomprehensible. 'You may be the first person to go to Canberra voluntarily. It's not finished, you know?'

She grimaced slightly. 'I may return to help build the nation.' She tried to make it sound sardonic.

'It'll do that all by itself.' He said this through the circular black, seemingly toothless hole of his mouth, a joyless laugh.

'I could give it a push,' she said.

They chattered lightly about the university days which helped her remember further, his brilliance and his gangly sort of handsomeness coming back to her.

He looked across at her and smiled, his smile now appearing like a crack in a plaster wall. He touched the flask which she didn't like him doing. 'An elegant flask. I like a woman who carries a flask. Of all that crowd you would've been the one I'd expected to carry the flask. And to wear a cape and gauntlet gloves.'

'Really?'

'You were "going places" even then.'

'I thought of myself as a rather earnest undergraduate.'

'You were that—and more than that. You were dashing. "Dashing" is the word.'

She was rather flattered to have a glimpse of her younger self and to have been remembered so. She looked down at her flask. She touched it as a talisman. 'A special memento.'

'And not for your husband.'

She smiled at his observation and at the same time had a flash of recall about Scraper. 'I remember now, you were friendly with Arthur Tuckerman.'

'That's right,' he said softly. 'Poor old Arthur.'

Ye gods, what dreadful thing had happened to Tuckerman that would make Scraper, in his condition, feel sorry for him?

'He was so impressive looking and he got those impressive marks for essays as well,' she said.

'He was a rare spirit. Old Tuck. He's dead you know, Edith.'

'I didn't know. What happened?'

'He did himself in.'

'But potential always *gleamed* out of him! He shone with it.'

'He had a breakdown in third year, remember, and then he went back a few years later.'

'From him, each conversation was a playlet. Everyone wanted to be around him and to talk with him.'

'He was doing brilliantly and then broke down again and went to work the land. He built something of a pretty little orchard out of nothing near Windsor. He thought "simple work" might save him but he slipped into the mental shadows and never recovered. He took his life with a shotgun.'

She found herself asking herself why Scraper hadn't taken his life.

'You are thinking why is it that I haven't taken my life?'

She opened her eyes wide. He was impressive. 'Oh, Scraper, you're dangerous. I know nothing of your life. Tell me.'

'It's a rotten life. And I often think of joining Tuck.'

'It must be hard. How'd you become a mind-reader?'

'Don't know if it isn't a curse. Mind-reading.'

'No need for me to speak then. I'll sit here and think and you can read it.'

He stared at her: 'You want to know how and where I live?'

That wasn't on her mind, but now it was. 'You have two sorts of occult: you can read minds; and you can implant thoughts in a mind.'

'I have a third sort of occult, as you call it, but that will be revealed.'

She didn't like the sound of that.

'Let me show you my poet's garret. I live around the corner in Macquarie Street.'

He stood up fumbling for money with his bent fingers. Probably exaggerated to avoid finding money in his pockets, she thought.

Don't be like that, Edith.

'Let me pay,' she said, reaching for her purse.

'Let the world pay? I like that idea. But a gentleman pays, crippled or not.' He found coins and a note in his pockets. He appeared to carry no wallet or coin purse. 'I'm not poor. I'm rather well off. I do not play a musical instrument on street corners and I do not have to operate a lift. Or run a tobacco shop.'

She apologized that she couldn't visit his garret that day, perhaps some other time? She was fagged from the talk and the whole damned day.

'Where are you staying, Edith?'

'At the Victoria Club. Which is also just around the corner.'

'I'll walk you home.'

She laughed.

'That's about all I'm capable of—walking.'

As they left she saw he limped in a lopsided way.

'What happened to you during the war?'

'I was blown up in France and when I landed everything was broken or missing.'

He was a walking entitlement for charity and indulgence. A requisition on humanity. He *was* the damned war.

'Macquarie Street's hardly a starving artists' garret.'

'Inherited the apartment. Come on, Edith, pay me a visit—for old times' sake. I want to hear abut the League and France as we walk. And let me in on the secret about when the next war is to start. I may rejoin. I have precious little to lose. A pre-dinner drink and then you can go. I haven't had a chance recently to talk with someone fresh from Europe.'

'I couldn't face a dinner table, I'm afraid.' The word *face* had jumped into her conversation.

'You meant to say you couldn't face me over dinner. I won't press dinner on you, promise.'

She let that pass, his bullying of the conversation was becoming tiresome. She was sick of his guesswork as well.

Scraper went on, 'We were mentioning Tuckerman. He was a conscious manipulator of glamour. I am a conscious manipulator of the gruesome. And I manipulate through close observation.'

His candour made her laugh genuinely and with relief. She reversed herself about him, for the first time she could see the possibility of liking him. But only the possibility. 'That is the first time I've ever heard anything honest about Tuckerman. When he was alive he was constantly given what he sought so desperately to get—popularity. You are so right.'

'Popularity instead of love. Charm instead of fame. I'd settle for it. Either.'

She tried to remember how popular Scraper was before. Not very. 'You had friends but you weren't popular.' He was at the fringes of her public affairs crowd.

'At university, no. In the army I was accepted. If you didn't shirk you were accepted and that was something special. It meant you were taken in and you belonged regardless. The army life was good for me. The belonging. I miss it more than anything. I think it was the nearest I got to marriage. Living with a platoon of men.'

She turned to him, 'Please, I don't like calling you Scraper and I can't think of your first name.'

'Warren.'

'I shall call you Warren. It's a little more grown-up.'

'No one ever does. I am now forever Scraper. It is perhaps easier for people. Makes me something other than a man.'

'I will call you Warren.'

His flat was surprisingly pretty. He had done much the sort of thing she would have done if she had been living in the flat. Curious. It had the smell of male hair oil and strong soap and shaving lotion.

'Oh,' she said, involuntarily.

'What is it?' he said.

'Nothing—I like the place—it's what I might do with it. If it were mine.'

He was opening a bottle of cognac and pouring over-large drinks for them both.

'That's more than enough for me. I was dosing the coffee all afternoon.'

He didn't accede to her request and went on, filling the glasses generously.

'That wasn't why you gasped,' he said. 'You gasped at the lithograph of *Les deux soeurs*. Why did you gasp?'

'I like the lithograph. I am surprised that you have a Laurencin print on the wall.'

He looked at her, head to one side, and with his damaged smile. 'You have the same lithograph!'

'Yes.'

She sometimes thought of the faces of the two sisters as Ambrose and herself. Ambrose's feminine self. At least Scraper had not been able to 'read her mind' about her strange, perverse affair with Ambrose back in Geneva. Knowing this gave her strength against his occult.

'You like her work?'

'Yes.'

She did not want to establish another 'connection' with this man. Establishing 'connections' was a flirtation. This man who was once a boy and then disappeared to reappear as…a wreck. 'May I ask why you are attracted to her work?'

'I was in France, you know.'

'You had time for art as well as soldiering?'

'I had time for art. During convalescence. Much time for art.'

She sat, deliberately choosing a chair rather than the couch. She had one sip of her cognac and then stood up again: 'I think you've made the flat a work of art.'

'I think that with my fastidious decorating of the flat I'm compensating for what I am.'

She looked again at the flat—and its resemblance to her own taste and its painful contrast with his disfigured self appalled her.

'I should be off. I've had a rather straining day.'

'Please stay. Indulge me for a few more minutes.'

She sat back in the chair. The flat was, in fact, another way he drew attention to himself, to his disfigurement.

He went on, 'Don't sit all the way over there. Come and sit beside me, here.'

'I'm comfortable where I am, thank you.'

'I am hard of hearing.'

She thought it a lie but there was no reason to think it a lie. She was being harsh. Why was she alternating between harshness and softness with him?

She tried to find a way of responding to this monstrous visage, which, in turn, had become something of a monstrous personality.

Reluctantly, she stood up and went to sit on the couch with him, as a nurse might.

'You are like Tuckerman. You are right to compare yourselves,' she said. Harsh.

'Manipulators?'

'Yes.'

What she had intuitively, but not consciously, suspected but had dismissed as beyond the bounds, now began to happen. Something so far from being humanly legitimate or acceptable as to be, itself, monstrous.

He had moved his leg next to hers.

She plunged into a confused swirling of feelings, of compassion and of indignation. And she felt a twitch of carnality in herself from the touch of his leg and the flesh.

She moved her leg away, and said, 'Regardless of how life has treated you, Warren, you should perhaps hold on to the conduct of a gentleman. And of an old mate.'

'I long ago jettisoned all that. It did not serve me.'

The conversation was faltering, if it had not already lapsed.

'I suspect you might be a tart, Edith.'

'I am not a tart in any way, shape, or form, Warren. Please remain…courteous.'

He then took her kid-gloved hand and placed it on his lap.

She felt his rigid, private part move under her open palm. He held her hand there as she tried to move it.

'Please, Edith. We're both people of the world, you and me. You've been in Europe long enough to know the ways of the world. We are miles away from Alva. And I'm forever placed beyond the boundaries of conventional nonsense. You know that people shun me. Have you ever been shunned?'

'Don't appeal to me, please, Warren.' She again tried to move her gloved hand, but he held it, and she felt his private part rise further and thicken into her hand.

'You were the sophisticate even back in university days, Edith. As a married woman you must understand the needs of a man—as *something* of a married woman.'

She had no time to deal with his observations about herself as she tried to find equilibrium in what had turned into a bizarre human skirmish.

She stared unseeingly at the Laurencin print. He was undoing his flies.

She said, 'Turn off the light.'

He rose and went to the wall to turn off the light.

This was her chance, to stand up and leave.

She didn't.

He returned to the couch and released himself from his trousers and replaced her soft kid gloves on his privates.

Still staring at the Laurencin print, without taking off her glove, she worked his privates with her fingers, it felt so stiff, so hard, sometimes she yearned for that sort of stiffness and hardness inside her, and sometimes Ambrose was like that when he was feeling less feminine and more masculine, and Robert—the completely masculine husband—had always been—very hard—sometimes too hard—and in a very short time she felt Warren spasm and finish.

She glanced at him. He had his eyes closed.

She felt none of the secret pride she sometimes felt when a man became erect for her and then gave out his semen to her.

She looked to her hand and was relieved that nothing of his fluids touched her or her glove. There in the dimness, she wasn't sure where the fluids had gone.

She stood up, took her handbag and went to the door of the flat. He stayed seated there alone in the half darkness.

At the door she said, 'I hope your life eventually finds some proper peace.'

'Please leave me your gloves.'

Was there to be no end to the bedlam of this day.

She took them off and laid the beautiful gauntlet gloves of kid leather on the arm of the couch. Wishing them well in their new life.

'My life has pleasures,' he said. 'But usually, as you see, I have to steal them.'

She closed the door behind her. In the lobby of the apartment block, she again searched her clothing for any sign of the fluids.

Oh God. There was a stain, it had come on to her sleeve. Her stomach clutched.

She walked out into the street, glad of the night air, the smell of the botanical gardens, but it scarcely kept her distaste in control.

She was rushing up the stairs of the Club when the receptionist called to her and she had to go back.

There was a cable waiting for her from Ambrose and, surprisingly, a letter from her psychiatrist, Dr Vittoz.

She opened the cable and read it as she mounted the stairs. Ambrose told her that her contract had been renewed. And there were some loving words in cable-ese, words which she found she needed dreadfully. She kissed the cable.

But was she going to renew *her* contract with the world? Out there so far away?

She took off the suit—one of her favourites from Italy—and underwear and put it all in the brown paper laundry bag and wrote on the bag, *Please dispose*.

She kept her cape and hat.

With resignation, she realized the maid would probably take the clothing and wear it. Oh.

Such was the world.

She wanted to think of the matter no more.

She saved Dr Vittoz's letter for the bath.

Sighing, immersed in the hot water and bath salts, she opened the letter.

It was simply a clipping and his card with *compliments* written in his handwriting and with his signature. The clipping was from the English magazine, the *New Statesman*. It was a letter signed by 300 psychiatrists from around the world—including Vittoz—who had declared 'war' to be a form of disease which infected communities, much as an epidemic would. The declaration proposed various 'treatments' which should occur if such epidemics broke out. That teams of psychiatrists should go to such places and work with those who had 'war fever'.

No personal message.

She put a finger on his signature. She found his communication rather cold.

And what would Dr Vittoz have to say about today?

She bathed and as she lay in the bath she wondered if she had lost forever the joy of the Laurencin lithograph. Would there be an intrusive third face there now? The face of a disfigured life.

As she soaked in the bath, Edith at last was able to laugh—bleakly.

She said aloud, 'It's a far, far better thing I have done—than all the knitting.'

This too had been a kind of war work. Eighteen years after the war.

But still, *war work*. □

GRANTA

MATE

Kate Grenville

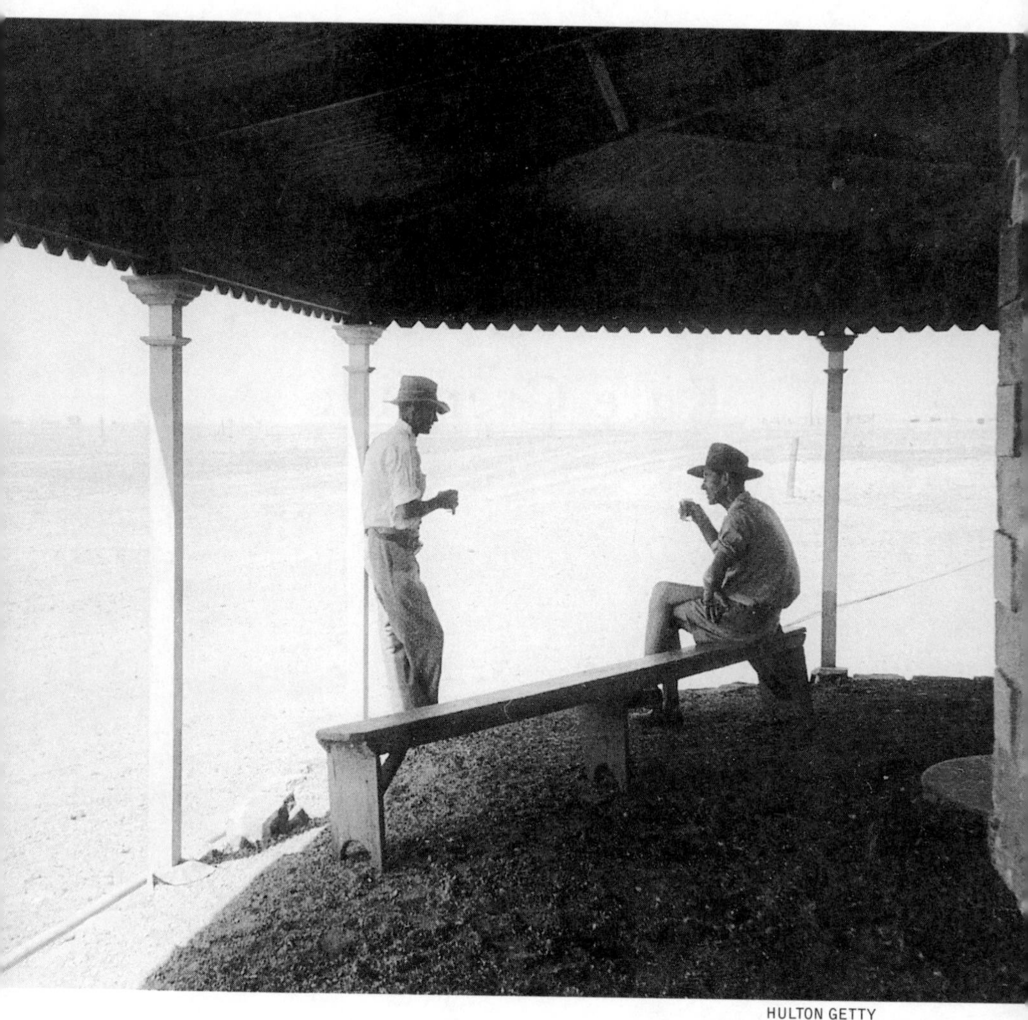

HULTON GETTY

He'd bought the Akubra and the elastic-sided boots but anyone could see he was a city bugger. Boolowa knew all about Will Bashford, the city bloke who'd bought the Phipps place as a hobby farm.

Hobby farm. He'd heard the way they said it.

The neighbour, Norm, would have told them all about him. *Nice enough bugger*, he'd have said. *Bit of a no-hoper, but*. Norm had seemed to know all about him as soon as they shook hands. You could tell Norm had never been a no-hoper. His grip was so strong that Will winced. 'Sharpe's the name, sharp's the game,' he'd said, and laughed, so Will had felt obliged to laugh too.

Will had stopped wondering how people knew straight away. It was like a smell he gave out, the smell of diffidence and uncertainty. He knew he smiled more than a man should, and knew it was the wrong kind of smile: too eager to please.

He was not stupid, he knew that. But his face often was.

Boolowa was a little town like dozens of others in the bush. Ridiculous wide main street, empty except for a dog crossing slowly from left to right. Shops all crammed up together outdoing each other with pretentious plaster facades. And over everything, the huge sky, pale with heat, and the crows taunting you.

There was a drought on—well, there was always a drought on. But over against the blue hills in the east, big heavy clouds built up every afternoon: heavier and bigger each day, dense-looking sharp-edged clouds with flat bases as if sanded smooth.

'Looks like rain,' he had suggested to Norm, that first day, meeting him at the gate down on the road. It was just for something to say, but Norm turned straight away to the men in the back of his broad dusty car.

'Will here reckons we're in for rain,' he said, and a man sunk deep in the back moved his mouth around his cigarette in something that could have been a smile.

'Rain, eh?' he said, and turned to tell the man next to him. 'Reckons we'll have rain.'

Then they all looked at him.

It was rather more response than Will Bashford would generally have wished for.

It was hard to get it right, with these country folk. You had to be *matey*, of course. If they thought you were *stand-offish*, you might as well pack up and go home. But getting the exact degree of matiness right was something Will never seemed to manage.

The country was another planet, though he had got to know the theory of it at Rockdale Public School in Sydney and some of it still stuck. He could almost remember the poem:

I love a sunburnt country,
A land of sweeping plains,
Of something something something,
Of drought and flooding rains.

They had made the cartridge-paper bullock-dray, the balsa Pioneer Hut, the cardboard shearing shed. They had learned that *Australia Rides on the Sheep's Back*. It had been explained that this was in the nature of a metaphor. Miss McDonald had made damper at home in her oven and brought it in. She had forgotten the salt and it had not been eaten, but they all knew after that what a damper looked like—scorched, unappetizing—and admired the pioneers all the more.

So the streets where they lived, the little houses cheek by jowl, the lawn-mowing, the rush-hour crowd in the bus, their fathers hot and cross from hanging on to the strap all the way from Central, the man in the back lane with his bag of lollies—all that was not really there. That was just an accidental, temporary thing. Australia was that land of sweeping plains. It was *Click Go the Shears* and *Once a Jolly Swagman*.

It brought on a certain guilt. Will Bashford's natural—almost pathological—diffidence was amplified here in the country, where the very air felt foreign in his nostrils. He was not a proper Australian, in spite of having once memorized what a snagger and a coolabah were, and he knew it showed.

He'd got it hopelessly wrong yesterday. He'd gone for a walk, along one of the back roads that led out of town. It was early enough to be cool and pleasant, the sun only just up, the flies half-hearted, the birds carolling away in the trees. The paddocks were soft and silvery in the early slanting sunlight, like something off a calendar. *Communing with nature* he told himself. *This is communing with nature.*

He was all alone. It was hard to be all alone in the city. Someone was always watching you from between the venetians. Whatever you did, you had to assume it was being done in public. This—being all alone on a little back road, not having to keep the right sort of expression on your face, or look as if you knew what you were doing—made a nice change.

Click go the shears, boys, click, click, click, he sang. It was exhilarating, belting it out into the stillness of the morning. *Wide is his blow and his hands mo-ve quick*. He heard his voice wavering, drifting up and down. 'Tone-deaf,' Miss McDonald had announced to 3B. 'William Bashford, you're tone-deaf,' and he had felt a clutch of fright, wondering if being tone-deaf was something you got sent to the principal for. 'Stand at the back, William, and just move your lips.'

He'd been an obedient boy. Being obedient was half of being a no-hoper. He had stood at the back and just moved his lips for years.

But he loved to sing. *The ringer looks around and dah-di-dah-di-dah, and curses the old something with the blue-bellied joe!* A cow lifted its head from the grass and stared.

Things had gone wrong when he saw a house he thought was derelict. He'd stopped, his hand on the cool metal of the gate, tempted to explore. This old place had its roofing iron curling at the seams, the grass was long around the rotting veranda, the house and the faded old red truck beside it all up to their ankles in dry grass. He liked poking around old places, but he'd been caught out before. You'd think a place was abandoned, but suddenly there'd be someone coming down off the veranda and you'd have to wave in a casual way, and call out *Morning, how's it going, mate*, and they'd come down to the gate and you'd have to have a conversation about who you were and what you were doing there. By the time you'd got through all that, any idea of communing with nature was well and truly finished.

There were cows in the front yard of this place, tearing at the grass around the water tank tilting dangerously on its stand. As he watched, an old woman in a long pink nightie ran around the corner of the house waving a stick at a few flustered cows that were lumbering along in front of her. In a surprisingly big voice for such a frail old thing she was shouting, 'Garn! Gaaaaaarn! Git!'

He watched, frozen to the gate, as she herded the cows down the side of the house and into a paddock. Her nightie, drenched and dark with dew along the hem, swung heavily around her bare feet as she strained to close the ramshackle gate. Her wispy white hair stood up in a ruff round her head, with pink scalp showing through.

She did not see Will, but disappeared around the back of the house. The cows gawped at the place where she had been. Will felt he was gawping too, and reminded himself to blink.

Coming back along the road later, the sun was in his eyes and he kept his head down. The dew had dried on the grass and the birds had been replaced by cicadas that were starting up one by one, each one drilling away a different note. The flies were taking it in turns to get up his nose.

As he came near the house he made his stride more purposeful and did not look around. The old woman was in her yard again, still in the pink nightie although there was a pink cardigan over it now. She was standing near the powdery old truck, looking up at the face of a young policeman writing in a notebook. Near them, another policeman bent over with a spring-loaded tape measure, stretching it out along the ground. As Will watched, the tape snapped back and the policeman grabbed his hand. His mouth made the word FUCK.

Will walked faster and did not glance over towards the house again, his neck stiff with the ungainly look of a tall person trying to be inconspicuous. He stared into the dusty bushes, at the dusty roadside grass, at the dust itself on the roadway. He was tremendously interested in the dust. But even a man as interested in the dust as he was could not fail to hear the old woman, speaking with one of those well-bred penetrating kinds of voices, 'If I was going to pinch his bloody cattle, d'you think I'd do it in my bloody nightie?'

He had not pinched any bloody cattle, had not been caught trespassing, had got no further than putting his hand on the gate. Had done nothing wrong, in fact. Why did he feel so guilty, scurrying along with bowed head?

The thing he had done wrong was going for a walk in the first place. Going for a walk was not something you did out in the country. That alone was asking for trouble. At least there had been no one listening to him sing.

He had the Akubra and the elastic-sided boots, but he had not thought to bring a raincoat with him from Sydney. But the clouds were there again, at the end of Hill Street, as they had been on the first day, big dramatic clouds with serious dark-grey folds that looked full of rain.

He imagined himself out on the paddocks—his own paddocks!—in the rain. He would have to huddle under a garbage bag. Word of that would soon get around. *That Bashford bloke, saw him out on his place in a bloody garbage bag!* It was easy to get off on the wrong foot in a new place.

Looking down Hill Street, he could see the Criterion Hotel and the Milk Bar. No raincoats there. There was the butcher, and a Draper and Mercer that looked as if it had been closed for years. Further along were the Stock & Station Est. 1919 and the General Store. The General Store had a window full of faded and flyspecked cornflakes boxes. It did not look a promising prospect for a raincoat. That left the Stock & Station, whatever that was.

As he walked along to the shop, a tall skinny bloke leaning on the War Memorial cairn, like a long drink of water, all chin and nose, watched him carefully as if he expected to have to give evidence. *Brown hair, brown eyes, big ears.*

Quickly, as if he knew exactly where he was going, Will crossed the road towards the Stock & Station. His walk felt jerky as he crossed the vast expanse of Hill Street under the gaze of the chin-and-nose man. *Funny kind of walk.* He forced himself not to look to the right and look to the left and look to the right again. Only a no-hoper would think a car could take you by surprise on Hill Street, Boolowa.

Inside the shop he paused, hearing the doorbell jangle above his head. He was going to be Norm Sharpe. Front up to the counter and say *mate* a lot. Easy.

The first problem was finding the counter. After the glare outside, the shop was dark. It would be easy to think those grey overalls were a person. That would get back to Norm. *Feller comes in here, says g'day to the bloody overalls.*

There had been a teacher at school called Mr Overall. Naturally, the kids had called him Mr Underpants.

It was the kind of thing you tended to remember at the wrong moment. He instructed himself not to laugh. *Feller comes in here, laughs at the bloody overalls.*

Beyond the overalls there were shoulder-shapes. It was hard to be sure of anything in the dimness, his eyes straining to adjust after the scalding light outside, but he thought the shoulder-shapes were not a *mate* either, just a row of checked shirts, with caps on a stand beside them.

He was working out that there must be a counter over on the far wall—there was a gleam of something horizontal cutting across the verticals of the shelving behind—when a voice came from the direction of the gleam.

'Help at all, mate?'

He thought of laughing and calling out *Bit dark in here, mate, nearly talked to the bloody overalls!* His mouth open for the laugh, he thought better of it. Over the years, he had learned that not everyone thought the same things were funny that he did. New place, new people, no offence intended. Better to play safe.

'Ah, yes. Mate.'

He dodged around a tower of brown blocks of cow-lick. He could see the man behind the counter now, two blanks of reflected light from glasses turned at him, another long nose, long chin, like the johnny over the road. Inbreeding. Small gene pool. Probably a lot of long noses and long chins in Boolowa.

After a moment he realized there was a customer at the counter too, a big solid man in a red check shirt, standing as still as a pair of overalls.

'Sorry, mate,' Will said. 'Didn't see you there.' He made an ushering gesture with his hand, palm up. 'Go ahead.'

But the man shook his head.

'You're alright, mate,' he said.

Will turned to the shopkeeper. The glasses sat cock-eyed on his face so you wanted to reach over and straighten them up. Tufts of grey hair unfurled from his nostrils. *Eye contact*, Will told himself. *Make eye contact.* But he could not look.

'I'm after a raincoat, mate,' he said. It sounded a bit on the loud side. 'Got a raincoat at all? Mate?'

Somehow it was not quite the way Norm Sharpe would have said it. The shopkeeper did a peculiar thing with his face that made the glasses twitch back up his nose. After a long blank-glassed stare, in which his hand smoothed over the empty counter, he said, 'Nope. No raincoats.'

It seemed that this was going to be all. Will nearly turned to go, but the image of himself under the garbage bag was vivid in his mind.

'Oh well,' he began. But the shopkeeper cut across him quickly.

'Not at the moment.'

There was another pause. Will started again. 'Oh well.'

But the shopkeeper might have been waiting for him to speak. 'Won't find a raincoat in Boolowa, mate.'

His words were like a force of nature. Will was silent. He did not think he would say *Oh well* again.

The glasses were slipping down the shopkeeper's nose again.

The man in the red shirt moved now. He turned slowly and methodically and had a good long look at Will Bashford, all the way from the elastic-sided boots to the Akubra. Then he crossed his arms over his big check chest and gave a short deliberate laugh like a cough.

'Not had a drop of rain here for three years.' He turned to the shopkeeper. 'That right, Lance?'

Lance nodded and stared at Will.

Before Will could explain about the big flat-bottomed heavy-looking clouds, and the way they were heaped up against the hills, the shopkeeper cackled and pushed his glasses back up with his thumb. You could see he was enjoying the anticipation. He was going to make a joke.

'Not a real lot of demand, for a raincoat, just at the minute.'

He and Lance both laughed thoroughly. Will tried to smile but was afraid it came out more like a snarl. He wished he could think of something else to ask for, so he could leave with dignity, but he did not want a cube of cow-lick.

He tried a joke of his own.

'Be prepared, that's what I always say!'

It was not what he always said, and it did not sound as if it was. His witticism was received in silence.

Will felt his mouth shaping a stupid meaningless smile.

'Oh well,' he found it saying again. 'OK, mate. See you later.'

He was turning away from the counter when Lance gave him a fright by saying suddenly, 'Pump's pressing charges, you know.'

Will was confused, his mind full of anxiety to get outside and check the clouds. Surely he had not imagined them. He felt as if his mouth was hanging open. *Pump? Pressing?*

The shopkeeper said loudly, as if he thought he was deaf, or slow, 'Charges. About the cattle.' He and Lance exchanged a tiny smirk. 'When you was out for your walk. This morning.'

Lance slapped his hand on the counter suddenly. 'Been bad blood there for years.'

Will turned from one face to the other as if he was lip-reading. 'Business about a right of way. Reckons he'll sue this time, but.'

They both watched Will. Even if he could still remember what came after *sweeping plains*, he had a feeling it would not help him now.

'Um,' he said, and wished he had not. They were both watching him as if he had something more to say.

After a long silence, the shopkeeper said kindly, 'So, if you saw, mate, you should say.'

Will was feeling congested, as if his pipes would burst from sheer incomprehension.

'Yes?' he tried.

'Don't want to see her go to jail, do you, an old thing like that?' He twitched the glasses up his nose again. 'Mrs Quincy, mate. You give a statement, she'll be right. Constable Small, in at Willoughby.'

He was speaking very slowly. Each word was beautifully clear. No problem at all with the words.

The man in the check shirt broke in impatiently. 'The cops, mate. Go to the cops, give a statement.'

'A statement,' Will repeated. 'The cops.'

They were waiting for him now.

He imagined himself going into Willoughby and finding Constable Small. Norm Sharpe had introduced him to Constable Small outside the Criterion. Gregory Small did not seem like a young man to hurry or cut corners. He had shaken Will's hand at length, as if testing it, and inspected his face closely.

'Bashford?' he had asked. 'Or Brashford?'

He would be slow on the big black Remington that the Willoughby Police Station would still be managing with. *I was proceeding along Seven Mile Road in an easterly direction at about seven a.m. on Tuesday the fourteenth of February.* Read out in Gregory Small's loud flat voice, it would make Will sound more of a no-hoper than ever. *At lot eighty-four, known as Braeside, I saw eight cows proceeding through a broken fence.*

The exact number of cows would cause a bit of a bottleneck. *About eight* or *approximately eight*, Will would want to say. But he did not think Gregory Small would be the sort of man likely to be comfortable with approximations. Cows were either eight cows, or nine cows, or seven cows. You could not have *approximately eight* cows.

They would sit there at the desk with the Remington between them and Will would feel himself going red in the face and his ears swelling, the way they did when he was embarrassed.

'Course, your mate Norm's on Pump's side,' the man in the check shirt suddenly said. 'They're cousins through old Grant Pump.'

'Plus Norm married the sister-in-law's girl,' the shopkeeper said. 'They own that, where you was going this morning. For your walk.'

There could have been another little smirk exchanged. *Click go the shears, boys, click click click.*

Will stared at the dusty boards between his boots. He could feel the blood pouring up into his cheeks, his neck, his ears. He seemed to be radiating heat, as if these two could warm their hands at him. *And curses the old something with the blue-bellied joe.*

There was a little jump on *blue-bellied* where his voice always cracked. It would have been funny if you had been a person behind a tree, listening.

'Well,' he said. 'OK.'

They did not ask him exactly what it was that was OK but

watched with interest as he backed away from the counter, turned himself round, and headed for the doorway. It seemed to have got lost among the shelves of dim things. Dodging a pyramid of big tins, he stumbled and had to put a hand out to save himself, knocking a big box of Ratsak on to the floor. His bottom felt a huge ridiculous target for the two faces watching as he bent over to pick it up. Then he could not find the right shelf for it and had to stuff it in next to a bundle of axe handles and some funny-looking leather appendages.

He felt he would never reach the hard white glare of the doorway. It seemed centuries ago that he had set off in the cool of the dawn, when he had not known that there was no such thing as a private walk in the country.

'Hooroo, mate,' the shopkeeper called, but he could not bear to turn. □

Order form

Subscribe and save:

❍ I'd like to subscribe and save:

❍ 38% with a 3-year subscription (12 issues) for £67.00

❍ 35% with a 2-year subscription (8 issues) for £46.50

❍ 30% with a 1-year subscription (4 issues) for £24.95

Please start the subscription with issue no:__________

My name: ____________________

Address: ____________________

Country/postcode: ____________________

Share and save:

❍ I'd like to give a gift subscription, for:

❍ 3 years (£67) ❍ 2 years (£46.50) ❍ 1 year (£24.50)

Please start the subscription with issue no:__________

Recipient's name: ____________________

Address: ____________________

Country/postcode: ____________________

Gift message (optional): ____________________

Postage The prices above include postage in the UK. For the rest of Europe, please add £8 per year. For the rest of the world, please add £15 per year. (Airspeeded delivery).

Payment Total amount: £________ by: ❍ Cheque (to 'Granta') ❍ Visa, Mastercard, AmEx:

Card no /__/

Expires /__/__/__/__/ Signature ____________________

Return You can either post ('Freepost' if you live in the UK), using the address label below. Or e-mail, fax or phone your details, if paying by credit card.

In the UK: **FreeCall 0500 004 033** (phone & fax).

Elsewhere: tel: 44 171 704 0470, fax 44 171 704 0470. E-mail: subs@grantamag.co.uk

00FBG700

❍ Please tick if you'd prefer not to receive information from compatible organizations.

Granta Magazine

FREEPOST
2/3 Hanover Yard
Noel Road
London
N1 8BR

GRANTA

GRANTA

VOYAGE SOUTH

Murray Bail

LONDON TO FREMANTLE:
EXTRACTS FROM A DIARY
1999

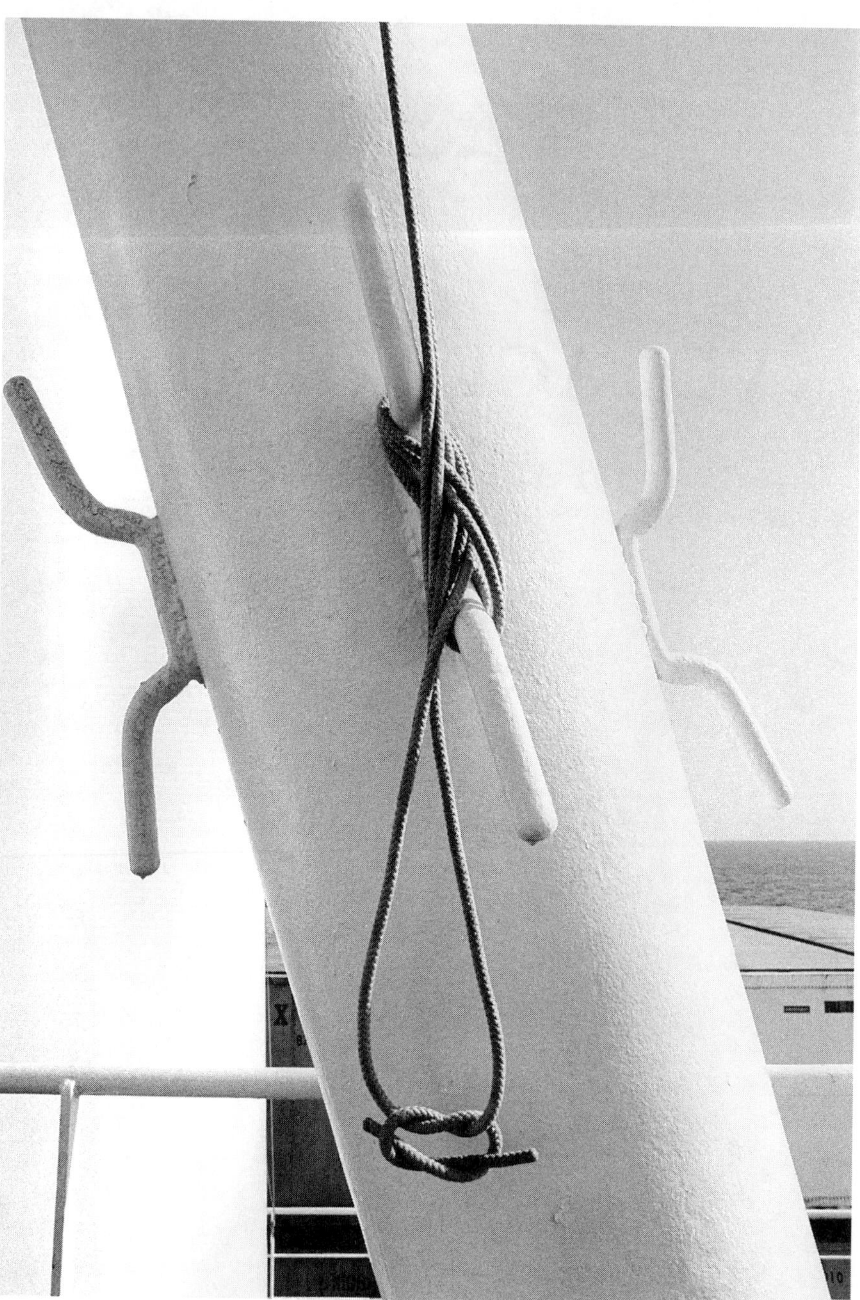

DAVID MOORE

19 July The container ship *Romance* parted from the wharf at Tilbury, 6.18 p.m. Men on wharf watchful, stepping back from the mooring lines as thick as their arms. As the ship moved away, parallel to the wharf, the land with its concrete, cranes, containers—bold colours—took on a broader, distant perspective; and distance made it look all the more empty. Then the ship was swung around by the tugs, and the tall wall of containers swung in a semicircle, as if on a vast turntable. The light, silvery. In one place the sun was aiming to come through—the feeble light of a torch. All was solemn grey, the river, land and sky. Of course, leaving early evening by the Thames would be like this. Industrial shapes of power stations, factories etc. lay in shambles along the river's edge, both sides, black against the general grey, as were the tapering strokes of the tallest chimney stacks. Now and then a green field or a vaguely yellow one sloped down. A goods train appeared parallel at mid-distance, trying to keep up like a little toy: it was brown and suddenly disappeared.

River now became wider, and wider still, until almost as grey as the sky, yellow buoys marking the channel. Ahead: imprecision of the broad sea. It was the greyness of breadth and immense distance. And out there the sea was only fractionally darker grey than the sky; was drawn into the gloom to establish the division myself, as in a grey painting by Rothko. Almost at the horizon the sun could not penetrate the grey. It settled for a seepage of orange, a glitter, then crimson-mauve which became wide and jagged; and—for all that demonstration—still couldn't penetrate the cloud. I held on to the butt of my cigar, as if holding on to a piece of land, or something representing my life on land.

The decks are brick red, the colour of old Australian verandas, as are the metal steps, the rails gloss white. Clamps and threaded rods which fasten the containers lie about in corners. There is the whiff of diesel and the smell of curry. The rails feel sticky with salt. And, before long, soot from the enormous dark funnel has speckled the surfaces, which is why hoses are coiled on the decks and each cabin has an ostentatious doormat, and in the bathroom a bucket and sponge for swabbing. There is a constant, even vibration of engine and steady forward motion, vibrating the water in a glass, rattling the cupboard doors, tingling and shifting small loose items.

Occasionally a larger unexplained vibration begins to rattle everything more. The ship expresses a groaning bodily irritation, or the adjustment of a life, as if it has scraped across a sandbar. To sleep is to enter this palsy of propulsion.

20 July Dawn: immediately a keenness to see something entirely new (a form of energy). The curtains are set on horizontal rods along the bottom to stop them vibrating apart. Through the porthole the waves are small, oily everywhere, same as yesterday yet different.

Three officers and an engineer, all German, and seventeen seamen control this large vessel. Most of the crew, including the impassive cook who cleans the cabins, are Filipinos. They wear orange boiler suits. On hours off they sleep or look at videos of blue movies. The Germans are friendly, working men, slightly overweight. The captain, his small hyperactive head and curt eye movements. He wears shorts, a striped short-sleeved shirt; he doesn't look like a captain at all. His cabin is directly below the bridge, two doors from mine. His door is always open. With him is his wife: short hair, pleasant intelligent face. Also their daughter with her boyfriend, either sunbaking or kissing.

FOURTH OFFICER is on the door of my cabin. It has built-in cupboards, fridge, desk and a table fixed to the floor, a lamp, also bolted down. The bed is against the wall, and has a strap—like a seat belt for when the ship rolls. Above the bed the porthole with the stiff curtain faces forward over the stacked containers, and two more portholes forward above the sofa in the small lounge. I noticed with satisfaction stains of rust around the portholes facing the weather. Otherwise it could be a motel room. On this, the first day, I slept five times; six, if the night is counted. Still I feel vague and foolish; and I look more than exhausted—something else.

Early evening. Escorted by tug up the Elbe: entering Germany through a soft opening, as it were. At regular intervals the metallic might of German industry comes down to the river's edge, the way animals in Africa drink at dusk. Chemical, paper, cement plants, power stations too, protrude fat pipes and jetties, and glass reflects the orange of the setting sun. These are rightly called 'complexes'. In the foreground is a manufactured geometry of lawns, flower beds and paths, which may have begun as an antidote to industry's untidiness, only to degenerate now into a national competition for the neatest, cleanest stretch of factory foreground, the names of each competitor spotlit in large capital letters, some of them familiar. The many tall chimneys (pleasing against the horizontality of the river). Pylons out there supporting drooping lines, lacing the land. All on the verge of overpowering the simpler spread of small white farms and villages.

I read *Independence Day* and kept strolling out on to the deck, avoiding the port side where the captain's daughter was sunbaking. Going slowly up the Elbe I counted the windmills. In fading light another container ship passed: a figure stood out on one of the decks, playing an accordion.

21 July Parted curtains, almost seven a.m: avenues of blue, red and orange container boxes, a regimented chaos; grey infrastructure here and there; yellow cranes. The first officer pointed out the portal cranes, gantry cranes, the wharf crane and the container crane. Hamburg here consisted of jibs and short horizontal movements on tracks, and flashing lights, all pointing to the one end.

At breakfast the captain loudly popped a paper bag. After the long voyage he was leaving ship and going home. 'You must be happy.'

'I am,' he said. 'I am very much. I will water the garden.'

The new captain introduced himself while seated at the table, calling out loudly. A handsome, watchful man, thin, with a bulging stomach, greying hair. Mournful eyes, mournful moustache—a slightly protruding bottom lip. Beside him at the officers' table was his daughter, about nineteen. She has a face lifted from a seventeenth-century Dutch painting (the rosy-cheeked waitress serving beer)—flat golden hair pulled back, smooth round face. In the company of men she was shy. The captain's son was there too. He didn't turn around. They were getting off at Melbourne.

Still reading at eleven p.m. Blue containers swung past my windows, before being lowered deep into the hold, shaking the ship. The whirring and the flashing lights, the loops of electrical wiring as rows of drooping breasts, of different sizes, on the overhead lifts. Will dismiss any thought of the busy yellow gantries as 'gigantic insects'.

22 July Windy, cold day. The sea, ruffled pewter. This is the North Sea. The foam from the bow left trails of lace. Clouds cast long shadows like seaweed or patches of oil. Oil platforms in the distance.

Lunch is the main cooked meal. Today vegetable soup, pork and rice, and a banana.

Slept twice before lunch and once in the afternoon.

I walked backwards and forwards on the deck behind my cabin. Rough, bumpy sea. It was necessary to keep grabbing the rail. Walking it sixty times is 1,800 yards, enough to think of Albert Speer in his prison garden. This is called the superstructure deck, but so too are the four decks below. Then there is the main deck.

Began the *Divine Comedy*.

Rotterdam, about five-thirty p.m.

The pilot climbed on board wearing a necktie. Why, in this part of Europe, the growth of the moustache?

The same single-bladed white windmills as in Germany. Otherwise, only factories and tall chimneys break the low horizon. Because of the flatness the pipes and taps and flames of the refineries spread along the ground without restraint.

Again the scale of Europe's industry displayed. Mile after mile of it. The earth has been altered with a purpose, to serve. On both sides of this port river, never-ending facts are displayed for inspection: paradise for men, a refuge for men.

Man in park alongside river throwing a boomerang.

23 July Overcast, cold.

Stood on deck as ship left port. The many small methodical movements, the slow drifting away before angling towards the direction to take.

Later it rained—a squall. The ship pitched a little, then went on as before.

24 July Sore throat. Coughed up during night. At four a.m. put on the light, first closing curtains (regulations), and read a few pages of Victor Klemperer's *Diaries from Germany 1933–41*, until tired of his methodical, though understandable complaints—not a pleasant man, an anxious watchful scholar.

Woke with headache.

Doors creak, ceilings creak.

Late for breakfast.

We were heading for Gibraltar, the Mediterranean. I asked the captain if we would land at La Spezia Tuesday.

'Tuesday, Wednesday. What does it matter here?'

One day flows into the next; all days the same here. Each day is the same, but different in its detail, like the sea. Only dates are used at sea. The present is the same as the past.

The perpetual cleaning of the decks: each morning before breakfast the hosing away of black soot, and along the lower decks and walkways salt. The crew always busy, walking with a purpose, a bucket, spanners, brush in hand. They have their own small dining room, facing the kitchen. A plastic tablecloth, and bottles of soya sauce and other hot items to douse the food.

Went back and forth along the main deck walkway, along the side of the ship from the beginning of the superstructure to the stern, which stops at a vertical ladder and an orange lifebuoy. This is sixty paces. Suede shoes and oil made the metal path slippery, I kept tilting and scratching my watch against the rails. With the ocean rushing past not far below and the ship tilting I had the absurd fear of losing something—sunglasses, car keys! Probably a small part of the idea of falling overboard myself. Several times I gazed about and appraised my chances; without a lifebuoy in the empty ocean, nil. The captain said it takes six miles for the ship to stop naturally, and 1.2 miles in an emergency.

After dinner I inspected the swimming pool—an empty tank. It is below the main deck, below the engine room and below the waterline, next to the laundry. Someone's washing slowly spinning in tune with the ship's turbines. From the main deck I looked out over the sawn-off stern. The white violence of the wake and the flow outwards and away was like water released from a dam.

Alone in my cabin I opened the last bottle of wine bought at the supermarket in Hamburg. Simple solitary pleasure at drinking two glasses, reading. Then like a champion I cut a cigar and although conscious of the sore throat went out on to 'my' deck, put both feet up on the rail, sat back and smoked. The captain passing commented on the cigar. I turned Klemperer's diaries face down on my knee, for the cover showed two Nazis in polished boots pasting boycott notices on a Jewish shop (one soldier has an especially repulsive nose and jutting jaw, legs apart).

For a moment the captain talked of the extra containers. 'The steering is heavier. It is less accurate. Deeper draught.'

I read more of Klemperer, more or less drugged by his difficulties, and the air became cooler. The cigar kept going out. No matter how I concentrated on throwing the dead matches overboard they landed on the lower decks.

Ten p.m. Describing a sunset. I would not want to try. Almost exactly at 10.10 p.m. it finally set, producing for a moment the glow of a distant cigar.

25 July Vivid thick semi-emblematic sub-violent dreams while at sea. Curiously knotted dreams.

Walked back and forth along one side of the main deck where all is painted grey, except for important taps and levers, and signs painted red—and the lifebuoy at the stern, attached to a torch on an orange nylon rope; walked until I'd done 2,000 yards. Found an orange/black ladybird crawling on my arm. Later a dark butterfly flew past. Now and then a single white bird skimmed the waves—so far from land on frail wings, and nothing solid to rest upon. Clear sky. Blue-black sea, choppy. A dramatic, powerfully elegant sea.

We have left the North Sea, the Channel, and are in the Atlantic without sight of land. The immensity of the achievement of British, Dutch, Spanish, Portuguese sailors who conquered the world in small wooden boats—to have reached out, then established and defended an empire by sea. Columbus's ship was as long as this ship is wide.

Read more of Klemperer complaining about lack of money, though he had a maid, a wine account and now a six-cylinder car.

At nine p.m. on the main deck, book under my arm. The captain came down the stairs from the bridge.

I asked if sailors loved the sea; it's what I'd often read.

'No, I don't. A few of the old ones do. The first officer probably loves the sea.'

'Do you find the sea boring?'

'The sea itself, no. This isn't boring,' he pointed. 'The sea is always changing. The ship is boring. Seventy-five per cent of my time is paperwork.'

'I could well imagine sailors growing to love the sea,' I insisted.

'Germans are not sea people. I'm from the mountains, in Bavaria. I love the forests. It's the English and the Dutch who love the sea—sea people.'

He wanted to retire to his house in Bavaria, in the forest. He also has a farmhouse in Austria.

How times have changed, he said. And in a short time. He had bought the place in Austria, because the village was untouched, was not modernized. He was the outsider from the modern world. Now all the houses have television and computers, and the villagers are like city people. And he is the old-fashioned one, wanting the old ways.

'Europe was at its best a thousand years ago,' he joked, almost serious.

A modest, likeable man; the mournful eyebrows, mournful grey moustache—pale blue, humorous eyes helping the face.

'Have you ever been frightened?'

'I'm frightened now,' he laughed and looked out at the sea.

But there were bad experiences.

Entering Singapore harbour with the pilot boat alongside he found he couldn't slow the engine. The pilot was screaming in Chinese. The captain began looking around at the small islands and ships to avoid. Then he did an emergency stop, just in time. To start again the engine would only go at medium speed etc.

At Port Said on a very hot day the Egyptian pilot came on board, climbed the many stairs to the bridge, and dropped dead of a heart attack at the captain's feet.

I could have listened to his stories all night.

In the Atlantic a storm came up so fast he couldn't turn the ship in time. He had large breaking seas coming from behind. Too dangerous to turn; he could only wait. The ship could have gone down.

'No, you can't panic. Even if you're afraid you can't panic. It wouldn't do. It cannot help.'

This captain's love is not for the sea, but the language and civilization of China. He can read and write Chinese and Mongolian. He is a member of various Chinese societies. His favourite book is Needham's *Science and Civilization in China*, a pirated edition bought in Taiwan for 110 marks.

26 July Woke 7.15, headache. Showered and went down the four flights for breakfast.

Read more of the *Divine Comedy*. As the ship was approaching Gibraltar Dante was also approaching Gibraltar. It marked the end of the world: 'And I and my companions were already old and slow, when we approached the narrows where Hercules set up his boundary stones that men might head and never reach beyond...'

Today the rock was covered in mist. The straits far wider than I imagined. The Mediterranean too is larger—for hours not a ship in sight.

Enormous tough T-bones (after soup), as oversized as the chains, ropes and spanners lying about on the ship. Amusement of the cook.

Afterwards went along the narrow lower-deck walk I hadn't known about, to the fore deck, a triangular area of unearthly stillness, made stranger and quieter still by the oversized anchor chain, winches, lines and bolts. Soft rushing of water, no wind, as the bow pushed forward; almost everything painted grey, objects resting in their place in the sunlight, waiting to be used. To walk the bow is about 150 yards. Rushing past, the waves are only a few yards below. I walked until I reached a mile.

I ordered four bottles of red wine (poor, French) from the Third Officer in charge of the store. Originally he'd gone to sea because of the 'romance'. Now all he wanted was a promotion.

Walked to bow again: keen to see the waves nearby, and the grey arrangement of the fore deck which somehow has the stillness of a vertical de Chirico. Wrote letters in cabin. The feeling here I should be writing letters, more letters. To be posted at La Spezia. The shadow of the radar scanner on top of the containers turned slowly like a ceiling fan. Still warm at eight p.m.

Decided, after elderly deliberation, on another cigar. Pleasure at this small freedom. After further hesitation I cut one, and went on to my deck. The chief engineer—a heavy bearded German—who had been sitting with his feet on the rail, engrossed in a book on the great tank battles of the Second World War, many colour photographs, had returned to his cabin where he usually played sad German songs. Soft, warm air. And soft blurry light. Sea flat, shifting about in folds like a woman's belly. Not far distant the mountains along the coast of Spain: darker, cleaner grey against the general softness. And dolphins in schools appeared darker still, black sharper shapes, solid against the softer sea—rising from the water, returning, not leaping; using their ocean. All this because of a Cuban cigar!

27 July Mild, long-lasting headache. Read in a languid sort of way all morning.

I paddled in the tank today: breaststroked backwards and forwards. I also walked along the lower deck clocking up about 1,000 yards, telling myself I would do another 1,000 after dinner.

In the afternoon a breeze made it difficult to walk to the bow. Waves whitened and multiplied, the ship rolled. It was hot. All day no sign of land, and for many hours no other ship.

At about eight p.m. I sat on the deck alone. Through half-closed eyes the sea was a vast burned field, with lumps of quartz showing through, swept by a wind. The wind rattles and whistles and hums the railings and wires. I searched for dolphins without seeing any.

At nine p.m., huge complex sunset. It was another land with islands in the sky, on fire.

Sunset: another land with islands in clear water in the sky, on fire.

Sunset: where the clouds stretched into another land in clear water in the sky, breaking off into long islands, all on fire.

28 July Again the direct relevance of Dante when he describes the steep cliffs along the coast around La Spezia. Approached the port just after one p.m.; a semi-stillness entered the ship as it slowed. Without the breeze the air became hot. Politely the ship dropped anchor outside breakwater, to wait for another one to leave, the way a man sits patiently in a barber shop, glancing around, or stands back with exaggerated tact waiting for a stranger to withdraw money from a wall bank. Where the anchor dropped in the green-blue water it produced a delicate spread of pale khaki, like northern Australia from the air.

Officers studied with binoculars the progress of the ship being loaded in the berth. After about three hours we were escorted in. Compared with Hamburg and Rotterdam, an untidy terminal. Stevedores have slick combed-back Fifties Hollywood haircuts, gold jewellery, mostly in shorts, bare-chested, no protective headgear. Two Italian immigration officers in full uniform on board, the captain's loud banter and laughter.

29 July The barber from the town scuttled around the corner of the main deck. Something about him caused everyone to laugh and shake their heads. A man not taken seriously. From a distance he had a medieval jester's stoop; also, on board to hustle a living, he needed to be visible. He cut the hair of several of the crew, seated on a stool by the railing. Someone said he was Irish, or part Irish.

Early afternoon. The ship left the wharf, two stevedores wiping their hands on a cloth, watching. In the harbour a yacht passed and a young man dropped his trousers and presented his pale arse to us—local custom?

Pause for sunset. Cloudless sky. A glowing coal, diminishing; then out.

30 July The tall bald chief engineer who climbed aboard at La Spezia carrying incredibly heavy black suitcases keeps to himself in the cabin adjoining mine. On his desk is a colour wedding photo of himself towering over his wife.

All decks were hosed by breakfast to clear off soot and muck from one and a half days in dock. Noticed while reading Victor Klemperer's *Diaries* his meal times in the 1941 German prison were hardly different from on this ship: lunch eleven-thirty, dinner five-thirty. And no music, no friends, no telephone: the rest of the world going about its business elsewhere. Movement confined to the small area of decks, all metal, and the narrow walkway to the bow, along the lower deck which often has large pools of water, and the shorter walk (forty-five yards) on the deck above, to the stern. No news from the rest of the world: all those stories in grey, and bits of information —the newspapers. There are gaps not replaced by much else, and here time itself is fairly featureless, replaced by a physical forward motion, taking many days for my own rhythm to establish itself. I had been sleeping too much—four, five times a day. I was eating large meals, unusual hours. Strange 'working' at a vibrating desk, one that keeps tilting ever so slightly.

Very hot on deck after lunch. For our passage through the straits between Italy and Sicily, a pilot came on board (completely unnecessary, according to the captain. Only one entrance needs a pilot and that is Port Phillip Bay at Melbourne). Here Sicilian fishing boats have long poles jutting from the bow, where a boy is perched, and another boy on top of the mast, spotting fish.

At dusk large pale brown fish—about a yard long—leaped out in groups from the foam of the bow. Sailfish?

With the captain on the bridge. Informed him I'd like to see three things on the voyage: a big storm, an albatross, a whale. In his booming, rhythmical voice, told of big seas near the Bay of Biscay, a few years ago. His ship and a Canadian ship were together; his with logs from West Africa on deck, the Canadian also stacked with timber, but cut to short lengths for mining. The storm lasted thirty-six hours. Big short waves pounded both ships, bending the rails and hatches. The logs loosened and were tossed end over end into the next stack, and vice versa, smashing the lifeboats and rails. All he could do from the bridge was watch. 'Nature was rearranging my load.' Not a single log was lost. But when they entered the calm of the Mediterranean sea he saw the Canadian ship had lost its entire load.

The swivel chair of the helmsman has a seat belt. In my cabin there is a seat belt at the desk, and one for the seat against the window, and there is a fixed stool in the shower.

Last night (10.40 p.m.) woken by ship rolling. Cupboard doors opened. Books and things slid off the desk and tables; wine glass broke on the floor.

31 July Still the Mediterranean; I had never considered its size before.

Lethargic from restless night. I go to bed too early, and am still not accustomed to the ship's movement.

Walked 1,000 yards to stern (bow walkway is awash). Unsteady progress, grabbing at rail with each step. Grey sea. Handwashed underclothes.

What is 'experience'? Is being more or less alone on a cargo ship 'experience'? It is fabricated experience. If something happened unexpectedly on this voyage it would add to the sum of experiences; then what? Are 'extreme' experiences better than the accumulation of 'ordinary' experiences? An extreme experience can suddenly have a person seeing themselves clearly—the weaknesses, strengths etc. Then other things one day appear more in proportion.

The 'ordinary' experience on board is an alteration in time, and the amount of time spent alone. Experiencing the sheer scale of the physical world is interesting—but useful?

At eight p.m. sat with the captain on deck. Very hot, humid. Genial gentle man, always ready—or is about—to laugh. This and constantly looking at the sea has left him with laughing eyes, though the German moustache has him appear initially mournful. Only fifty-three, looks older. Spoke of the irrational use of pilots: if they're unable to get on board in bad weather they're not used. Seamen still tend to be superstitious. He himself will not allow whistling on board; it attracts strong winds. Smiled and shrugged at himself. He also will not use certain numbers on charts. Once in the Indian Ocean his ship replied to a distress call. A fishing boat had run out of fuel. After they were supplied the Indian captain asked if payment was required. What do you have?—the first officer looked into the boat. He saw a dolphin. But when the captain later saw the dolphin on board, being cut up for meals, he ordered it thrown overboard. And the crew, he said, would have thought him mad.

Uncomfortable in the plastic chair. Heat rash.

1 August Slept well. Very hot.

To the bridge, mid-morning. Lavish space in the wheelhouse, rubber flooring, the feeling here of all things having evolved to their rightful place. All equipment including binoculars at rest has its place, to be used. Such a tiny helm high above the waves to steer this enormous vessel, the wheel as small as the steering wheel of a modern racing car. Oddly the wheel is slightly to one side of the ship's centre, as marked by a port and light on the bow. Tilted windows to reduce glare, filtered blinds, large windscreen wipers. Muted colours: grey, brown, cream. No decoration, anywhere. A poster illustrating cloud formations with their codes. Comfortable swivel chairs. Hard surfaces. An alcove on the port side holds the communication equipment. Directly behind the helm a low wide counter forms the chart room, and there's a small sink and coffee machine. Here is a door to the internal stairs down to the deck below, just near the captain's cabin. At each side of the bridge is a door with lever handles which opens on to the flying bridge, open to all weathers, with steps down to the deck below.

Sat with the captain. It costs $55,000 US dollars for the *Romance* to use the Suez Canal; $500,000 for an American nuclear aircraft carrier. The ship costs $25,000 a day to charter. Taking the canal saves three to four days. Still we have to wait at anchor for over twelve hours for a convoy to form behind us, and the convoy from the south to come through the canal.

Canal (on radio): 'Don't forget our usual gifts to the pilot, thank you. Over.'

Captain (winking at me): 'Two cigarettes. Over.'

Canal: 'No! No! Four cartons and soft drinks!'

Captain (aside): 'He accepts more than anyone.'

Concentration of young Filipino helmsman in yellow boiler suit, a trainee. His flickering eye-movement.

Acquisition of facts (as when on a ship, which is nothing less than a concentrated mass of assembled facts) gives only an illusion of gaining experience. When things are seen, what actually is being added? And experience acquired from the experiences recorded by others—including intellectual experiences—remain minor experiences, until given proper consideration.

An unexpected experience—i.e., a true experience—may prepare a person for the next time.

A minor sunset.

2 August Dreamed of disembarking from stern at Suez, moving along the wharf, then unable to rejoin the ship. Saw the ship going away. Unusual hectic running about in bare shadowy town trying to reach telephone etc.

Had woken several times as we entered canal after 1 a.m: a strange straight line interrupts the voyage, the open sea. We are the second ship in the convoy. Very hot, thirty-eight to forty degrees, and no breeze from the ship. For the first time, flies. Slowly passing mounds of grey sand, in low broken hills, to infinity. Because it is 'desert' it all becomes a mirage. On the port side, which is the Nile side, brief bitumen roads now and then among the settlements, palms and other green, white buildings; the starboard side, barren hot wrecked grey-yellow sand. On both sides, war wreckage scattered along the edge, allowed to remain, piles of barbed wire, pontoons ripped open with shell-holes, lengths of twisted steel, all rusting. Egyptian army strung out at regular intervals: lookouts, huts with one or two soldiers in shade, checkpoints, compounds, trucks in formation; and large anti-tank hills of sand, and memorials to the dead.

Eucalypts and palms line the canal on the side where the settlements appear; red gums, by the look. Ferry engine started up like a camel roaring. Trucks waiting in line for the ferry—ready to cross quickly between ships. Flat hot-looking buildings. Man in white singlet waving. How the heat has surely held the place back.

Sand-coloured mosque in the middle of nowhere. It suggested coolness—beckoned in that way.

Otherwise, barrenness and heat, the lassitude.

The Bitter Lakes, dividing the Canal—how biblical ('bitter').

At Port Suez: the 'Red Sea Hotel'.

All doors on the decks had been locked on the inside.

Young man whistling at ship. Men sitting in shade. A soldier began running to give a message, but stopped to walk.

In the wheelhouse the Egyptian pilot in white shirt over dark trousers, large rimless sunglasses, pacing behind the helmsman, calling out sonorously, melodramatically, 'One point seven-two!' More pacing, glance up at the channel. 'One point seven-eight!' Repeated by helmsman. Later, as his boat came bobbing alongside, the captain handed the pilot two cartons of Marlboro. Once he saw an Egyptian pilot drop his carton, and the boat left him dangling on the ladder to retrieve the cigarettes in the water.

3 August Red Sea. It is not red; but, rather, dark brown. Oily.

Main reason for voyage: to feel what it is like travelling steadily on water, in a different self-contained world.

Captain announced contest of estimating arrival time at the equator. Such is his modesty he admitted that usually it was the steward who won.

Mid-morning in the wheelhouse with the captain. He said during a sinking he would put women and children first—weaker. He had no doubts. Women weaker? Fire is the fear, not sinking. Every few paces on the ship is some sort of fire equipment, fire information, instructions.

Captain's father was an officer, captured by Russians in 1945, released 1946; mother in northern Poland, a believer in the Third Reich—told her son she had known nothing of the Holocaust. An uncle was captured on Russian soil in 1956, after years of working in mines in Siberia—very hard, cold. He died a year after release, 1957.

Captain speaks in a loud voice, as if into a wind. A moist bottom lip. He is a Taoist. Not one life is worth losing for a political idea, he said.

The Filipino helmsman said he saw whales two evenings ago, in the Mediterranean, about three miles away. He didn't especially 'love' the sea. It was a job, a good job; he had followed his cousins. Prefers new ships. His worst storm was a typhoon in the Indian Ocean, force twelve, at night. Horizontal rain, sea all foam. A plump cheery man, thin moustache, who lives with wife and children in village, in hills away from Manilla. Doesn't like the Red Sea. Always misty: dust from the desert, on the rails and decks.

Read bits of *The Mariner's Handbook*—the hierarchy of waves, ice, etc., the Beaufort Wind Scale, the system of names.

'Almost all waves at sea are caused by wind, though some may be caused by other forces of nature such as volcanic explosions, earthquakes or even icebergs calving. ...The area where waves are formed by wind is known as the generating area, and Sea is the name given to the waves formed in it. ...The height of the sea waves depends on how long the wind has been blowing, the fetch, the currents and the wind strength...'

4 August Restless night. Humid. Too hot to sit on deck. I leaned on the rail and gazed at the sea. Every wave different; little point following one, before it dissolves into another, or anticipating the emerging of another. For this, and the general repetitiousness, soothing.

To estimate time we meet equator I added to the captain's figure of 8 August, 17.26 hours, gambling on his optimism and stronger weather in the Indian Ocean: 22.80 hours.

Sat with the captain in wheelhouse. Told of sister ship that lost two plates at the waterline in storm; a captain he had served under, who phoned shore, 200 miles away, he was abandoning ship. A helicopter just in range lifted them all off. The ship drifted eight days without sinking; towed ashore, it was inspected, taken out to sea, scuttled. Captain survived an Inquiry.

The matter-of-fact modesty of the seamen. No need for the exaggerations.

This ship is 42,000 tons, holding about 2,000 containers. Each container about twenty-five tons. Europeans never say 'boat'—an American term. Captain took it off automatic pilot and allowed me to steer for a while. Stiff, jerky; a matter of steering ahead, of anticipating possibility. The ship changes direction slowly, then more rapidly. It felt large, almost cumbersome. When I looked behind I saw the meandering wake of my inexperience.

Example of increased worldliness. 'I have steered a container ship of 42,000 tons for ten minutes. It was in the Red Sea.'

Many dolphins at dusk. Too hot and humid for the deck.

5 August Still the Red Sea. Monotony. Sand and salt on the decks, rails. Hot and humid. Mist.

Walked backwards and forwards diagonally across cabin for 2,000 yards and felt suitably self-satisfied.

Talked with Filipino third mate at helm. His first ship was 4,000 tons and narrow. It rolled easily. And the containers were stacked so low he could see the ship bending. From west Africa they went to the United States. During storm in the Atlantic he wanted to leave the ship, and the sea-life. On the bridge he was vomiting into a paint bucket; but he couldn't stop working. German captain: 'Why are you talking to the paint bucket?' The first mate had advised: burned toast, liquid, stay vertical, face the weather outdoors. Otherwise he would always be seasick. Filipino said he had never been frightened at sea. It depended not on weather, but first mate and captain.

First Officer (bearded, tattoo from Hawaii): 'I don't see the sea any more.'

Of the crew: 'I wouldn't have them on hooks in the freezer.'

'I hate the sea. But after three to four months on land I want to get back.'

For twenty-five years was married; then spent three years working the American coast—and wife left. One son.

He has friendly brown eyes, and pleasant crinkles which come more from checking the weather than smiling encouragement. Has exquisite neat sloping handwriting. Pleasant watching him write up the log.

Quickly read Powell's *A Time to Be Born*. The sort of American novel hammered out on a Remington in a professional, efficient way. Fear of lack of books; I counted the days, counted the books.

6 August Horn of Africa, 5.40 a.m. Woken by pitching and rolling, the entire large ship shifting about, as if skidding and sliding on the surface. Then it would be met by a vibrating bump, the engines still driving on. Doors swung open, everything loose rattling or sliding, glass broke, suitcase slid across floor. The floor shuddering and tilting. The noise: loud rattling and whistling, the moaning. Clear sky through the porthole, but the sea grey-black, with white crests—many short waves. The horizon tilting, bow rising and falling.

Difficulty reaching the bathroom: thrown against wall, clutching at anything.

Difficulty climbing to the bridge, and force needed to open the door. The captain was standing with his officers. We looked down at the ocean. He was cheerful to me. It was a 'disorganized' sea. Force eight to nine.

Went out on to the flying bridge, into the weather; had to hold on to the rail, the ship kept rolling. The entire visible sea had aroused into irrational activity, short big waves without consistency. Three huge waves began approaching at forty-five degrees, about half a mile away. Unable to take my eyes off them, as the ship held its course. The bow met the first, shuddered, and plunged—perhaps thirty feet. Nothing for a moment. Then mass of water flew up and drenched my face and the windscreen to my right. Bridge is 150 yards to the bow, and over six storeys to the waterline.

At breakfast, tablecloths made wet to prevent plates, glasses etc. sliding. Through the forward portholes the horizon tilting, things falling in the kitchen.

All day on the bridge watching the sea, grey-black with streaks of foam along the direction of the wind. The ship shuddering as it met a huge rolling weight of water, spray shooting up and over the containers below, occasionally drenching the wheelhouse windows. Or else erupting like a decorative fountain and floating into white smoke, producing two or three brief rainbows. Anger of the sea; grey with streaks of white; it looked old. Ship rolling seventeen degrees.

Lunch with captain and first officer. They told of other storms, matter-of-fact.

Asked if he had ever been frightened the first officer immediately answered, 'Yes!'

He saw a thirty-one-year-old in his first command in a typhoon off Japan, running from one side of the bridge to the other, covering his face with his hands. 'What are we going to do?' Other officers: 'It's not so bad.' Two containers had shifted.

Captain told of a captain he had served under who had been in a typhoon when a container was thrown up, all twenty-five tons, and its corner smashed into the captain's cabin.

His own worst experience was in the Atlantic during a hurricane (force eleven). After standing at the wheel for twenty-six hours he needed to go below. Carefully he told the Filipino helmsman to keep the speed ahead of the waves. He repeated those instructions. In less than ten minutes below he felt the ship turn. He had a rush of nausea. On the phone the helmsman was screaming, 'I've lost steering! The steering's broken!' Captain ran up to the bridge, doing up his trousers. He shoved the helmsman to the floor. He increased speed to regain steering then began turning the ship 360 degrees in enormous seas, hoping it wouldn't capsize. As it turned it began tilting to what seemed an impossible degree; he waited for the worst or containers to fall off. Gradually the ship righted and continued on.

For hours I sat alongside as he sat in his swivel chair at the helm, or he'd join me outside on the flying bridge, holding on to the rail, where surveying the sea he broke the silence, 'Do you consider classical Stoicism is akin to Taoism?'

As the gale continued the noise, bumping instability of surfaces had a tiring effect—assault on the senses. In the cabin the ship appeared to tilt even more.

Without necessarily meaning to I have acquired dozens of new facts—of no use to me.

7 **August** Rolling pitching night. Little sleep.

The sea is like the land with its contours changing all the time. Still rough this morning, uneven; less wind.

'In the old days,' the captain said, 'ships were made of wood and the men of iron; today ships are of iron and men of wood.'

Some ships are heavy, dull etc., each with different personalities, 'like women'. 'Yes,' the first officer nodded, 'just like women.'

Second officer has a girlfriend back in village outside Cologne, but 'she tells me she's pregnant'. He won't get married, 'it's too expensive'.

'Does she want to get married?'

'I did not ask her. Anyway, I'm on board this ship.'

Sailor's soap, for use in sea water. Many sailors still prefer it.

In bed at 8.05 p.m.

8 August Sat with captain in wheelhouse, 206 miles north of equator, twenty-one knots, after watching large school of dolphins. Talking about China when the plump third officer, Filipino, interrupted from the helm: 'Excuse me, Captain. Could you look at this?'

On the computer chart one bar was high and red, flashing. A cylinder overheating, broken piston rings.

The engine was stopped, the ship gradually slowed, drifted. Engine crew began repairs. It would take seven hours. The ship had simply stopped in the empty ocean, the way a truck stops in an empty paddock—for repairs. The ship rolled and pitched a little. In four hours it drifted five miles. Sirens sighed and moaned through the wires.

Barbecue intended for equator crossing still went ahead. Winner of estimated time announced by captain: me, assisted by the breakdown. Hot, humid. False gaiety. The Filipino crew began singing Sinatra songs around a guitar. Drank too much. Left for bed early (9.30 p.m.).

9 August Slept well. Tropical dawn: of long narrow flat-bottomed clouds along the horizon. Twisted cotton wool and pipe cleaners came to mind.

Glassy sea of the darkest, deepest blue. The ocean felt deep here. Again the ship stopped twenty-nine miles from the equator, the rings in another cylinder broken. All day the ship wallowed. Walked to bow and back eight times (1,200 yards), until saturated; faintly pleased at the achievement. Any activity felt superior to the stationary, overweight ship. Later I hoped to join the crew fishing; all were asleep.

With the captain in the wheelhouse, the ship silent. 'It's like a marriage,' he said. 'Nothing is spoken. There is no news.' Second officer: 'Women have complaints.'

Captain said little can be done to speed up the engineers. Only careful encouragement. He and the chief engineer don't like each other. 'It is unfortunate.' Told of the German oiler who gave harsh order to Indonesian oiler in an engine room. The Indonesian went to the kitchen and returned with a box of knives and scattered them on the floor: 'Choose one!' The German ran to the captain, banged on his door.

At about 7.30 p.m. from the bridge ink of clouds streaked the sky. A few minutes later the ship crossed the equator in complete blackness, the second officer calling out: 'Now!'

10 August Mariners developed the habit of keeping a log to remind themselves of actual differences in the days passing in apparent similarity.

Rain in night, light showers in morning. Entirely cloudy: thick robust clouds.

11 August Restless night: rolling, pitching. Ship creaking like someone creeping about in the cabin and above, opening cupboards; a person or persons trying to find a way in. And someone is cracking almonds; someone else tapping their fingernails.

Sat with captain on the bridge all morning. He talked of his favourite authors—the Austrian novelist Stifter, Jane Austen and Virginia Woolf. He has read *Orlando* three times. He met his wife at Cologne University. He'd enrolled as a ship's captain who'd decided he'd finished with the sea. She was one of five in a class studying Mongolian.

Captain's father died at eighty-nine; lived alone, almost blind; sat in chair listening to light music and TV, nodding off. Would not talk about the war. Only once did he mention it, late in life, to his son. He regretted sending out a young soldier on reconnaissance: he was killed by a Russian sniper.

Returning from Russia as a POW he was uncomfortable with his children. He couldn't talk to them. The three daughters in the house each had intense 'conversational relationships' with their mother, excluding him. Only alone with his wife did he begin to be natural with her. One daughter whose favourite book then and now is *Les Misérables* could never find perfection in many men, and for hours discussed her unsatisfactory love affairs with her mother. She is still unmarried, and has become 'very fussy'. The father lost interest in everything; no interest at all in his children, or grandchildren.

Large waves began to form, occasional rain. After lunch went forward along the catwalk to see I don't know what: size of sea. Mountains and ruffled valleys, dark grey, long white tops, approaching, always approaching, striking or lifting the steel ship. Towards the bow much spray, and all awash, water flowing along the floors. Necessary to hold on to the rail. It was like hanging on to the mane of a huge grey horse, rearing and spitting foam back at me.

12 August Captain's sister, the unmarried one—he was telling me—is a woman who is constantly rearranging things, like Cézanne with a host's bowl of fruit, so that any visit soon became nerve-racking.

Sunset made puffy clouds mauve, the colour of a galah's breast.

13 August Dressed by six a.m. for sunrise which didn't appear until 7.20. Until then a black ink cloud slashed across pink sky. And a single bright morning star.

In the afternoon the long narrow shadows of clouds on the water looked more like oil slicks.

About five p.m. I looked over the rail—and saw a flying fish. It was white, wings towards the front, and it landed and disappeared. There was something human about it flying to avoid the ship.

14 August Common words of sailors: 'were', 'was' and 'once.'

Captain patiently answered questions about typhoons etc.

In Japan watched as containers on wharf were blown over, one falling and dislodging others. His chief engineer wanted to go ashore to see a girlfriend in the red light district. He kept phoning the bridge while the wind was at its highest, 'Can I go ashore now?'

First Officer: 'I was married to a force twelve for twenty-five years. Day and night.'

At captain's table he told of albatross that had followed the ship for five days. First officer said one had landed on his ship in the Atlantic. He had put on gloves and protection for his arms and crawled out along the containers. Managing to grab the large bird and as it snapped at his arms etc. threw it into the air, where it managed to fly away.

15 August Woke six a.m.; Saturday, which means nothing on board.

Woke only once in the night. The rocking and pitching of the ship has me pissing more, sometimes three or four times a night. Last night: just once. Southern Indian Ocean, clear sky at sunrise; Jupiter clear, above the stern. Clouds were cities and icebergs along the horizon, puffy islands above. Following the ship an enormous compact Ayers Rock, white with shadowed underbelly; it came very low and close, threatening to overwhelm the ship. Very strange, ominous.

16 August The helmsman, calm and measured until talking about his country. Quick to say Filipino coffee, especially made by his father in the village, is superior to any Italian coffee; and from what he had seen of bullfighting on TV, cockfighting is far more interesting.

Finished *Aeneid*. Tremendous thrilling work, very strong throughout. As in Homer—and Dante—not a single trace of humour.

Huge rainbow appeared ahead. The ship approached, intending to sail through it (and the rainbow forever kept out of reach). In ancient times a rainbow would have appeared as something from god, an omen; the rainbow is so 'manufactured', so celestial. And yet do rainbows appear in the myths? Not that I recall. This one was out to sea, north-west of Australia.

Then, directly ahead, about a dozen sperm whales, brownish, quite clear shapes, swimming across our course. The way they blew was like boulders landing in water, sending up a spray.

Docked Fremantle, nine p.m., after long approach past distant lights. Ship going slowly, gliding, almost silent. Pleasure, excitement at seeing land after sixteen days. Smell of land; a more solid smell. First words from Australia: wharfies handling ship's lines, 'Fuckun idiots!' □

GRANTA

MY FATHER'S AUSTRALIA

Thomas Keneally

MACLEAY RIVER HISTORICAL SOCIETY

My Father's Australia

My ninety-two-year-old father, like many of his generation, grew up in the bush and lives in Sydney, an integer in the process which saw Australia transformed during the twentieth century from a rustic to a markedly urban society. It is not, however, too harsh an urban environment he confronts. He lives with my mother in a block of characteristic cream-brick Sydney flats 200 yards from the Pacific to the east and a lagoon to the west. He is visited daily by rainbow lorikeets and sulphur-crested cockatoos, whom he feeds. He has retained from his infancy a devout and jaunty contempt for authority, and at his age doctors and other practitioners represent authority.

'They wouldn't know shit from clay,' he tells me. 'A man goes to a doctor healthy and comes out with four bloody diseases!' His grandchildren have always loved this unredeemed urchin defiance in him.

In the rural Australia of his childhood, more than nine out of ten inhabitants derived from Britain and Ireland. Today his fellow residents on that strip between sea and lagoon have ancestry in Holland, Greece, Croatia, the Pacific Islands, the Philippines, Italy, Canada, Cambodia and China. The suburbs in which he worked and lived until some twenty years ago, in the west of Sydney, have become Turkish and Arab enclaves. Having spent two and a half years in the Middle East during the Second World War, he was not a little astounded that the Middle East had come to him in Sydney.

Yet despite this diverse ethnicity, the Australian questions remain what they were on the day he was born. How does Australia relate to the rest of the world? How does it deal, even in the age of the internet, with isolation? What peculiar duties and perils are presented by its geographic location, this huge lummox of a place in the south-west corner of the Pacific Rim? What does it make of Aboriginality, that tower of ancient and violated culture rising more than 40,000 years into the past? And what is an Australian?

Once a year, generally in the mild winter of the Macleay Valley, we go 300 miles up the Pacific Highway to my father's home town in New South Wales; to the Keneally store in East Kempsey, which he won't enter for fear of ghosts and, to quote him, 'memories that bless and burn.' Then we visit the remains of his father Tim, his mother Katie, and sundry former school and girlfriends, in West

Kempsey cemetery. 'There's Billy Walsh,' he'll say, pointing out a gravestone to my mother. 'He was after you, Elsie.' My mother says not to be ridiculous. 'Yes, he was,' says my cock-sparrow father. 'I nearly had to declare the bastard on at a dance one night.' He's been 'declaring people on', offering to fight them, all his life.

My father, Tommy, is the last survivor of nine brothers and sisters. He was first raised to the light in the valley of the Macleay river in 1907. The river ran through a valley of magnificent and sacred hills, flexed itself like a languid serpent around the town of Kempsey, and then surged on with tranquil muscularity to disgorge into the Pacific. The climate was subtropical and the vegetation lush. Thus among the things my father first smelt was the nurturing mud and the bracing odours of a variety of tall eucalypts and wattle, and of jacaranda, frangipani and camphor laurels growing in the town's front gardens. Thus among the things he first heard was the suck of river against the banks of dark soil by the general store in which he had just been delivered. He heard cicadas shouting their way through their frantic six-week life in summer, and querulous magpies and sentimental curlews in their journeys across the green body of the Macleay. All this in a dairy and timber town of some 5,000 people, and a valley of ten.

As she felt his avid little hands and lips at her breast, his mother was aware that her contract with history and her husband had been fulfilled. Kate Keneally, my grandmother, had come from Cork on the White Star Line to marry her husband and be delivered of a decent quotient of children. Now, approaching forty, she had already given birth to eight children. First there was Molly, then came Maude, Johnny, Frankie, Nellie, Annie, Danny and Jimmy—whom she called by the Gaelic name Taidy, transmuted by the Australian tongue to Tardy. Tommy was the last Australian she intended to produce. Tim, my grandfather, could consider his days of procreating over.

The Macleay Valley was in its way a model of Australia itself in the first half of the twentieth century. All of the ethnic components, including the Aboriginal, were vividly in place. All the rivalries and twitches imported on immigrant ships from other places were in play. Questions of capital and labour, questions of race and immigration, questions of nationalism and imperialism were all argued here in passionate, isolated microcosm—no less so than at the counter of my grandfather's Harp of Erin Store.

The town was also like Australia in its isolation. Many broad rivers and harsh, sharp-ridged ranges lay between the Macleay and the coastal mining town of Newcastle to the south, let alone between the Macleay and Sydney. In the year of my father's birth some of the old, verminous, creaking steamers which had connected Kempsey to Sydney went out of commission. Two new 500-ton passenger and freight steamers, the *Kempsey* of Kane's Cooperative Coastal Steamship Company Limited, and its rival the *Yugilbar* of the North Coast Steamship Navigation Company (accommodating seventy saloon and twenty steerage passengers along with a hundred head of stock), had come into service to connect Kempsey to the newspapers, books, ideas and produce of Sydney and the world. The *Yugilbar* tied up within yards of Tim Keneally's Harp of Erin store. This was 'the head of navigation' on the Macleay, as far as a coastal steamer could sail upriver. During my father's childhood, the *Yugilbar* and the *Kempsey* would arrive once (or in busy times, twice) a week, to puncture what would otherwise have been the hermetically sealed world of the Macleay. Even today, Macleay people value their discreteness from the rest of the world. When they use the phrase 'He or she is from the Macleay', they are conferring a special order of humanity upon the person they speak of.

Soon after my father's birth, his family moved across the river to East Kempsey, where on a hill a short distance above the steamer mooring, they took over a store—business downstairs, residence upstairs. Perhaps little Katie, the matriarch, liked the move across the river because the children would be safer here from the infections of Central Kempsey, such as the diphtheria and enteric fevers which rose periodically out of the sewage-impregnated mudflats. (In the year of my father's birth, the bubonic plague had also visited Kempsey, carried by shipboard rats and believed to have originated in Calcutta; its appearance left in the minds of Macleay people a fear of the infectious and complex strangeness of Asia, which intervened between them and the centres of all earthly good in Northern Europe).

The new store also had the benefit of being close to the river but out of range of its regular flooding. In cyclonic storms it flooded biblically. It swept across mudflats north of the town, drowning some of the finest land, making a straight road for itself, 'carrying away horses, cattle, snakes, logs, even houses, and on one occasion people asleep in their homes' according to the recollection of my father's sister Annie. The people in question had been friends and customers of the Keneally store—an Irish sister and brother, the Coadys, sober, Mass-going, reclusive people who farmed the mudflats. Deaf with age, they had not heard the police knocking to tell them to evacuate, and 'the two poor creatures were swept twenty-five miles down the river and out to sea'. To my father, the righteous Coadys swept away in this flood in his infancy were the most graphic index of the Macleay's ferocity.

The new business in East Kempsey bore my grandmother's name—*K* for Kate Keneally. The truth is that my grandfather had built up some debts in East Kempsey. He seems to have been the sort of man of whom hard-nosed and competent women like my peasant granny said, 'He's too generous for his own good.' But his pride was wrapped up in generosity too. Kempsey was full of hard luck stories, on top of which it was an insult not to offer respectable people credit, and the credit was not always honoured. My grandfather, a lean and melancholic man, hated the indignity of chasing people for money. Some angry letters were exchanged by steamer between my grandfather and the Sydney wholesalers, the settlement of whose bills was overdue. Ultimately, somehow, they were persuaded to supply a new business entity bearing my grandmother's name.

Why were there hard luck stories in a town where pawpaws and plums grew on trees, where choko vines adorned every garden and lane way, and where meat was inexpensive and pervasive in comparison with Europe? Again, the river was an explanation. Because crops of maize and sugar cane were regularly destroyed by flood, the people took to dairy farming—the theory was that the cattle could at least walk to high ground in flood time, something beyond the powers of a corn crop. A dairy cooperative factory began to operate at Smithtown, downriver from Kempsey, from which steamers could collect milk and take it to Sydney. In country encountered eastwards on the way to the sea, on broad mudflats, and across the river at Euroka, dairy cattle—Jerseys and Guernseys—flourished. But up the valley, along Nulla Nulla and Hickey's Creek where share-farmers ran their dairy cattle on holdings of only forty acres or so, there was bush poverty. Stark-eyed parents, coming to town in drays to attend to business and buy groceries, would bring their underfed, shoeless children with them. The family myth is that my grandfather was a sucker for such people.

Sometimes I can see my father's childhood as that of an antipodean Huck Finn, surrounded as he was by children who largely spent their summers diving from the town's bridge and swimming in the river's green, strenuous waters. When my father was still an infant, his eldest brother, Johnny Keneally, and his sister, Maude, were honoured with medals of the Royal Humane Society for dragging a drowning child named Gough out of the river's deep channel. (The accompanying bravery certificate is on display today in the historical museum in Kempsey.) Gangs of kids from East Kempsey, among whom some of my father's siblings were notable generals and lieutenants, would swim the river and have fights on the mudflats with kids from Central, at other times defending their own turf from trans-riverine forays in the opposite direction. My Irish-born grandparents, who came from a country where even the fishermen could not swim, looked with resigned astonishment at their seal-like children.

When they were not in the river, they were in the swamp, which lay behind the hill on which the store stood and where my grandfather's delivery-cart hack, a demoted, temperamental but long-living racehorse named Pee Dee, grazed between excursions. The swamp's acres of paperbark, soggy earth and reaches of water were a resort for egrets and ibises. Here my father and his friends could conduct experiments with gunpowder from bullets shoplifted from the family store, investigate such universal questions as whether bullfrogs liked to smoke, and watch out for snakes—the aggressive brown snake, the striped bandi-bandi, the more timid red-bellied black snake, all venomous in varying degrees, and endowing my father with a horror of snakes which has never left him.

And when, during summer, the Keneally children were neither in the swamp nor the river, they were frequently in the store, pressed into service especially on those Fridays once a month when cedar-cutters and farmers came in from their remote shacks for supplies. Seen from high above, the Macleay valley would have resembled a map of the brain, complicated with arteries and sub-arteries and veins. A thousand streams fed its creeks before the water reached the main, majestic channel. My grandfather's once-a-month customers came from obscurer branches of this map. They were ageless men, seamed with wood smoke and sun and labour, and eccentric from their bush torpor and chosen loneliness. They liked to binge-drink at the Federal Hotel down near the steamer dock, as Tim and Kate Keneally and their children filled their scribbled monthly or two-monthly grocery orders. Sometime late on Friday night, these womenless men would stagger back to their drays, confident that their supplies lay behind them, packed in by the Keneallys. Occasionally, the boys would take a man's dray horse out of its shafts, lead it into the adjacent paddock, and re-harness it, leaving the small impediment of a slab timber fence intervening between horse and carriage. My father once found a flying fox—a fruit bat—hanging from one of the succulent fruit trees on the edge of the swamp, and placed it under the saddle of one of his father's customers. The bat slept tranquilly until the horseman emerged from the Federal Hotel to climb aboard his docile horse, sure that it knew its way home. Under the rider's sudden weight, the flying fox dug its claws into the horse's flesh, and the best-trained mount on earth bucked, rooted and threw its rider. These manufactured accidents were considered the height of fun by Tardy and Tommy, and were typical of the children they were—sportive, of broad bush humour, colonial princelings of mischief, or—as people said—utter larrikins.

But into the life of Huck Finn comes the slave, Jim. In the Macleay there was a pervasive Aboriginal presence. Kempsey itself had been named after a village in the Vale of Severn, with which Mr Enoch Rudder, the Birmingham man who founded Kempsey as a cedar shipment depot in 1834, had associations. There were other English place names such as Five Day Creek, Innes Creek, Stony Flat, Hickey's Creek, Sherwood, Bellbrook. But the landscape was peppered also with names which came from antiquity: Willawarrin, Dungay Creek, Nulla Nulla, Wabra, Toorooka, Temagog, Moonaba, Dongdingalong,

Clybucca, Bellimbopinni, Yarrahapinni. In my father's boyhood Aboriginal families who wanted to be independent of the upriver Aboriginal reserve named Bellbrook settled in shanties at Green Hill, on the edge of West Kempsey. Other Aboriginal clans lived on a reservation south of town named Burnt Bridge. Both these sets of people were from different groups of the Danggadi People, and had at one time shared common blood and ceremonies. Initiations were still taking place in my father's childhood, though without the knowledge of white people, in the ancestral country north of town. The predictable impact of livestock-farming and timber-gathering on native, nomadic peoples has been much written about, but here, as elsewhere in Australia, it was never presumed that the apparently aimless Danggadi nomads had any title to the land.

The Danggadi were dispossessed in other ways too. The Australian Federal Constitution promulgated in Sydney on 1 January 1901 made no mention of the Aboriginal people except for a clause which said that in reckoning the population of the Australian Commonwealth or any its component States, Aboriginals would not be counted. In 1902, under a federal electoral act, Katie Keneally and other women were awarded the vote by a progressive and optimistic parliament, but even the Labor members opposed the extension of the franchise to the Aboriginals. It was considered in Darwinian fashion that the race was doomed, and that it was the duty of the civilized community to soothe the dying pillow. Disease and demoralization marked the Aboriginal people of Green Hill and Burnt Bridge, the 'blacks' camps', as townspeople called them. It was common for Aboriginal women, gins, to hire themselves out as washerwomen in town. When, in my father's boyhood, Aboriginal families came into Kempsey to attend the flicks at the Adelphi in West Kempsey or the Victoria in Central, they were required to sit up front, near the screen. As with all such arrangements, it seemed totally natural to the townspeople, who argued that the arrangement suited the blacks; Aboriginals enjoyed Charlie Chaplin more if surrounded by their own. As for saloons and bars, they were banned from them, an exclusion which provided the opportunity for an informal market in liquor. Often whites, even policemen, would genially acquire liquor for an Aboriginal they liked, though commission might be charged.

The thirst of this dislocated people was sometimes fed with methylated spirits, rendered sherry-like with boot polish or sweet with syrup. My aunts used proudly to claim that their father never sold methylated spirits to an Aboriginal, for he feared the use to which it would be put.

Of course, the social traffic between whites and blacks did not stop with drink. Men might buy the sexual favours of some Aboriginal women with a bottle of sherry or port, and sometimes the consequence would be a half-caste baby. The blacks' camp contained several children who resembled certain men in town. Those who had a reputation for going with Aboriginal women were referred to with some derision as 'gin jockeys'. There must have been wives who noticed their husbands' likenesses in half-caste children, and who made private adjustments of denial or marital protest. The enigmas of trans-racial distance and intimacy, however, were sucked deep into the social fabric of Kempsey and spoken of only in lowered voices.

Above the ancient substratum of Aboriginality, the town had a complicated social structure of which my father grew up very conscious. Storekeepers and their children were in some ways the confessors of a community. They knew who, on a particular day—the poor, the pretentious, the asset-rich and the cash-strapped—could afford to push money across the counter in return for a pound of tea or a bag of flour. Knowledge of these realities made them particularly suspicious of social pretension, of which there was as much in Kempsey as there was in every town in the bush. My father claims that in his boyhood, at certain dances, there was a line across the hall, and the valley's toffs danced on one side of it, and those of lesser public standing on the other. The distinctions were not merely economic. As in North America, there was a vigorous sectarian divide, and suspicion and derision of Catholics was a national sport. The Catholics in the Macleay came largely but not exclusively of Irish descent. Italians were scattered through the coastal towns, and in the valley itself there were a number of German families—my Aunt Maude would marry into one of them, the Bolsters—who were in part refugees from Bismarck's anti-Catholic Kulturkampf. Then—another mystery common to country towns—a few families of Lebanese Maronite Christians had settled in. They ran fabric businesses and sent their consistently clever children to schools staffed by Irish and Australian nuns, and frequently intermarried with the children of Irish immigrants.

Catholics were suspect for the usual reasons: because of their baroque religion; because people said it was hard to see how they could be obedient to the Pope and the Crown at the same time, and because they were suspected of Irish Republicanism. There were subtle signs of their untrustworthiness. On Empire Day, when children from the state school and from the convent marched together to the Kempsey showground to celebrate their good fortune in being subjects of an Imperial Crown, the state school children carried the Union Jack, while those from the convent school bore the less august Australian flag, in which the stars of the Southern Cross were predominant. Catholics, it was muttered, always voted Labor, because the priests told them to vote that way. They thus represented a possible phalanx of social unrest and anti-civic feeling. But, as in the fountainhead of all such prejudice—Ireland—wealthy Catholics were accepted as 'good people despite being Catholics'. When the twin daughters of the owner of the Hotel Royal, Mr O'Neill, were to be married, their trousseaux went on display in the salerooms at the back of the hotel, and women of all backgrounds queued up to admire the finery. And to be a Catholic was in any case to be much more superior in the creation than an Aboriginal. The convent school was attended by an Aboriginal child named Harry Mumbler, of whom a nun told the children, 'Harry Mumbler may have black skin, but he has a white heart'.

At the same school, my father's reputation for larrikinism was enlarged. His best friend was a boy called Jackie Piggot, a madcap himself. Muscular school-boys were sent out to ring the angelus at noon at the open bell tower outside the Catholic church and convent. Three tolls, three tolls, three tolls and then nine. One day my father suggested to Jackie Piggot, or vice versa, that at the end of the next toll they should let go of the rope. The result was that a solitary third boy, still affixed to the rope, was swept high in the air in imitation of the ascension of Christ and hung howling from the rope's end. Father Morris had to be fetched from the presbytery with a ladder to get him down, and Keneally and Piggot were thrashed.

Impishness, adventure, disciplinary pain were between them no ultimate protection from the bush torpor which sooner or later overtook everyone in that valley so discrete in its geography. When his sisters went to Sydney on a trip in 1911, Johnny, my father's brother, wrote to them, 'The old town is so dead that they've arranged the funeral for next Thursday.' When Johnny eventually found excitement it was elsewhere, and then much too much of it.

When the great European war began in August 1914, Andrew Fisher, Labor Prime Minister of Australia, committed the country 'to the last man and the last shilling'. By late September, Private Rowley Egan of Kempsey was sailing to New Zealand as a member of an Australian battalion which was to collect New Zealand forces and take them wherever they were needed. The Kempsey-Macleay Patriotic Fund was founded. One hundred and three men volunteered at the courthouse to drill for the defence of the coastline. By the *Yugilbar*, the Kempsey branch of the Red Cross forwarded 120 blanket mufflers, ten hand-knitted mufflers, thirty-one flannel shirts, eight cholera belts and fifty-seven pairs of lambswool socks, all provided by the women of the Macleay. From Hickey's Creek alone, dairy farming country, five men volunteered and, with their womenfolk and fiancées, stared, gawkily innocent, at the photographer from the *Argus*.

My grandfather, along with other Irish folk of the Macleay, mistrusted the imperial fervour of the early war. Let Britain fight for itself! Tim Keneally came from a particularly Republican area of north Cork. His uncle, John Kenealy (the Keneallys were never consistent in transliterating their Gaelic name), had been transported to Western Australia with a ten-year sentence for sedition—later, pardoned by Gladstone, he went to California. But if Tim Keneally doubted whether it was necessary, just or wise for young Australians to die in Britain's war, his sons had different attitudes. For young Australian men, the war was their current test of worth. The Kaiser was a barbarian, and hadn't nuns been raped in Belgium? There was also a paradoxical anti-Britishness at work. The British were too runty to deal with the Germans; let the boys from the Macleay show the world what Australians were made of! The children of Irish immigrants could show the rest of Australia their prowess. No more milking, or in Uncle Johnny's case, no more hitching of that turbulent horse, Pee Dee, to the grocery cart. No more cooling of heels, and wondering whether to get half a pound of wurst (soon to be patriotically renamed devon) from Mottee's Greek cafe, or to go to the flicks at the Victoria.

My father was only seven when the Australians landed on Gallipoli in 1915. But he was aware of the contest between the Irish father, Tim, and the Australian son, Johnny, the classic conflict between the immigrant, to whom the politics of the country of origin were paramount, and the native-born child. The pressure on Johnny to enlist grew as the recruiting band of 'Dungarees' or 'Coasters' descended the coastline from Grafton and arrived in Kempsey in the February of 1916. Marching under a lieutenant, they were formally welcomed at the Kempsey showgrounds by Mr Morton of the New South Wales Legislative Assembly who said that Australians had already shown that they could play the game on bigger fields than the sports arena. Either then or soon after, young John Keneally enlisted. My father took his side instinctively. The mystique which attached to the Diggers—a generic name for Australia's soldiers—would influence his own later decision to volunteer in the Second World War, which meant that, in being fatherless for two and a half years myself, I too would pay my dues to the myths of Diggerhood.

My Uncle Johnny's enlistment created a tragic division between him and my grandfather. He sailed away in late 1916. My father was at the time a colonial urchin of eight years, rankling under the control of the West Kempsey Sisters of Mercy.

Along the Pacific coast of New South Wales, either side of the mouth of the Macleay, are some of the most splendid beaches in creation. In 1915 at Trial Bay, within walking distance of the Macleay Bar, an old stone prison became home for 500 German internees, 'men of education and substance', as the local history described them, engineers, doctors, hotel managers, colonial civil servants from now-seized German territories throughout South East Asia and the South West Pacific, including German New Guinea and the German concession on the coast of China. Some were German Buddhist monks—an extraordinary photograph exists which shows Macleay farmers watching them disembark from a prison steamer. Cultivated, energetic, these Germans swam, played tennis, staged for their fellow prisoners German dramas and farces, for which they designed their own elegant posters. Some Kempsey people spoke darkly of how the prisoners had devised a means of communicating with the German raider, Wolf, by magic lantern shows. (Ultimately, fears that this uncaptured raider would land at Trial Bay and liberate all the prisoners led to their removal to Holdsworthy military camp, outside Sydney.)

The contradiction between the closeness of the German prisoners and the distance at which Johnny now lay would tease my father's child mind.

By the spring of 1917, Johnny was in France, facing the kinsmen of the Trial Bay internees. He and most of his friends from the Macleay were reinforcements for the Nineteenth Infantry Battalion, part of the Second Australian Division which had suffered at Pozières the previous summer. His letters arrived intermittently. They were eagerly read by Katie, and then read aloud by her to her youngest child, my father, as they sat in the kitchen together drinking tea. Along with news of France and Flanders he would absorb her rural aphorisms, which in some cases he would go on using long after they had lost their currency. Thin folk: 'straight up and down like a yard of pump water'. The fashionably attired: 'dressed up like a pox-doctor's clerk'. Advice to the dreamer: 'Wish in one hand and shit in the other, and see which gets full first.'

Since she combined her gift for earthy imagery with an unaffected belief in the tenderness of the Mother of All Mothers, the Virgin Mary; since she was dutiful at novenas, sieges of worship spread over nine days, and had a missal crammed with cards on which were prayers to which 300 or 400 days of indulgence—that is, time off purgatory—were attached; and since she said the rosary daily, she had faith that Johnny was under the Virgin Mary's special protection. Johnny's notes home were generally written during rest periods out of the line, and only from our knowledge of the nature of that frightful war do they seem poignant. Even his complaints were jaunty. He gave the impression that the Western Front was full of boys from the Macleay. He regularly saw Frank Wedlock and athletic Joe Lalor and someone named Young Lawrence.

He went into action at Bullecourt in April 1917. The Nineteenth's objective was to capture some trenches of the Hindenburg Line to the west of the town, but it and the other regiments of the Fifth Australian Brigade came under a ferocious crossfire from machine guns. Later he wrote to one of his brothers, Danny perhaps, that he had 'been in some stunts where you wouldn't see how a fly could live let alone a man'. He had a thorough education in this mystery that summer at Passchendaele, Glencorse Wood, Black Watch Corner, Polygon Wood—during the entire tragedy of the 400,000-casualty battle named Third Ypres. By September, he was 'having a bit of a spell in hospital with Trench Fever', and again the Macleay motif: George Gilfillan and a man named Bates from East Kempsey had been killed in action—'It's a bit of bad luck.' Young Lawrence, meanwhile, had met Billy and Bert Piggot in the gardens just a little way from the hospital.

At home Billy Hughes, the new Australian Prime Minister, wanted conscription. Immediately, the Labor Party began to split over the issue. In the light of the Easter Rising in Dublin in 1916, the idea of conscripting young Australians enraged people like my grandfather. Billy Hughes's wonderful British army had executed the wounded rebel, Connolly, as he sat in a chair in an enclosed courtyard of Kilmainham Gaol. So to hell with them! Archbishop Mannix of Melbourne perfervidly expressed the opposition of the Irish Catholic faithful, thereby convincing most loyalists that they had been right about the Catholics all along. In a referendum on 28 October 1917, the proposal to conscript men was defeated. Hughes called another referendum for 20 December, but it was defeated by a greater margin still. Johnny, in letters from France, was himself trenchant about Hughes: 'We are waiting very anxiously for the result of the referendum and see what sort of a time Mr W Hughes has got for his trouble.' Volunteers themselves, the Australians at the front believed they could trust only other volunteers. Many of them thought of younger brothers and the need to spare them from the mess and waste.

Johnny went back to the trenches in time for the fighting of October and November 1917, which caused 38,000 Australian casualties. In a spell behind the lines on 25 November, he met Jack Goggins of the Macleay at Mass, which was said by a very martial Irishman, a warrior priest named Father Clune, who had won the Military Cross for capturing a German machine gun nest and killing several Prussian guards. He was always with the boys in the trenches, Johnny wrote, and they had the rosary nearly every night. He kindly reassured his mother that godliness could still persist in the ungodly havoc: 'Myself and two young Walshes from the Macleay go every chance we get.'

In the same year the railway came to Kempsey. It had been advancing towards the town for some time, and my grandparents had a contract to provision the tracklayers. Tardy and my father would take a laden dray, pulled by Pee Dee, down to Smith's Creek where the Maltese railwaymen lived under canvas and where, made nostalgic for their own sons by my wild father's angelic looks, they pressed holy pictures on him. At last, these men concluded their work and the rail ran south as far as Wingham and northwards to Macksville. The steamers which had ruled the coast would now have to compete for freight and passengers. The valley's isolation was penetrated. Trains arrived—though not yet all the way from Sydney—in a town which only a few months before had received the wonder of electric light. Those who could afford it had electricity installed in one room of their houses. Many Macleay people considered the bare incandescent globe harmful to the eyesight, but one shone in the Keneally living room, and letters were written by it, with postcards enclosed of the new Kempsey railway station.

'Well by this time you have the railway completed to Kempsey and [you're] swanking it to the train,' Johnny wrote from the Western Front. 'I have had all the trains I want—from Red Cross to cattle trucks...'

My father faced his own battles in 1918. For all his life he would carry a sense of injustice at having become his convent school's whipping boy. He struggled for self-esteem in the face of the nuns' apparent conviction that he must be perpetually watched for his behaviour, and strenuously punished for the smallest acts of defiance. He had none of the good spirits and confidence that his elder brother brought to the great German spring assault in the last year of the war. 'Old Jerry...has bitten off much more than he will be able to chew this time...his losses are terrible—they come over massed and it is quite a treat for our gunners to get going on them in the open...'

But of course Johnny was suffering more than he told his mother or little brother. In a state of battle fatigue after the crisis around Amiens, he consoled himself by looking at his postcards of Kempsey's new railway again. 'I would not mind if I was speeding over the lines just now. I've had enough of travelling to do me a lifetime. I'll settle down in some quiet spot when this bit of a squabble is over.'

In the light of the lonely and solitary state in which he would spend the rest of his life, his projection of hopes rings pitiably.

He soldiered on. He fought in the battle of Hamel, designed in part by the remarkable Jewish-Australian general, John Monash, to demonstrate his belief that losses could be minimized with the proper use of tanks and infantry. He took part in the famous forward push which General Ludendorff called 'the black day of the German army in this war', when—helped by fog—the Allies overran artillery positions south and north of the Somme. It wasn't the end of it though, and in September 1918, writing to Katie, Johnny reported that the Nineteenth Battalion's Lieutenant Jack Plummer from Smithtown, just downriver from Kempsey, had been killed at Mount St Quentin. The Nineteenth Battalion, down to a third of its strength, was taken out of the line and amalgamated with the remnants of the Twentieth Battalion. 'By the way I lost one of my old mates—Barny Heffernan—you have his photo I think I sent on which we had taken when we first arrived in England. He had a fairly hard knock and died of wounds.' Johnny could lose his friend and consider it a mere 'hard knock', whereas my child father felt he was losing his very soul at the place that was meant to save it—the West Kempsey convent school.

He combined his inner bewilderment with a continuing rebelliousness of a kind which would now seem relatively mild. He was no delinquent, but, rather like the young Commonwealth of Australia itself, he had a superficial raucousness which caused strangers to miss a potential nobility of spirit. Tim, my grandfather, still had enough control to demand total silence at meals, and my father did not defy him. But in other ways, perhaps because my grandparents had other cares and were nearing middle age, my father ran rings round his parents. Confined to the residence above the store, and told by his father not to 'go off with those other blackguards of yours', he would simply climb over a balcony and shimmy down a drainpipe. He possessed a raw athleticism. He was muscular and wiry, a sportsman. He swung clubs, he was good at Rugby League. He descended poles. He was fast over the ground, quick in the water. And he would soon be too old for the nuns to thrash.

As another Australian summer set in, and the afternoon thunderheads hung above the exquisite blue mountains to the west, official news of the Armistice was received in Kempsey by telephone shortly before 9 a.m. on 12 November 1918. People wandered into the streets, shopkeepers closed their stores, Katie received congratulations. Johnny's younger brother, my Uncle Danny, had already joined up and was on his way to France; his ship lay in Cape Town when news of the Armistice came through. Johnny's letters had become franker when he knew Dan was on his way. He wrote to him: 'Don't you bloody-well come to France. If you do I'll shoot you myself rather than let you go into the trenches.'

On the day peace came, a large effigy of the Kaiser was erected near the post office in Smith Street. The mayor, Alderman Lane, a pharmacist, declared that for his crimes against mankind the Kaiser had been condemned by the whole world. He announced the sentence: that the Kaiser be shot and then burned at the stake. To my father's delight, a firing squad commanded by Lieutenant Daly fired a salvo of blank cartridges in the direction of the effigy, and then one Alderman Brown sprinkled it with benzine.

In 1919, after an ecstatic summer, not even the worldwide influenza epidemic could put a dent in the rail-connected, electrically-lit exhilaration of Kempsey. The town was exuberant in its gratitude to its sons for fighting history's last war. But even my eleven-year-old father noticed that the men who came back showed none of the military confidence which had shone from their letters. They woke at night, sweating from remembered bombardments, the waft of chlorine and mustard gas on their tongues and pricking their nostrils. Many of them stuck together, drank together, often excessively, and found it hard to settle in. Johnny, who had seen so much, would find it hard to recycle his unsettled warrior soul into a state appropriate to that of a grocer's son in the Macleay. When he eventually came home that year, arguments with his father erupted. The Black and Tans, another mercy of the British, had been unleashed in Ireland, not least in rebellious north Cork, in Mallow, Kanturk, Newmarket—Tim's native soil. This was the work of an Empire Johnny had gone thousands of miles to preserve. One day soon Johnny would disappear.

Before that happened, though, several Kempsey citizens, including its patriotic undertaker, Jos Walker, began gathering dynamite to blow up the twenty-foot memorial above Trial Bay to the few German internees who had died of natural causes in the prison camp there. Where on the coast, asked the disgruntled veterans, was a monument to their dead? In the same hearse in which Katie herself would, in a later decade, be conveyed to her grave in West Kempsey, dynamite was transported to the German monument at Trial Bay. Perhaps the blowing up of the German memorial was a petty act of xenophobia; but the TNT in the hands of these harmed young men was also a prayer for the restoration of their world, and for the resurrection of their dead. Johnny was believed to have been involved. The explosion turned out to be his most strident statement before he vanished forever to the backblocks of Queensland.

My father was involved in a final gesture of rebellion too. As he waited at the convent to be flogged yet again for some mischief, he saw his brother Tardy draw up in the grocery cart with Pee Dee, delivering produce to the convent. My father walked out of the schoolroom where he stood awaiting blows, ran to Tardy and sought asylum. 'You can't come home,' said Tardy. 'I bloody can. I've had it!' My father was barely twelve. Out of the Jansenist shadow of the convent, he rode away in a cart pulled by an eccentric horse, back to East Kempsey where he knew that by force of personality he could make his harried parents grant him liberty. He meant to become a state school boy.

The world looked splendid that day. Everywhere in town, there did seem now to be a sense of sanity restored and illimitable promise, at least for those who had not seen Barny Heffernan take a bad knock. Billy Hughes, the Prime Minister, was in Versailles, signing the peace treaty for Australia, asserting his country's independent sovereignty. And my father felt himself to be a child restored to possibility as he and Tardy progressed down Belmore Street towards the bridge of their infant aquatics, the frank Australian sun on their faces, towards East Kempsey and tea with Katie. □

NOTES ON CONTRIBUTORS

Murray Bail was born in Adelaide and lives in Sydney. His novels include *Homesickness* and most recently *Eucalyptus,* which is published by Text Publishing in Melbourne, Harvill in London and Farrar Straus Giroux in New York.

Georgia Blain lives in Sydney. Her novels *Closed for Winter* and *Candelo* are published by Penguin Australia. *Candelo* is published in the UK by Transworld under the title *Snake in the Grass.*

Polly Borland's exhibition *Australians* is at the National Portrait Gallery in London until 17 September. Her book *The Babies* will be published by Powerhouse Books (UK and US) at the end of the year. She is working on a book based around the lives of the people photographed in her essay for this issue.

Peter Carey's novels include *Illywhacker* and *Oscar and Lucinda,* which won the Booker Prize in 1988. 'The True History of the Kelly Gang, First Part' is taken from *The True History of the Kelly Gang*, published later this year by University of Queensland Press in Australia, Faber in the UK and Knopf in the US. Peter Carey lives in New York.

Peter Conrad was born in Hobart. He teaches English literature at Christ Church, Oxford. He is also a reviewer and feature writer for the London *Observer*. His most recent publication is *Modern Times, Modern Places* (Thames and Hudson/UK, Knopf/US); his next will be *The Hitchcock Murders*, published this Autumn by Faber.

Robyn Davidson's book *Tracks,* her account of her journey across the Western deserts of Australia by camel, first appeared in 1980 and is now published by Picador (UK) and Vintage (US). Her most recent book *Desert Places* is a chronicle of two years spent with nomads in north-west India (Viking Penguin/US, Penguin/UK and Australia). She lives in London.

Kate Grenville was born and lives in Sydney. Her novels include *Lilian's Story, Dark Places* (Picador Australia) and *The Idea of Perfection* published by Picador Australia and this year by Picador in the UK.

Howard Jacobson worked as a lecturer in England and Australia before becoming a novelist, critic, and columnist for the London *Independent*. His most recent novel *The Mighty Walzer* was published last year by Jonathan Cape.

Thomas Keneally's novels include *The Playmaker* and *Schindler's Ark,* which won the Booker Prize in 1982. His most recent novel is *The Great Shame* (Heinemann/UK, Doubleday/US). His new novel *Bettany's Book* will be published later this year by Sceptre. He lives on the coast of New South Wales.

Roger Law was the co-founder and co-designer of one of the most successful satire shows on British television, *Spitting Image*, which ran between 1983 and 1997. He studied painting at Sydney's National School of Art and now divides his time between London and Sydney. His paintings on the cover of this issue will form part of his exhibition at the Rebecca Hossack Gallery in London from 26 October until 25 November this year.

David Malouf's novels include *An Imaginary Life* and *Remembering Babylon,* which was shortlisted for the Booker Prize and won the IMPAC Prize. His short-story collection *Dream Stuff* is published by Chatto and Windus/UK, Pantheon/US. He has also written a libretto for Michael Berkeley's opera *Jane Eyre,* which receives its world premiere at the Cheltenham Music Festival this year. He lives in Sydney.

David Moore's collections of photographs *Fifty Photographs* and *From Face to Face* will be published this year by Chapter & Verse in Australia.

Frank Moorhouse was born in Nowra, New South Wales and currently lives in France, the setting for his last novel *Loose Living* (Picador Australia). 'War Work' is an extract from *Dark Palace,* which will be published this year by Random House in Australia in October and by Picador in the UK.

Les Murray lives in New South Wales. His verse novel *Fredy Neptune* and many other collections are published by Duffy & Snellgrove in Australia, Carcanet in Britain and Farrar Straus Giroux in the US. He won the T. S. Eliot Prize in 1997 and the Queen's Gold Medal for Poetry in 1999.

Ben Rice was born in Devon in 1972. *Pobby and Dingan* is his first published work and will be published later this year by Jonathan Cape in the UK and Knopf in the US. He lives in London.

Paul Toohey is the Darwin correspondent of the *Australian* newspaper. His non-fiction books *God's Little Acre* and *Rocky Goes West* are both published by Duffy & Snellgrove in Australia.

Tim Winton's novels include *Cloudstreet,* and *The Riders* (published by Picador/UK, Scribner/US) which was shortlisted for the 1995 Booker Prize. He lives in Perth, Western Australia.